CUSTOM EDITION
WEST CHESTER UNIVERSITY

HOW WRITING WORKS:
A Guide to Composing Genres

Jordynn Jack
Katie Rose Guest Pryal

Source material from:
Jack and Guest Pryal, *How Writing Works: A Guide to Composing GenreS*
978-0-19-985985-6

Oxford   New York
OXFORD UNIVERSITY PRESS

Oxford University Press is a department of the University of Oxford. It furthers the University's
objective of excellence in research, scholarship, and education by publishing worldwide.

Oxford New York
Auckland Cape Town Dar es Salaam Hong Kong Karachi
Kuala Lumpur Madrid Melbourne Mexico City Nairobi
New Delhi Shanghai Taipei Toronto

With offices in
Argentina Austria Brazil Chile Czech Republic France Greece
Guatemala Hungary Italy Japan Poland Portugal Singapore
South Korea Switzerland Thailand Turkey Ukraine Vietnam

Copyright © 2016 by Oxford University Press.

Published by Oxford University Press.
198 Madison Avenue, New York, New York 10016
http://www.oup.com

ISBN 978-0-19-046770-8

CONTENTS

1. Asking Questions   2
    A. What Is a Genre?   2
        Frederick Douglass, "My Bondage and My Freedom"   2
        Abida Sultaan, Memoirs of a Rebel Princess (excerpt)   6
        Amy Tan, "Mother Tongue"   8

    B. "What Is It?": Identify Shared Conventions   12
    C. "Who Reads It?": Identify an Audience   15
    D. "What's It For?": Identify a Genre's Purpose   17
    E. Conclusion   18
    F. Chapter Project: Write a Literacy Narrative   18

2. Discovering Rhetorical Situations   19
    A. Discovering Your Rhetorical Situation   19
        Aliyah's "Public Problem"   19
        Aliyah's "Observations"   21
        Lewis and Clark Journal [excerpt]   25

    B. Considering Your Purpose   27
    C. Identifying an Author's Role   29
    D. Analyzing an Audience's Needs   30
    E. Discovering Timing   32
    F. Conclusion   33
    G. Chapter Project: Write Journal Entries   34

3. Writing New Genres   36
    A. Writing a New Genre   36
        Claire Zhang, "Amy Tan Phase" (excerpt)   36
        Louisa Rodriguez, "Identity in Context"   39
        Russell Johnson, "Identity in a Material World"   41

    B. Finding Examples   44
    C. Identifying Conventions   45
    D. Locating Options   48
        Foxxy, "The Way of a Cherokee"   49

    E. Conclusion   52
    F. Chapter Project: Write a Response Essay   53

4. Developing a Writing Process   55
   A. Discovering Your Writing Process   55
   B. Composing a Personal Essay   57
      Maisha, "Two Worlds, One Great Nation"   57
      Mark, "I Believe in the Senses"   58

   C. Prewriting   61
   D. Drafting   65
   E. Revising   66
   F. Editing and Proofreading   69
   G. Publishing   70
   H. Conclusion   71
   I. Chapter Project: Write a Personal Essay   72

5. Profiles   74
   A. Profile Mini-Genre: Social Network Profile   74
   B. Portfolio   77
   C. Program Profile   81

      Stephanie Gottschlich, "The New Recruits: Students Answer the Call for Next
         Generation of Air Force Scientists"   88

   E. Strategies for Profiles   92
      Sarah Creek, "Profile of an Engineering Professor: Dr. Grace Yang"   92

   F. Chapter Project: Write a Profile Article   97

7. Inquiries   129
    A. Inquiry Mini-Genre: Student Class Notes   129
        Josephine Perry, "St. Augustine on Love"   129

    B. Blog Entry   133
        Brandy, "Disappointment: *Rizzoli & Isles*"   133
        Lucia Gonzalez Hernandez, "Straw-Man Fallacy and the 'Anti-Antiterror Left'"   135

    C. Reading Notes   137
        Mei Lin, "Aristotle, *On Rhetoric*"   138
        Terrence B., "Notes on Pamela Lewis Reading"   138
        Michael M., "Elizabeth Barrett Browning Response: 'The Cry of the Children'"   139

    D. Observation Notes   141
        Zachary Fitzgerald, "Observations of the Campus Courtyard"   141
        Belinda W., "Peer Classroom Observations: Sierra M."   142

    E. Strategies for Inquiries   146
    F. Chapter Project: Write Observation Notes   148

8. Analyses   149
    A. Analysis Mini-Genre: Keyword Analysis   149

    D. Rhetorical Analysis   174
        Cody M. Poplin, "Rhetorical Strategies and Effectiveness in the Declaration of
            Independence"   174
        Kelly Simpson, "*Kairos*, Violence, and *The Hunger Games*"   176
        Carlos Fernandez-Smith, "Appraising *The Help*: *Ethos* and *Logos* in
            Critical Accounts"   177

E. Strategies for Analyses   184
    Association of Black Women Historians, "An Open Statement to the Fans of
        The Help" (excerpt)   185

F. Chapter Project: Write a Rhetorical Analysis   190

D. Website Review   208
    Megan M., "Forum: Redesign Critiques"   208
    Hester Cho, "Healthcare.gov: Website Review"   209
    Jonas Webber, "Website Review of Ravelry.com"   211

E. Strategies for Reviews   214

10. Argumentative Genres   218
    A. Argument Mini-Genre: Print Advertisement   219
    B. Column, Op-Ed, or Letter to the Editor   223
        Nate Rushing, "UF's Meatless Mondays Are Ridiculous"   223
        Amelia Jensen, Letter to the Editor   224
        Rini Sampath, "Insults against Disabled People Must Be Eradicated"   225

D. Satire   242
    Pia DiGiulio, "Uncontrolled Study Orgies Break Out in Gender-Neutral Dorm"   242
    Dr. Jonathan Swift, "A Modest Proposal: For preventing the children of poor people in
        Ireland, from being a burden on their parents or country, and for making them
        beneficial to the publick"   243
    The Onion, "Professor Deeply Hurt by Student's Evaluation"   249

E. Strategies for Argumentative Genres   252

12. Workplace Genres   315
    A. Workplace Mini-Genre: Company Slogan   315
    B. Email   318
        Joe Smith, "Reference Request"   318
        Maria B. Hernandez, "Agenda for Biology Majors Club Meeting"   319
        Editorial Staff of *Undergraduate Research Journal*, "Journal decision declining
            to publish your article"   319

13. Proposals   333
   A. Proposal Mini-Genre: Elevator Pitch   333

   C. Student Proposal   339
      Victor Egbukichi, Student Event Proposal   340
      Leticia Garcia-Rodriguez, Student Organization Proposal   341
      Tyler Williamson, Independent Study Proposal   342

15. Developing a Topic   398
    A. Genre Toolkit: What Are You Writing?   398
    B. Browse for Topics   399
    C. Narrow Topics with Initial Research   400

16. Prewriting   402
    A. Freewriting   402
    B. Question-Dialogue   404
    C. Audio-Brainstorming   405
    D. Concept Mapping   406

17. Drafting   410
    A. Try Out Different Drafting Strategies   410
    B. Digital Composing: Find Tools that Work for You   416
    C. Writing Collaboratively   421

18. Generating Arguments   423
    A. What Is an Argument?   423
    B. Examining the Topic   425
    C. Researching Arguments   426
    D. Developing a Thesis (or Claim)   427
    E. Finding Good Reasons   429

    G. Rhetorical Appeals: *Ethos*, *Pathos*, and *Logos*   432
    H. Addressing Counter-Arguments   434
    I. Arguing Ethically: Avoiding Fallacies   435
    J. Argument Troubleshooting   439

19. Using Rhetorical Modes   441
    A. What Happened? Narration   441
    B. What Is It Like? Description   444
    C. What Is It? Definition   445
    D. What Kind Is It? Classification   447

E. How Is It Similar/Different? Comparison/Contrast   447
F. What Causes It? What Are Its Effects? Cause/Effect   448

20. Organization   449

E. Ordering Sections or Topics   459
F. Introductions   460
G. Conclusions   462

21. Developing Style   464
A. Matching Style to Genre, Audience, and Purpose   464
Maya Schenwar, "The Prison System Welcomes My Newborn Niece to This World"   464
Ann Booker Loper and Elena Hontoria Tuerk, "Improving the Emotional
   Adjustment and Communication Patterns of Incarcerated Mothers:
   Effectiveness of a Prison Parenting Intervention"   465
Ashley McAlarney, "Access for All: Federal Funding and Regulation of For-Profit
   Higher Education"   466

B. Choosing a Persona   467
C. Choosing Tone   468
D. Making Vocabulary Choices   468
E. Choosing a Level of Formality   471
F. Using Rhetorical Figures   472
G. Tips for Developing Style   478

22. Polishing It Up   480
A. Revising   480
B. Self-Editing: Creating Fresh Eyes   481
C. Conducting Peer Review   482

29. Choosing Visual Elements, Layout, and Design   624
    A. Matching Design to Genre   624
        Centers for Disease Control, "HIV Among Women"   625

American Public Health Association, "Are You Ready?" 626

B. Matching Design to Audience, Purpose, and Situation 627
University of North Carolina, "20th Century Women at UNC" 628
U.S. Department of Agriculture Report (excerpt) 629

C. Putting Things in Place: Layout 630
D. Types of Visual Elements 633
E. Principles for Visual Elements 644
F. Using Electronic Tools 651

30. Getting It Out There 652
A. Delivering Oral Presentations 652
B. Developing Multimedia Presentations 657
C. Creating a Portfolio 659
D. Submitting Your Work for Publication 662
E. Self-Publishing Your Work 664

S1 How Verbs Work 668
A. What Is a Verb? 668
B. Common Problems 668

S2 How Nouns and Pronouns Work 673
A. What Is a Noun? 673
B. What Is a Pronoun? 673
C. Common Problems 673

S3 How Modifiers Work 677
A. What Is a Modifier? 677
B. Common Problems 678

S4 How Sentences Work 681
A. What Is a Sentence? 681
B. Common Problems 681

S5 How Punctuation Works 684
A. What Is Punctuation? 684
B. Common Problems 685

S6 How Usage Conventions Work 690
A. What Are Usage Conventions? 690
B. Common Problems 690

Asking Questions

The word *genre* refers to a group of documents that all share similar features. As a college student, you will be expected to write a number of different genres—essays, reviews, letters, presentations, and so on. As an employee of a business, you might encounter a different set of genres, such as proposals, profiles, reports, and more. We can't fit all of these different genres into one book, but we can give you tools: tools to help you learn about genres and tools to help you write them.

This chapter will teach you to identify a genre by asking questions.

A. What Is a Genre?

Read the passage below, published in 1855; it is an excerpt from an autobiographical narrative written by Frederick Douglass, an American author, orator, abolitionist, and escaped slave.

EXAMPLE 1: Frederick Douglass, "My Bondage and My Freedom" (excerpt)

Once in Baltimore, with hard brick pavements under my feet, which almost raised blisters, by their very heat, for it was in the height of summer; walled in on all sides by towering brick buildings; with troops of hostile boys ready to pounce upon me at every street corner; with new and strange objects glaring upon me at every step, and with startling sounds reaching my ears from all directions, I for a time thought that, after all, the home plantation was a more desirable place of residence than my home on Alliciana street, in Baltimore. My country eyes and ears were confused and bewildered here; but the boys were my chief trouble. They chased me, and called me "*Eastern Shore man,*" till really I almost wished myself back on the Eastern Shore. I had to undergo a sort of moral acclimation, and when that was over, I did much better.

My new mistress happily proved to be all she *seemed* to be, when, with her husband, she met me at the door, with a most beaming, benignant countenance. She was, naturally, of an excellent disposition, kind, gentle and cheerful. . . . I hardly knew how to behave toward "Miss Sopha," as I used to call Mrs. Hugh Auld. I had been treated as a *pig* on the plantation; I was treated as a *child* now. I could not even approach her as I had formerly approached Mrs. Thomas Auld. How could I hang down my head, and speak with bated breath, when there was no pride to scorn me, no coldness to repel me, and no hatred to inspire me with fear? I therefore soon learned to regard her as something more akin to a mother, than a slaveholding mistress. . . .

Mrs. Auld was not only a kind-hearted woman, but she was remarkably pious; frequent in her attendance of public worship, much given to reading the bible, and to chanting hymns of praise, when alone. . . . The frequent hearing of my mistress reading the bible for she often read aloud when her husband was absent soon awakened my curiosity in respect to this *mystery* of reading, and roused in me the desire to learn. Having no fear of my kind mistress before my eyes (she had then given me no reason to fear), I frankly asked her to teach me to read; and, without hesitation, the dear woman began the task, and very soon, by her assistance, I was master of the alphabet, and could spell words of three or four letters. My mistress seemed almost as proud of my progress, as if I had been her own child; and, supposing that her husband would be as well pleased, she made no secret of what she was doing for me. Indeed, she exultingly told him of the aptness of her pupil, of her intention to persevere in teaching me, and of the duty which she felt it to teach me, at least to read *the bible*. Here arose the first cloud over my Baltimore prospects, the precursor of drenching rains and chilling blasts.

Master Hugh was amazed at the simplicity of his spouse, and, probably for the first time, he unfolded to her the true philosophy of slavery, and the peculiar rules necessary to be observed by masters and mistresses, in the management of their human chattels. Mr. Auld promptly forbade continuance of her instruction; telling her, in the first place, that the thing itself was unlawful; that it was also unsafe, and could only lead to mischief. To use his own words, further, he said, "if you give a nigger an inch, he will take an ell;" "he should know nothing but the will of his master, and learn to obey it;" "if you teach that nigger—speaking of myself—how to read the bible, there will be no keeping him;" "it would forever unfit him for the duties of a slave;" and "as to himself, learning would do him no good, but probably, a great deal of harm—making him disconsolate and unhappy." "If you learn him now to read, he'll want to know how to write; and, this accomplished, he'll be running away with himself." Such was the tenor of Master Hugh's oracular exposition of the true philosophy of training a human chattel; and it must be confessed that he very clearly comprehended the nature and the requirements of the relation of master and slave. His discourse was the first decidedly anti-slavery lecture to which it had been my lot to listen. Mrs. Auld evidently felt the force of his remarks; and, like an obedient wife, began to shape her course in the direction indicated by her husband.

The effect of his words, *on me*, was neither slight nor transitory. His iron sentences— 5 cold and harsh—sunk deep into my heart, and stirred up not only my feelings into a sort of rebellion, but awakened within me a slumbering train of vital thought. It was a new and special revelation, dispelling a painful mystery, against which my youthful understanding had struggled, and struggled in vain, to wit: the *white* man's power to perpetuate the enslavement of the *black* man. "Very well," thought I; "knowledge unfits a child to be a slave." I instinctively assented to the proposition; and from that moment I understood the direct pathway from slavery to freedom. This was just what I needed; and I got it at a time, and from a source, whence I least expected it. I was saddened at the thought of losing the assistance of my kind mistress; but the information, so instantly derived, to some extent compensated me for the loss I had sustained in this direction. Wise as Mr. Auld was, he evidently underrated my comprehension, and had little idea of the use to which I was capable of putting the impressive lesson he was giving to his wife. *He* wanted me to be *a slave;* I had already voted against that on the home plantation of Col. Lloyd. That which he most loved I most hated; and the very determination which he expressed to keep me in ignorance, only rendered me the more resolute in seeking intelligence. In learning to read, therefore, I am not sure that I do not owe quite as much to the opposition of my master, as to the kindly assistance of my amiable mistress. I acknowledge the benefit rendered me by the one, and by the other; believing, that but for my mistress, I might have grown up in ignorance.

Now that you have read this passage, ask yourself the following questions:

- What is it?
- Who reads it?
- What's it for?

Let's try to answer these questions by examining the text more closely.

What Is It?

Looking at Douglass's story, we see that it is an excerpt of an autobiography. We know this because the introduction to the text tells us so, and because the story uses a key feature of the genre of autobiography: it is written in the first person (using "I"). This excerpt focuses on the subject of learning to read and write: Douglass became a "master of the alphabet" and he learned "to read *the bible.*" The excerpt thus tells the story of how Douglass became literate.

Douglass's story of achieving literacy also highlights the connection between literacy and power. Douglass points out the ways that his white slave-owner used "ignorance" to keep Douglass in slavery: "[T]he very determination which he expressed to keep me in ignorance, only rendered me the more resolute in seeking intelligence."

Given these observations, we can say that the genre of this excerpt is a *literacy narrative*, which is a first-person story about learning to read or write that often highlights the power the narrator gains from literacy.

Who Reads It?

Frederick Douglass's autobiographies—he wrote more than one—are widely read. *My Bondage and My Freedom* is often read today in high schools and colleges in the United States, usually to teach students about the history of slavery.

This specific excerpt, however, is also widely taught as a classic example of the genre of the literacy narrative. Literacy narratives are used by students of education, English, language acquisition, and other academic disciplines to explore the powerful impact that learning to read and write can have on individuals as well as on groups.

At the time Douglass wrote his autobiographies, however, the books were important political documents. Douglass and other abolitionists used an autobiography to educate readers about slaves' experiences. Often, these readers would never have known an enslaved person, so Douglass's book would be their only insight into the mind of a former slave. Today, literacy narratives continue to serve a political purpose: for example, to help argue for improved access to educational resources in underserved communities.

What's It For?

At the time he published this autobiography, Douglass would have had multiple purposes for the book. He would have wanted to educate northern, white readers about slavery. He would have wanted to persuade these readers to support abolition of slavery. Many of these readers would have been unfamiliar with the practice of slavery in the American South.

This excerpt, in particular, persuaded readers about the importance of education in the abolition of slavery. As a literacy narrative, the excerpt highlights how slave-holders deliberately withheld education from enslaved people in order to keep them enslaved. When Douglass wrote that "[education] would forever unfit [a slave] for the duties of a slave," he suggested that educating slaves would be a powerful form of rebellion. In this way, Douglass's book also served as a guidebook for escaping slavery.

Congratulations: You Have Just Discovered a Genre

These three questions—*What is it? Who reads it? What's it for?*—will guide you whenever you encounter a new kind of document, or genre.

This book introduces you to the notion of genre as a way to advance your writing skills. In simple terms, a genre is a group of documents that share similarities (called *conventions*).

By studying a genre, you can learn about the goals of writers, the needs of readers, and the kinds of information to include. You can learn about how best to organize a document, how to format it, and what kind of words to use. You can also learn about *why* people write a genre in a particular way.

The conventions of a genre arise in response to situations in which a certain kind of author needs to communicate a certain kind of a message to a certain kind of audience. When situations recur over and over again, they often give rise to genres. The literacy narrative has become a genre in response to situations in which people are excluded or oppressed on the basis of their ability to read and write.

Situations create a need to communicate, and genres arise to fill this need. We call these situations *rhetorical situations* because they present a particular need or opportunity for communication. By *rhetoric*, we mean any attempt to communicate something to an audience—to inform, persuade, challenge, or argue (Chapter 2).

Here are two more literacy narratives to consider. As you read them, think about the genre toolkit questions. What is it? Who reads it? What's it for?

EXAMPLE 2: Abida Sultaan, "Memoirs of a Rebel Princess" (excerpt)

> This excerpt is from the autobiography *Memoirs of a Rebel Princess* by Abida Sultaan (1913–2002), an Indian royal and statesperson whose diaries of the twentieth century histories of India and Pakistan present a unique portrait of a vibrant, active life: she was a hunter, a pilot, a sportswoman, a leader, a mother, and a scholar. The following excerpt relates the story of Sultaan's coming to literacy, when she first learned to read the Koran, and how her family celebrated her feat. As you read, think about any preconceptions you might have about gender, Islam, and politics.

Among Muslims, a child's formal education used to start with the Holy Quran when the child reached the age of 4 years, 4 months, and 4 days; the ceremony being called the Bismillah. Born on 28 August 1913 the fateful beginning of my formal education began on New Year's Day 1918. I was at an age when I had begun to appreciate the significance of dates and looked forward to birthdays, Eids, Christmas or New Year, which brought presents, toys and Christmas trees for us children. For the New Year, I had been promised the "greatest gift" of my life—the Bismillah—and I had been looking forward to it as another joyful celebration. Little did I realize what the event held in store for me. Whatever blessings this auspicious New Year may have spelt for Sarkar Amman [Sultaan's grandmother, and the ruler of Bhopal], the drudgery, torture and misery that I suffered from that day onwards was a long nightmare that had a defining influence on my personality and my attitude to life.

Ever since my birth, I had shared Sarkar Amman's apartments and had been put to sleep in a cot placed next to her bed. Now, with the Bismillah, she started waking me up before dawn to perform the *namaz-i-fajr* [early morning prayers]. I was supposed to do the *wuzoo* [ablutions] in ice-cold water and after prayers, report to her for the Quran.

Still half asleep and with eyes closed, I would stagger into the bathroom and promptly put myself to sleep in the empty bathtub until some anxious attendant pulled me out and splashed water on my face, and hurried me off to an impatient Sarkar Amman.

"Have you said your prayers?" she would sternly demand.

5   "Yes." I would lie!

"Then get your Quran." She would growl.

There never seemed to be an end to my Quran. Either I had to recite my lesson to Sarkar Amman's complete satisfaction, or be kept sitting in front of her, chanting and swaying in typical *mullah* style. As we had no electricity, I would read my lesson under a kerosene lamp until daybreak while Sarkar Amman would remain on her *janamaz* [prayer mat] telling her beads or performing additional prayers until 9 a.m. The slightest mistake would draw an angry response, or a slap, from Sarkar Amman. Further mistakes would lead to pinching, tweaking my nose, ear bashing or even knocking my head against the wall.

Then she would transfer me, my Quran and herself, to her little white mattress spread on the floor in the main courtyard. Surrounded by visitors, petitioners, secretaries, Dr. Johory (her personal physician) and several black boxes containing state papers, she would attend to all of us at the same time. The slightest mistake did not escape her notice and no matter how intensely she was occupied, she would react to any mistake with another sharp slap across my face in full public view.

When I started crying, I would be unable to stop and the more I cried, the more I was slapped. Almost tearing off my ears, she would swing my head from side to side and knock it against the wall. To introduce more variety to her punishments, she would pull at my eyelids, pinch my cheeks, or twist my nose, leaving dark bruises and hard lumps all over my face, my nose, behind my ears and on my eyelids. . . .

On the other hand, there were days when I rebelled after the first slap or two and stopped reading. Then no matter how I was tormented, slapped or pinched, I would not utter a single word even though it meant missing my lunch or dinner. It became a test of wills between grandmother and granddaughter. I would go on strike by standing silently without uttering a sound while Sarkar tried to pinch, slap or shake me into submission. Even as a child the rebel in me could not be suppressed and the standoff usually ended with Sarkar Amman giving up—and starting my lessons later. At 9 p.m. sharp, I had to be in bed, next to Sarkar Amman's, where she would be sitting with several of her ladies, cutting *chhalia* [betel nut] until she was ready for her *tahajjud* prayers. No one spoke unless spoken to by Sarkar Amman. So my early childhood was filled with memories of drudgery and interminable torment at the hands of my grandmother. 10

However, by the tender age of six I had earned the distinction of being the first and only member of Sarkar Amman's family to have completed the Arabic version of the Quran. Bursting with pride and affection, Sarkar Amman generously distributed sweets and rewarded me with a one-day holiday and a kiss! No one had ever kissed me before! Briefly, a light had appeared at the end of a dark, grim tunnel.

By 1921, I had earned my second distinction. I had memorized the *lafzi tarjuma* [the word for word translation of the Quran] before my eighth birthday. As the Quran is in Arabic, which was not taught as a language, the completion of the *lafzi tarjuma* amounted to a remarkable feat of memory achieved by me between the age of six and eight.

Now Sarkar Amman really did explode with pride, "My Abida is incomparable and will be rewarded with a *Nashra* [a ceremony held on completing the first reading of the Quran] ceremony that will put all royal weddings to shame," she announced. I was given a whole week off. It was my first long holiday since the Bismillah four years earlier! After four dark years it seemed that I had stepped out into the sunlight.

EXAMPLE 3: Amy Tan, "Mother Tongue"

> The literacy narrative excerpted here, titled "Mother Tongue," is written by nov-
> elist Amy Tan, daughter of Chinese immigrants. Tan's novels, including *The Joy
> Luck Club*, have won numerous awards. "Mother Tongue" was originally pub-
> lished in *The Threepenny Review*, a literary journal, in 1990.

Recently, I was made keenly aware of the different Englishes I do use. I was giving a
talk to a large group of people, the same talk I had already given to half a dozen other
groups. The nature of the talk was about my writing, my life, and my book, *The Joy
Luck Club*. The talk was going along well enough, until I remembered one major difference that made the whole talk sound wrong. My mother was in the room. And it
was perhaps the first time she had heard me give a lengthy speech, using the kind of
English I have never used with her. I was saying things like, "The intersection of
memory upon imagination" and "There is an aspect of my fiction that relates to thus-
and-thus"—a speech filled with carefully wrought grammatical phrases, burdened,
it suddenly seemed to me, with nominalized forms, past perfect tenses, conditional
phrases, all the forms of standard English that I had learned in school and through
books, the forms of English I did not use at home with my mother.

Just last week, I was walking down the street with my mother, and I again found
myself conscious of the English I was using, the English I do use with her. We were
talking about the price of new and used furniture and I heard myself saying this:
"Not waste money that way." My husband was with us as well, and he didn't notice
any switch in my English. And then I realized why. It's because over the twenty years
we've been together I've often used that same kind of English with him, and sometimes he even uses it with me. It has become our language of intimacy, a different
sort of English that relates to family talk, the language I grew up with.

So you'll have some idea of what this family talk I heard sounds like, I'll quote what
my mother said during a recent conversation which I videotaped and then transcribed. During this conversation, my mother was talking about a political gangster
in Shanghai who had the same last name as her family's, Du, and how the gangster in
his early years wanted to be adopted by her family, which was rich by comparison.
Later, the gangster became more powerful, far richer than my mother's family, and
one day showed up at my mother's wedding to pay his respects. Here's what she said
in part: "Du Yusong having business like fruit stand. Like off the street kind. He is
Du like Du Zong—but not Tsung-ming Island people. The local people call putong,
the river east side, he belong to that side local people. That man want to ask Du Zong
father take him in like become own family. Du Zong father wasn't look down on him,
but didn't take seriously, until that man big like become a mafia. Now important
person, very hard to inviting him. Chinese way, came only to show respect, don't
stay for dinner. Respect for making big celebration, he shows up. Mean gives lots of
respect. Chinese custom. Chinese social life that way. If too important won't have to
stay too long. He come to my wedding. I didn't see, I heard it. I gone to boy's side,
they have YMCA dinner. Chinese age I was nineteen."

You should know that my mother's expressive command of English belies how much she actually understands. She reads the *Forbes* report, listens to *Wall Street Week*, converses daily with her stockbroker, reads all of Shirley MacLaine's books with ease—all kinds of things I can't begin to understand. Yet some of my friends tell me they understand 50 percent of what my mother says. Some say they understand 80 to 90 percent. Some say they understand none of it, as if she were speaking pure Chinese. But to me, my mother's English is perfectly clear, perfectly natural. It's my mother tongue. Her language, as I hear it, is vivid, direct, full of observation and imagery. That was the language that helped shape the way I saw things, expressed things, made sense of the world.

Lately, I've been giving more thought to the kind of English my mother speaks. 5 Like others, I have described it to people as "broken" or "fractured" English. But I wince when I say that. It has always bothered me that I can think of no way to describe it other than "broken," as if it were damaged and needed to be fixed, as if it lacked a certain wholeness and soundness. I've heard other terms used, "limited English," for example. But they seem just as bad, as if everything is limited, including people's perceptions of the limited English speaker.

I know this for a fact, because when I was growing up, my mother's "limited" English limited my perception of her. I was ashamed of her English. I believed that her English reflected the quality of what she had to say, that is, because she expressed them imperfectly her thoughts were imperfect. And I had plenty of empirical evidence to support me: the fact that people in department stores, at banks, and at restaurants did not take her seriously, did not give her good service, pretended not to understand her, or even acted as if they did not hear her.

My mother has long realized the limitations of her English as well. When I was fifteen, she used to have me call people on the phone to pretend I was she. In this guise, I was forced to ask for information or even to complain and yell at people who had been rude to her. One time it was a call to her stockbroker in New York. She had cashed out her small portfolio and it just so happened we were going to go to New York the next week, our very first trip outside California. I had to get on the phone and say in an adolescent voice that was not very convincing, "This is Mrs. Tan."

And my mother was standing in the back whispering loudly, "Why he don't send me check, already two weeks late. So mad he lie to me, losing me money."

And then I said in perfect English, "Yes, I'm getting rather concerned. You had agreed to send the check two weeks ago, but it hasn't arrived."

Then she began to talk more loudly. "What he want, I come to New York tell him 10 front of his boss, you cheating me?" And I was trying to calm her down, make her be quiet, while telling the stockbroker, "I can't tolerate any more excuses. If I don't receive the check immediately, I am going to have to speak to your manager when I'm in New York next week." And sure enough, the following week there we were in front of this astonished stockbroker, and I was sitting there red-faced and quiet, and my mother, the real Mrs. Tan, was shouting at his boss in her impeccable broken English.

We used a similar routine just five days ago, for a situation that was far less humorous. My mother had gone to the hospital for an appointment, to find out about a benign brain tumor a CAT scan had revealed a month ago. She said she had spoken very good English, her best English, no mistakes. Still, she said, the hospital did not apologize when they said they had lost the CAT scan and she had come for nothing. She said they did not seem to have any sympathy when she told them she was anxious to know the exact diagnosis, since her husband and son had both died of brain tumors. She said they would not give her any more information until the next time and she would have to make another appointment for that. So she said she would not leave until the doctor called her daughter. She wouldn't budge. And when the doctor finally called her daughter, me, who spoke in perfect English—lo and behold—we had assurances the CAT scan would be found, promises that a conference call on Monday would be held, and apologies for any suffering my mother had gone through for a most regrettable mistake.

I think my mother's English almost had an effect on limiting my possibilities in life as well. Sociologists and linguists probably will tell you that a person's developing language skills are more influenced by peers. But I do think that the language spoken in the family, especially in immigrant families which are more insular, plays a large role in shaping the language of the child. And I believe that it affected my results on achievement tests, I.Q. tests, and the SAT. While my English skills were never judged as poor, compared to math, English could not be considered my strong suit. In grade school I did moderately well, getting perhaps B's, sometimes B-pluses, in English and scoring perhaps in the sixtieth or seventieth percentile on achievement tests. But those scores were not good enough to override the opinion that my true abilities lay in math and science, because in those areas I achieved A's and scored in the ninetieth percentile or higher.

This was understandable. Math is precise; there is only one correct answer. Whereas, for me at least, the answers on English tests were always a judgment call, a matter of opinion and personal experience. Those tests were constructed around items like fill-in-the-blank sentence completion, such as, "Even though Tom was ____, Mary thought he was ____." And the correct answer always seemed to be the most bland combinations of thoughts, for example, "Even though Tom was shy, Mary thought he was charming" with the grammatical structure "even though" limiting the correct answer to some sort of semantic opposites, so you wouldn't get answers like, "Even though Tom was foolish, Mary thought he was ridiculous." Well, according to my mother, there were very few limitations as to what Tom could have been and what Mary might have thought of him. So I never did well on tests like that.

The same was true with word analogies, pairs of words in which you were supposed to find some sort of logical, semantic relationship—for example, "Sunset is to nightfall as ____ is to ____." And here you would be presented with a list of four possible pairs, one of which showed the same kind of relationship: red is to stoplight, bus is to arrival, chills is to fever, yawn is to boring: Well, I could never think that way. I knew what the tests were asking, but I could not block out of my mind the images already created by the first pair, "sunset is to nightfall"—and I would see a burst of colors against a darkening sky, the moon rising, the lowering of a curtain of stars. And all the other pairs of words—red, bus, stoplight, boring—just threw up a mass of confusing images, making it impossible for me to sort out something as logical as saying: "A sunset precedes nightfall" is the same as "a chill precedes a fever." The only way I would have gotten that answer right would have been to imagine an associative situation, for example, my being disobedient and staying out past sunset, catching a chill at night, which turns into feverish pneumonia as punishment, which indeed did happen to me.

I have been thinking about all this lately, about my mother's English, about achievement tests. Because lately I've been asked, as a writer, why there are not more Asian Americans represented in American literature. Why are there few Asian Americans enrolled in creative writing programs? Why do so many Chinese students go into engineering? Well, these are broad sociological questions I can't begin to answer. But I have noticed in surveys—in fact, just last week—that Asian students, as a whole, always do significantly better on math achievement tests than in English. And this makes me think that there are other Asian-American students whose English spoken in the home might also be described as "broken" or "limited." And perhaps they also have teachers who are steering them away from writing and into math and science, which is what happened to me.

Fortunately, I happen to be rebellious in nature and enjoy the challenge of disproving assumptions made about me. I became an English major my first year in college, after being enrolled as pre-med. I started writing nonfiction as a freelancer the week after I was told by my former boss that writing was my worst skill and I should hone my talents toward account management.

But it wasn't until 1985 that I finally began to write fiction. And at first I wrote using what I thought to be wittily crafted sentences, sentences that would finally prove I had mastery over the English language. Here's an example from the first draft of a story that later made its way into *The Joy Luck Club*, but without this line: "That was my mental quandary in its nascent state." A terrible line, which I can barely pronounce.

Fortunately, for reasons I won't get into today, I later decided I should envision a reader for the stories I would write. And the reader I decided upon was my mother, because these were stories about mothers. So with this reader in mind—and in fact she did read my early drafts—I began to write stories using all the Englishes I grew up with: the English I spoke to my mother, which for lack of a better term might be described as "simple"; the English she used with me, which for lack of a better term might be described as "broken"; my translation of her Chinese, which could certainly be described as "watered down"; and what I imagined to be her translation of her Chinese if she could speak in perfect English, her internal language, and for that I sought to preserve the essence, but neither an English nor a Chinese structure. I wanted to capture what language ability tests can never reveal: her intent, her passion, her imagery, the rhythms of her speech and the nature of her thoughts.

Apart from what any critic had to say about my writing, I knew I had succeeded where it counted when my mother finished reading my book and gave me her verdict: "So easy to read."

EXERCISE 1.1: Evaluate a Literacy Narrative

For Sultaan's or Tan's text, answer the following questions:

1. What is it? Is it a literacy narrative? Why or why not? What features does it share with Douglass's narrative?
2. What kind of person authored this literacy narrative? What can you tell about her personal history just from this story about literacy?
3. Who reads it? (List all possible audiences of this literacy narrative.)
4. What is it for? Why might the author have written this literacy narrative? What kind of message is the author trying to get across with this literacy narrative? Are there multiple messages? What are they?
5. In what ways are literacy and power connected in this literacy narrative?

GROUP ACTIVITY 1.1: Compare Literacy Narratives

Compare all three literacy narratives using the chart below:

	DOUGLASS	SULTAAN	TAN
What is it? (Describe the text.)			
Who reads it? (Name the audiences.)			
What's it for? (List the purposes and messages.)			

B. "What Is It?": Identify Shared Conventions

In the first part of this chapter, you learned how to ask the right questions in order to analyze a genre. Writers analyze genres in order to write more effectively. If you know what you need to communicate in your document and who will be reading it (and what they expect to see), you will write a better document. Asking the right questions helps you to write the most effective document.

In the rest of this chapter, we're going to delve more deeply into these three questions in order to better understand how a genre works.

Experienced writers know that any document they write has to conform—at least somewhat—to the conventions of the document's genre. Otherwise, readers may be confused by the document. Experienced writers familiarize themselves with conventions in order to know what they need to write—and where they can bend the rules.

When you compare the three preceding literacy narratives, can you identify any qualities (or conventions) that the narratives have in common? Let's make a list:

- All three literacy narratives tell a story.
- All three literacy narratives use the first-person singular pronoun "I."
- All three literacy narratives emphasize the connection between literacy and power: Douglass connects education with freedom; Sultaan connects her learning to read the Koran with power struggles with her grandmother; Tan discusses how her limited English "limit[ed] my possibilities in life."
- All three literacy narratives tell a story of transition from illiteracy and disempowerment to literacy and empowerment.

Can you think of anything else?

Although these three literacy narratives cannot fully represent the range and diversity of all existing literacy narratives, we are already getting a picture of what sorts of conventions literacy narratives tend to share.

Despite these similarities, though, the exact form a literacy narrative can take depends on a range of choices an author can make based on readers (or audience), where the document will be published (if applicable), who the author is, and so on.

Accordingly, when you are asked to compose a genre that is new to you (such as a literacy narrative), your best first step is to do a little research. This approach works for academic assignments as well as for workplace assignments. If you look at samples of an unfamiliar genre, you can figure out a lot about your audience, the format your document should take, what to include, and what kind of style to use.

You may be tempted to look for cookie-cutter templates for each genre, like the document templates that come with many word-processing programs. While there are commonalities between examples of a genre, simply filling in a template with your ideas makes writing a pretty boring process. Boring writing leads to bored readers, and bored readers do not pay attention to what they are reading. In addition, templates don't tell you much about the choices you can make to get your message across or to interest your readers.

Everyday Genres

While the literacy narratives you just read were published in books and magazines and intended for wide audiences, other genres are more common.

You may be surprised by how many genres you use for different writing tasks every day. For example, a text message is a genre, as is an email. A grocery list is also a genre, one that has a variety of conventions that a writer can choose from.

When you write these genres, you probably don't follow a template, but you probably do use some shared conventions. For example, your grocery list will obviously include the different items you plan to purchase because listing those items is the purpose of the genre. But the list may be bulleted or numbered, handwritten or typed into a smartphone, organized by supermarket section or according to the recipes you plan to make. These choices make the grocery list genre more flexible than a rigid template.

You might even ignore some of the conventions—perhaps you mix "to do" items in with your grocery list, or maybe you have your own unique way of remembering what items to get.

EXAMPLE 4: **Numbered Grocery List**

Groceries
1. Produce
   - Apples (4)
   - Grapes (1 lb)
   - Bananas (1 bunch)
   - Tomatoes (6)
2. Starches
   - Bread (1 loaf)
   - Tortillas (1 package of 12)
3. Meats
   - Ground beef (2 pounds)
   - Bratwurst (6)

EXAMPLE 5: **Plain Grocery List**

Milk
Eggs
Ice cream
Cheese
Spaghetti sauce
Penne

The next time you write something—anything—think about how many times you have written the same type of document before. Are you writing a genre with shared conventions? What conventions do you tend to follow, and what ones do you ignore? Which conventions are optional, and which ones are necessary?

EXERCISE 1.2: Discover Conventions of Everyday Genres

Make a list of three or four genres you write on a daily or weekly basis (such as a text message, grocery list, or journal entry). For each genre, answer the following questions:

1. What is it?
2. What conventions do you repeat every time you write this genre?
3. What conventions do you change or ignore?
4. How do you decide to change or ignore certain conventions?

MULTIMEDIA EXERCISE 1.1: Compare Written and Digital Conventions

Think of a traditional print genre (such as a letter). Next, think of a genre that is similar to the traditional print genre that only exists online or in a digital format (such as email). Answer the following questions:

1. How are the conventions of the online/digital genre different from the print genre?
2. What conventions does the digital genre share with the print genre?

C. "Who Reads It?": Identify an Audience

Experienced writers know that an effective document satisfies their audiences' expectations for that genre. For example, readers of literacy narratives expect stories that describe how an author learned a new language and simultaneously gained power (financial, political, or cultural).

Thus, when you write any genre (not just genres for school), you must always keep your audience's expectations in mind.

In the workplace, for example, you might prepare a résumé. No audience expects to read a résumé written in crayon on construction paper. Instead, because résumés are usually written by people seeking employment, readers expect résumés to present a polished and professional image. Indeed, readers expect that a résumé will provide information about the writer's work experience, education, and relevant skills in a professionally designed document. However, this does not mean that the résumé is just a template to fill out. Instead, you can creatively shape a résumé to fit within the parameters of the genre based on what your *particular* audience might want to see (Chapter 2).

For instance, you may place your work experience before your education, if your audience is interested in applicants with significant work experience. You may or may not include an "Objective" statement depending on whether résumés in your desired profession tend to use them, or whether you want to highlight a particular skill for your readers. You may include many items about yourself (and write a longer résumé) or you may select only the most persuasive elements to include (and write a shorter résumé). Employers usually expect longer résumés for more advanced positions, since applicants tend to have more work experience. All of these choices depend in part on your audience and what effect you hope to have on it.

For any writing task, you should start by considering your audience, thinking through who your readers will be.

EXERCISE 1.3: Identify the Audience

Pick one of the everyday genres that you identified in Exercise 1.2, or pick another genre that you write on a regular basis. Answer the following questions about the audiences for that genre:

1. Who will read this document? Yourself? Others? A large audience, or small?
2. What will the reader do with this document?
3. How will the reader read it? In print? Online? In a book? On a bulletin board?

MULTIMEDIA EXERCISE 1.2: Identify Your Preferences as a Reader

Think of a genre that you read online on a regular basis, such as a blog or an online newspaper. Answer the following questions from the perspective of the genre's audience:

1. Why do you enjoy reading this genre?
2. When do you usually read this genre and on what device? (For example: On a mobile phone? Tablet? Laptop or desktop computer?)
3. How do the genre's conventions make it easy and/or difficult for you to read the genre on your preferred device?

D. "What's It For?": Identify a Genre's Purpose

When analyzing examples of a genre, think explicitly about the genre's purpose or purposes. Why does this genre exist? What need does it fulfill, or what task does it accomplish?

Genres emerge when writers and readers need to address a situation that occurs over and over again. For example, one of the recurring needs met by the literacy narrative genre today is the validation of nonstandard language practices and immigrant dialects, as Amy Tan does in "Mother Tongue."

Now, think about the purposes of some everyday genres that you are familiar with. For example, the purpose of an invitation is to inform readers about the place, time, and reason for an event, and to encourage them to attend. The genre of the invitation is continually evolving to keep pace with new kinds of technology (like Evites or Facebook "events") and changing social conventions (like parties to celebrate divorces, or funerals for pets).

The purpose of another everyday genre, the restaurant menu, is to inform diners about the food options available at the restaurant and to encourage customers to purchase them. Again, dining out is a common event, so it is not surprising that the genre of the menu has developed to address that purpose and that it continues to evolve as technology evolves (for example, ordering food from an online menu to have delivered to your home).

When you are assigned to write an unfamiliar genre (either in a course or in the workplace), and you are examining samples of the genre for guidance, think about what other authors who have written the genre intended their documents to do.

EXERCISE 1.4: Identify a Genre's Purpose

Pick one of the everyday genres that you encounter often. Answer the following questions:

1. What need does this genre address? What problem does this genre seek to fix?
2. How do you know, based solely on the document you are reading?

MULTIMEDIA EXERCISE 1.3: Identify an Online Author's Purpose

Pick one of the online genres that you read every day (such as a blog or social network newsfeed). Answer the questions in Exercise 1.4.

E. Conclusion

In this chapter, we have discussed three basic questions you can use when you encounter a new genre. These three questions are the basis of the "genre toolkit."

Ask Questions

What is it?

Who reads it?

What's it for?

The three genre toolkit questions help you begin to analyze a genre. But what happens when you are in a situation where you need to write a document yourself? In Chapter 2, you will learn how to assess your own rhetorical situation and figure out where you stand.

F. Chapter Project: Write a Literacy Narrative

For this chapter project, you will write a literacy narrative. Remember, a literacy narrative is a first-person story about learning to read or write that often highlights the power the narrator gains from literacy.

Start by thinking of moments in your life when you encountered barriers posed by language. These moments might have occurred when you were a child, before you learned to read or write. They might have occurred as you learned more advanced literacy skills in school. They might have occurred when you encountered a foreign language or unfamiliar dialect.

Then, think about your audience and purpose. Who might read your narrative? What message do you want to get across?

Take another look at the examples of literacy narratives in this chapter (and perhaps search online for additional examples of literacy narratives) to determine what conventions of literacy narratives you'd like to use—and which you might like to ignore—based on your own purpose and audience for this project.

Multimedia Version

A narrative can be told using a combination of text, images, and sound. Using software that allows you to combine multimedia features, such as Microsoft PowerPoint or Prezi, tell your literacy narrative in a multimedia fashion.

Discovering Rhetorical Situations

In Chapter 1, you learned the three genre toolkit questions: "What is it?" "Who reads it?" "What's it for?" You learned how to use these three questions when you encounter an unfamiliar genre for the first time to discover a genre's conventions, audience, and purpose.

This chapter will walk you through the steps to perform before writing any genre. You will need to discover your *rhetorical situation*: your purpose, role, audience, and timing.

A. Discovering Your Rhetorical Situation

In this chapter you will learn how to identify a rhetorical situation when writing a particular document. First, read the sample student writing in Example 1, written for an English composition class, and then use the three genre toolkit questions from Chapter 1 to discover the genre.

EXAMPLE 1: Aliyah's "Public Problem"

Aliyah Forsyth
English 102
Week 11

> Prompt: What contemporary public problem do you, as a college student, feel most prepared to do something about, and why?

As a college student, I don't have a lot of power. I don't have a lot of money, and I don't

have a job. I don't even have a car. I can't get a job that would give me money or societal

power without a college degree, so right now I have to just focus on school.

However, I am very aware of public problems such as climate change, animal abuse, domestic violence, racism/sexism/heterosexism, and others. I read about these problems online, on my favorite news sites such as Jezebel.com and through links my friends share on Facebook. I like to think that I'm a politically aware person. I just feel powerless because of my place in life.

That being said, I do think there are ways that college students can help address public problems and make the world a better place, despite our lack of power/money/transportation (ha ha). For example, even just educating our fellow students about a cause that is important is an important first step in changing things. Holding "teach-ins" in the student union, for example, about climate change, can help teach people that climate change is a real scientific fact, and not "just" a "theory" as deniers argue. Hosting screenings of documentaries on climate change and discussions afterwards would help too. We could even invite climate scientists and researchers to come give talks on campus to help educate students and the wider community further.

Basically, although I'm not prepared to spend a lot of money or use powerful influence to get things done, I can organize a relatively large community of young people—and young people have energy and the desire to shape the world to make it better for us. In many ways, this desire is the greatest power there is.

EXAMPLE 2: Aliyah's "Observations"

Aliyah Forsyth
English 102
Week 12

Prompt: Go to a place on campus that you have never visited before and observe for thirty minutes or more, taking notes. Reflect on your observations.

Today I went to the lobby of the nursing school on campus. The nursing school is a newer building, with lots of tall windows that create an atrium feeling when you first enter the lobby. There are plants all over the atrium-lobby, and benches too. I sat on one of these benches to observe.

The nursing students were easy to spot. They all wear the same green scrub uniforms with the logo of the nursing school embroidered on their chest pockets. The nursing professors were harder to spot. Some were obvious, because they wore scrubs and name-tags, but their scrubs were navy blue like the scrubs of the nurses that work in the hospital. There were also professors that were dressed in suits or other dress-clothes; these professors went into lecture halls to teach more traditional classes. Mostly, people in the lobby were coming and going from classes and other rooms in the building. But some people sat on benches and talked, or went into the snack bar area to grab cups of coffee together.

The most striking thing I noticed was the racial and gender diversity among the students. I think that most people have a preconceived notion that all nurses are older white women. But the nurses I saw were of all different races, and more surprising, they were both men and women. Yes, the women outnumbered the men, probably 60-40 if I had to guess, but for a field that has historically been dominated by women, that break-down was a surprise to me. I'd be interested in learning more about how men's entrance into the nursing profession has affected the profession in terms of public respect for nursing, but also how it has affected women's ability to get good jobs in nursing. In other words, do the male nurses tend to get the better jobs in nursing like they do in other professions?

USE THE TOOLKIT

Let's use the three genre toolkit questions from Chapter 1 to learn more about the genre of the student writing just presented.

What Is It?

These two sample texts were written by a college student, Aliyah Forsyth, for her English composition class. Aliyah labeled each piece of writing by week ("Week 11" and "Week 12"), which suggests that this kind of writing was something she did on a weekly basis for class. At the beginning of each piece is a prompt from the instructor.

The pieces themselves are relatively short (about 300 words) and are written in an informal style (Chapter 21). Aliyah uses the word "I" a lot, focusing on her own thoughts, observations, ideas, and reflections.

These two pieces of writings are *journal entries*, excerpted from Aliyah's weekly journal that she wrote for her composition class. A typical journal entry uses a two-step sequence. First, the author describes or observes something, and then the author reflects upon that description or observation.

Who Reads It?

In composition courses, typically only the author of journal entries and the author's instructor will read them. For example, Aliyah's journal will be read by Aliyah and by Aliyah's instructor. Some instructors allow students to keep their journals entirely private.

Other types of journals are more widely read, as we will see later in the chapter.

What's It For?

A journal for a composition class can have many different purposes. One purpose is to practice writing and build good writing habits. Another is to help the student to discover his or her ideas about a topic. Yet another is to prepare for longer writing projects for the class. For example, Aliyah's journal entry for Week 12 might be laying the groundwork for a research paper (Chapter 11) on gender changes in the nursing workforce.

Now that we have discovered the genre of the journal entry, let's turn to the tools that you will need in order to write one yourself.

Use the Rhetorical Situation

Every time you write a genre, you need to pay attention to your rhetorical situation. An author's rhetorical situation is made up of these four things:

1. the author's purpose (Chapter 1)
2. the author's role
3. the audience's needs
4. the document's timing

Let's say that your instructor has asked you to write a journal entry that reflects upon a reading for class. In this situation, the journal entry will only be shared with your instructor.

The author's purpose arises from the situation. The rhetorical situation helps create the purpose for a writer. A good communicator *recognizes* the rhetorical situation, *selects* the appropriate genre for the situation, and *considers* how to use that genre to fulfill his or her purpose.

Let's consider our hypothetical journal entry. While the general purpose of a journal entry is to describe and reflect upon the topic at hand (for example, a reading, an event, a current issue, or a film), you might narrow down that general purpose to fit a particular situation.

You can ask yourself, "What is my own goal for this document?"

For example, you will want to relate your journal entry to the themes, concepts, and vocabulary discussed in the particular class you are writing it for. You might use the journal entry in preparation for other, more formal writing, such as a longer essay.

Your role as an author determines the stance you take when writing. The rhetorical situation also influences your stance as a writer—the attitudes and roles you are likely to take on.

If you are asked to write a journal entry for a class, then your role is one of student. However, journals serve a variety of other purposes as well and are written by a variety of authors. Novelists, researchers, investigators, and others use journals to describe and reflect on their writing, their research progress, and their discoveries.

Depending on the subject area of your class, you might be asked to keep a research journal, a reading journal, an observation journal, or another kind of discipline-specific journal. The type of journal your teacher asks you to keep helps determine the stance you will take as the author of the journal. An observation journal for a criminal justice class might be more objective in tone, for example, whereas a reading-response journal for a world literature class might be highly reflective and opinionated.

The audience's needs impose limits on how a document is created and shared.   The rhetorical situation also suggests how your audience will respond to and use your document.

Many journal entries are only read by the author and, perhaps, the author's supervisor (or instructor). If the only reader of a journal will be the author, then the author has freedom to create a document that is meaningful only to him or her. Many authors keep journals that are only read by the author. The journal is a place where the author can generate ideas, reflect on current issues, and discover ideas that the author might want to write about. If the only audience of a journal is the author, then the author need only write in a fashion that the author can understand. Be sure that you can read your handwriting; if you use abbreviations, be sure that you will be able to understand them later when you revisit your journal entries.

If a journal entry will be shared with other readers, even with only *one* other reader, then the author has a duty to ensure that the document will be easy for an audience to understand. Write neatly, or type. Avoid abbreviations except for those that you are certain your audience will understand.

The document's timing determines what is "appropriate."   As an author, you always want to have good timing.

For example, your journal entry may have a deadline. Your professor may ask you to turn something in by a certain time so that he or she has time to read it before class.

As you will learn later in this chapter, sometimes timing is out of a writer's control.

Here is an entry from the journal of the Lewis and Clark Expedition, written by co-leader Meriwether Lewis on Monday, September 17, 1804. Keep in mind that the spelling and other "errors" in the document are original to the journals. Spelling and punctuation were less standardized in the era of this journal. The authors kept this journal as a public record of an important exploration of the North American continent.

EXAMPLE 3: **Lewis and Clark Journal (excerpt)**

Having for many days past confined myself to the boat, I determined to devote this day to amuse myself on shore with my gun and view the interior of the country lying between the river and the Corvus Creek—accordingly before sunrise I set out with six of my best hunters, two of whom I dispatched to the lower side of Corvus creek, two with orders to hunt the bottoms and woodland on the river, while I retained two others to acompany me in the intermediate country.

one quarter of a mile in rear of our camp which was situated in a fine open grove of cotton wood passed a grove of plumb trees loaded with fruit and now ripe. observed but little difference between this fruit and that of a similar kind common to the Atlantic States. the trees are smaller and more thickly set. this forrest of plumb trees garnish a plain about 20 feet more lelivated than that on which we were encamped; this plain extends back about a mile to the foot of the hills one mile distant and to which it is gradually ascending this plane extends with the same bredth from the creek below to the distance of near three miles above parrallel with the river, and is intirely occupied by the burrows of the *barking squril* hertefore discribed; this anamal appears here in infinite numbers, and the shortness and virdue [verdure] of grass gave the plain the appearance throughout it's whole extent of beatifull bowlinggreen in fine order. it's aspect is S. E. a great number of wolves of the small kind, halks and some pole-cats were to be seen. I presume that those anamals feed on this squirril.—

found the country in every direction for about three miles intersected with deep revenes and steep irregular hills of 100 to 200 feet high; at the tops of these hills the country breakes [off] as usual into a fine leavel plain extending as far as the eye can reach. from this plane I had an extensive view of the river below, and the irregular hills which border the opposite sides of the river and creek. the surrounding country had been birnt about a month before and young grass had now sprung up to hight of 4 Inches presenting the live green of the spring. to the West a high range of hills, strech across the country from N. to S and appeared distant about 20 Miles; they are not very extensive as I could plainly observe their rise and termination no rock appeared on them and the sides were covered with virdue similar to that of the plains this senery already rich pleasing and beatiful, was still farther hightened by immence herds of Buffaloe deer Elk and Antelopes which we saw in every direction feeding on the hills and plains. I do not think I exagerate when I estimate the number of Buffaloe which could be compreed at one view to amount to 3000.

my object was if possible to kill a female Antelope having already procured a male; I pursued my rout on this plain to the west flanked by my two hunters untill eight in the morning when I made the signal for them to come to me which they did shortly after. we rested our selves about half an hour, and regailed ourselves on half a bisquit each and some jirk of Elk which we had taken the precaution to put in our pouches in the morning before we set out, and drank of the water of a small pool which had collected on this plain from the rains which had fallen some days before. We had now after various windings in pursuit of several herds of antelopes which we had seen on our way made the distance of about eight miles from our camp.

5   we found the Antelope extreemly shye and watchfull insomuch that we had been unable to get a shot at them; when at rest they generally seelect the most elivated point in the neighbourhood, and as they are watchfull and extreemly quick of sight and their sense of smelling very accute it is almost impossible to approach them within gunshot; in short they will frequently discover and flee from you at the distance of three miles. I had this day an opportunity of witnessing the agility and superior fleetness of this anamal which was to me really astonishing. I had pursued and twice surprised a small herd of seven, in the first instance they did not discover me distinctly and therefore did not run at full speed, tho' they took care before they rested to gain an elivated point where it was impossible to approach them under cover except in one direction and that happened to be in the direction from which the wind blew towards them; bad as the chance to approach them was, I made the best of my way towards them, frequently peeping over the ridge with which I took care to conceal myself from their view

the male, of which there was but one, frequently incircled the summit of the hill on which the females stood in a group, as if to look out for the approach of danger. I got within about 200 paces of them when they smelt me and fled; I gained the top of the eminece on which they stood, as soon as possible from whence I had an extensive view of the country

the antilopes which had disappeared in a steep revesne now appeared at the distance of about three miles on the side of a ridge which passed obliquely across me and extended about four miles. so soon had these antelopes gained the distance at which they had again appeared to my view I doubted at ferst that they were the same that I had just surprised, but my doubts soon vanished when I beheld the rapidity of their flight along the ridge before me

it appeared reather the rappid flight of birds than the motion of quadrupeds. I think I can safely venture the asscertion that the speed of this anamal is equal if not superior to that of the finest blooded courser.

EXERCISE 2.1: Discover the Situation of a Journal Entry

Answer the following questions to help you figure out the rhetorical situation of Lewis's journal entry.

1. What is the author's purpose?
2. What is the author's role and potential stance?
3. Who are potential audiences? What are the audience's needs?
4. When would this document's timing be best?

MULTIMEDIA EXERCISE 2.1: Discover Other Kinds of Journals

Journals can be used in a variety of contexts. Using an Internet search engine, search for "famous diarists." ("Diary" is another word for journal.) Select an online diary or journal stored on a reliable website (such as a government, library, or university website), and read some entries.

Answer the following questions about the journal entries that you read:

1. What is the author's purpose?
2. What is the author's role and potential stance?
3. What are the audience's needs?
4. When would this document's timing be best?

B. Considering Your Purpose

In most cases, your purpose as an author will fit into one of the following categories:

- To persuade
- To argue
- To inform
- To entertain

- To explain
- To express
- To analyze

You'll find that these purposes tend to arise from different kinds of rhetorical situations and match with certain kinds of genres.

For example, what kind of document would you write if you wanted to express yourself? A journal entry, blog post, or even a status update on a social networking site would all be likely choices. You probably wouldn't write a formal report to express yourself.

When you are in a particular rhetorical situation, though, your purpose will be even more specific. Let's say you are upset that your roommate has left her dirty dishes in the sink for the fifth time this week. You might write an angry entry in your diary with the purpose of expressing your frustration at your roommate.

It is especially important to think about purpose when a college teacher gives you a writing assignment. Sometimes, the purpose may be embedded in an assignment description, and unless you can identify what that purpose is, you may miss the mark completely.

EXERCISE 2.2: Identify an Assignment's Purpose

Here are a few sample assignments. Can you identify the purpose(s) for each?

1. "Write an editorial for the school newspaper in which you support or dispute the current proposal to cut the budget for recreational sports."
2. "Write an essay in which you interpret the symbolism in *The Lord of the Flies.*"
3. "Create a cartoon that pokes fun at a stereotype of our campus."
4. "Design a brochure to inform students about a health issue they may encounter."
5. "Write a paragraph in which you describe how RNA transcription works."
6. "Write a blog post in which you share your personal experience with volunteering."
7. "Design an advertisement to encourage students to attend the health fair next week."

EXERCISE 2.3: Match the Purpose with a Likely Genre

For each of the purposes listed here, suggest one or two genres that might fit that purpose.

Purpose	Likely Genre
Persuade	
Argue	
Inform	
Entertain	
Explain	
Analyze	

C. Identifying an Author's Role

The author's role is the position an author occupies when writing. Often, in college classes, you will write in the role of "student." In other cases, both in class and out of class, you may take on a different kind of role—as an expert, a member of a particular community, a citizen, an employee, and so on. These are all different roles that shape how you write.

When you write a document, you should also think about how you want to come across to your readers. Here are three questions to ask yourself to help you identify your role as an author in any particular rhetorical situation:

1. Do I come across as likeable? Does it matter if I do?
2. Am I an expert or authority on the subject I'm writing about? (And, do I want to be perceived as one?) Do I come across as accurate, reasonable, and rational?
3. Do I come across as fair, ethical, and trustworthy?

Let's use an example to examine the kinds of choices you might make as an author. Suppose you purchased a pair of expensive sunglasses while on vacation in another state. As soon as you returned home, the frames broke during normal use. You can't return the sunglasses to the store because it is a small boutique and doesn't accept returns. Your only recourse is to write to the manufacturer to convince them to send you another pair.

This type of letter or email is often called a "product complaint" or simply a "complaint." There are different strategies that you might want to take with such a complaint, including how you want to come across as an author.

Let's look at the three author questions.

Likeability

You are writing this email complaint because the company sold you a defective product. On one hand, you have a right to be angry, or at least annoyed. On the other hand, if you come across as unlikeable in your message, then the person who receives the message may be less likely to help you.

Expertise and Reasonableness

In this situation, you will want to describe with a degree of certainty and reasonableness just how the sunglasses broke. You want to convince your reader that the breaking is not your fault. Since you are the expert in how the sunglasses broke you need to convey this information accurately to your reader.

Fairness and Trustworthiness

You want your reader to believe what you have written about their product's flaws. Therefore, you need to come across as fair and trustworthy. You don't want to be perceived as a person who would lie about how the sunglasses broke and blame the company unfairly.

As you can see, writing an effective complaint requires a lot of thought about your role as an author.

Additionally, you will need to take into account the best way to deliver your complaint to the company: via mail, via fax, or via email. Often, companies provide information for how they would prefer to receive a complaint, often on their websites. But, you might choose to bypass an online automated complaint system and send a paper letter instead, because sending a paper letter carries a certain weight, even in our digital age.

EXERCISE 2.4: Examine the Author's Role in a Cover Letter

Suppose you are writing a cover letter for an internship. Using the three author questions, think about how you would write an effective cover letter.

1. Do I come across as likeable? Does it matter if I do?
2. Am I an expert or authority on the subject I'm writing about? (And, do I want to be perceived as one?) Do I come across as reasonable and rational?
3. Do I come across as fair, ethical, and trustworthy?

D. Analyzing an Audience's Needs

Figuring out your role as an author is closely tied to your audience's needs. Before selecting an appropriate genre and creating an appropriate communication, an author must ask the following questions:

1. What level of expertise does the audience have? (Are they scientists, nonscientists, or policy makers? Managers? Executives?)
2. What attitudes does the audience have to this topic?
3. What does the audience know already? What don't they know?
4. What responsibilities do they have? How much decision-making power do they have?

Let's return to the product complaint to examine each of the audience's needs.

Expertise

Your readers will have good expertise of their sunglass product, or at least they should. In fact, in this rhetorical situation, they are the experts and you are the non-expert—at least when it comes to sunglass technology. Now, if you were an expert in high-tech plastics, you might have more expertise than your readers in that area, and you might be able to explain a weakness in their sunglass design.

Attitudes

You can probably expect that your readers will have some degree of pride in their product, and this pride might cause them to be defensive (in the worst-case scenario). Or, your readers might be very interested in keeping you happy as a customer (in the best-case scenario). You can write a more effective letter if you keep your audience's potential attitude in mind, and try to address those concerns. You might try to avoid criticizing the product in overly negative terms (call it "faulty" rather than "a piece of junk"), or you might mention your high opinion of the company in general.

Knowledge

Your readers will have good knowledge about their product in general but will not have good knowledge of how your particular pair of sunglasses broke. You can build on their expertise about their products to explain how and where the break occurred.

Responsibility and Power

If you've ever asked to "speak with someone's supervisor," you were seeking an audience with responsibility—that is, power. When writing your complaint letter, you will need to be sure to address the letter to the proper person or group—the readers with the appropriate level of responsibility and power. Ask yourself: who is capable of replacing my sunglasses? You might need to research the company's website in order to find the right audience for your letter.

EXERCISE 2.5: Analyze Your Audience

Let's return to the audience of the cover letter for the internship: the committee that is responsible for hiring you for the internship. Conduct an audience analysis for this audience.

1. What level of expertise does the committee have?
2. What attitudes do committee members have to the topic?
3. What does the committee know or not know?
4. What responsibilities does the committee have?

E. Discovering Timing

Good communication has good timing. For example, say you are an expert on hurricanes. If you publish a book on hurricanes at the same time as a major hurricane event, then your book will probably sell more copies. This is because more readers will be interested in your topic due to its timeliness.

Thus, when you are evaluating the rhetorical situation of a document, you need to examine when the communication occurs and what else is occurring at the same time. Does the communication have good timing?

Sometimes a communication has terrible timing—and often by no fault of the authors. For instance, in June 2011, the government of Northern Ireland ran a large, expensive advertisement in an issue of a national magazine in the United States encouraging tourism to Belfast. The advertisement was probably designed and arranged for publication weeks or even months before it appeared.

Then, one week before the publication of the advertisement, violent riots broke out in Belfast, making the international news. Few people would want to travel to Belfast given this risk of unpredictable violence. Thus, through no fault of its own, the advertisement had terrible timing.

This example also demonstrates how timing can be affected by place. Suppose the authors of the tourism advertisement chose to focus on another part of Northern Ireland instead of Belfast—say, Antrim or the Walled City of Derry. The audience of the advertisement would be less likely to associate the advertisement with the violence in Belfast (which is only one city in the region), and the advertisement would have had better timing.

Remember, certain rhetorical situations call for certain timely communications. Unlike the authors of the Northern Ireland advertisement, authors often have control over the timeliness of a communication. As an author, strive to have good timing—but remember that timing is not always under your control.

For example, if a friend has a birthday in two weeks, you might mail a birthday card, knowing that there is adequate time for the card to arrive before your friend's birthday. If the birthday slipped your mind and you only have one day, you might send an e-card instead, because it will arrive on time.

EXERCISE 2.6: Discover Timely Genres

Suppose that you own a stationery store. Three clients come in for assistance with each of the following wedding situations. Brainstorm any timely genres that you can imagine would be appropriate. You might list multiple answers for each situation.

- Client #1: A large wedding occurring in six months
- Client #2: A small wedding occurring in three weeks
- Client #3: An elopement that occurred last week

MULTIMEDIA EXERCISE 2.2: Discover Timely Genres Online

Scientists, contrary to popular opinion, do a lot of writing. But you might not be familiar with the type of writing that a scientist might do in the following situations. Research each of these situations, using reliable online resources, and list the types of genres that would be appropriate. Notice that each of these situations occurs at a different *time* in the research process.

- Situation #1: A scientist has a new scientific research project that needs funding.
- Situation #2: A scientist has results of a research project that need to be vetted by other experts.
- Situation #3: A scientist has findings of a research project that need to be publicly shared.

GROUP ACTIVITY 2.1: Timely Genres in Advertising

Suppose that your group owns a public relations firm. You have been approached by an ice cream shop for help launching their business. As a group, brainstorm the types of genres that you might design for your clients at different times. Use the Internet to conduct research on possible genres.

- Situation #1: The company wants a document to create interest in their ice cream shop—the month before it opens.
- Situation #2: The company wants a document to advertise a special they are having for their first week of business—next week.
- Situation #3: The company wants a document to get people to attend their Grand Opening—today.

F. Conclusion

In this chapter, you have learned that you need to take into account your rhetorical situation whenever you write a genre. You learned how to think about your purpose within a rhetorical situation, how to think about your role as an author, how to analyze an audience's needs, and how to take into account timing when writing. These four elements, along with the document's purpose, make up a rhetorical situation.

In Chapter 1, you learned about the three genre toolkit questions to ask when you encounter an unfamiliar genre for the first time. Here, you learned how to assess your rhetorical situation when sitting down to write a genre. In Chapter 3, you will learn how write a new genre with confidence.

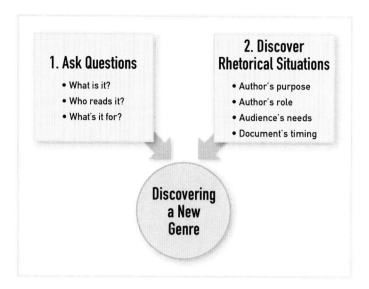

Figure 2.1
The Genre Toolkit

G. Chapter Project: Write Journal Entries

Keeping a journal for yourself can be a good way to practice writing, to keep track of observations and research, and to generate ideas for future writing projects.

Remember, the two basic steps for writing a journal entry are these: first, describe or observe; second, reflect on your description or observation.

For the first part of this chapter project, write three journal entries about three recent movies that you have seen, three recent books that you have read, or three different songs that you have listened to. After you have written your three journal entries (each a minimum of 300 words), do the following:

- Revise your journal entries as though you were going to publish them on a blog for others to read.
- Pay attention to how your journal entries change as your audience changes.
- Assess the rhetorical situation for your journal entries using Table 2.1.

Table 2.1 Journal Entry Analysis Chart

	Private Journal Entries	Blog Journal Entries
What is the purpose of this journal entry?		
What is your stance as author?		
Who will your audience be?		
How can you best address your audience's needs?		
How can you make these journal entries timely?		

Writing New Genres

In the previous chapters, you have learned how to discover a new genre and to discover the rhetorical situation surrounding it, including the purpose, role, audience, and timing. In this chapter, you will learn how to study, in more detail, examples of a genre to determine its design, organization, content, and style features so that you can write that genre yourself.

A. Writing a New Genre

First, read this short essay.

EXAMPLE 1: Claire Zhang, "Amy Tan Phase" (excerpt)

Sometime in the past school year, a group of Chinese tourists stopped me as I was crossing Elm Street to walk back to Old Campus. A woman asked me, in Chinese—"你会说中文吗?" *Can you speak Chinese?* I nodded vigorously and answered, "可以!" *I can!* The exclamation point is telling. That this woman recognized that I was Chinese, simply from my appearance, excited me. I was thinking *yes! Yes! I am like you! I speak your language, my language, our language!* She asked me where they could eat lunch. The moment I tried to point them in the direction of Church Street, I realized I had forgotten how to say some very basic things like *turn right*, and it took me a few seconds to remember. The words tripped out of my mouth and felt foreign and awkward on my tongue. I felt ashamed and sad, though they understood me and tottered off to where I had directed them, I suddenly noticed the rust forming on the language that had been my first. The language that is supposed to be mine. I'm losing it. I've been losing it. Little things will continue to remind me of this. I will try to write a basic sentence and find I can't remember the simplest characters. I won't recognize or be able to read some phrases in the level 1 Chinese textbook. Perhaps one of the biggest jolts is to realize that so many of my friends, who aren't Chinese—外国人 *waiguoren*, foreigner,— can speak Chinese better than I can, know more than I do. Being away from home for the year also made me realize another thing—I *miss* Chinese-ness. [. . .]

Growing up, I never felt exactly torn between two different cultures, the way characters in novels frequently described. I wasn't aware enough to notice it at the time. I naively invited all my American friends over to my home. Friends would occasionally make faces and ask what random dishes in our refrigerator might be, but it never bothered me. [. . .]

Looking back on it now, the most amazing thing is how all these events failed to make me realize that I was somewhat different from everyone else. My neighbor would ask me why I didn't wear Limited Too clothes, and I would quite candidly tell her that they were too expensive, which is what my mother told me, and hence, must be true. I marveled at the fact that my neighbor had a drawer full of at least 20 different swimsuits, when I only had two swimsuits, and how she had a room littered with Beanie Babies and Build-A-Bear bears, when I only had one Build-A-Bear bear that I got as a birthday present. But I believed it wholeheartedly and genuinely when my mother said that that was a waste of money and I didn't need it. I got into a fight with my neighbor about whether college was necessary to be successful in life, she insisting that she knew people who didn't go to college and had good jobs, and I deafly repeating the very stereotypical mantra of my Chinese parents—you have to get good grades and get into a good college. My obliviousness and naiveté saved my early childhood self-esteem.

This wouldn't last long. I slowly began to notice the differences. It came at first, when I missed pop culture references that were clearly obvious to everybody else, such as discussion about the latest Lizzie McGuire episode or when Avril Lavigne's new album was blasted at a birthday party. I would simply pretend I knew what everybody was talking about and then learn what I needed to in the privacy of my home, using the internet or television. I learned the common, socially accepted opinions about various things. I would repeat these when the subject came up. I observed how my friends or television characters interacted or acted in certain situations and mimicked them. I went on a Limited Too shopping spree before middle school with my mother. This was enough for me, and I felt that I fit in decently—though again, in retrospect, I don't think I did nearly as good a job as I felt at the time. The learning process was still very slow going. I wore tourist t-shirts and skirt ensembles with ugly sneakers to middle school, again completely unaware of how dorky I clearly was.

It was somewhere in late eighth grade, though I couldn't point to a specific moment, where I gained some sort of consciousness at realizing that I was rather socially awkward because I just didn't *know* things and wasn't comfortable with what a lot of my classmates thought was fun and cool. In middle and elementary school, I had never indulged in the weird American thing called "hanging out." No one had ever invited me, and I had always been busy and unwilling to attend even if I was invited to a birthday party. I felt uncomfortable at these things, and I preferred to spend time with my Chinese friends. I went to Chinese parties, went on vacations and trips with my Chinese friends, and played tennis with them. I felt comfortable in their presence, more confident and sure of myself. I wasn't putting on a play or mimicking anyone, in fact I was the popular and cool one. A middle school friend kept inviting me to see the Harry Potter movie with her over the summer after middle school, but I made up all sorts of excuses and then flat out ignored her until she stopped asking. 5

In high school, I made new friends, and I was invited to hang out—a lot. At first, it was foreign, but my old plan of pretending I knew what was going on and then going home to research, if necessary, worked well. I learned that movie and a meal were common ways to hang out, and that girls liked to go shopping together at the mall—a novelty considering my mother and I typically only went shopping at big discount stores like Target or Ross or JCPenny, and shopping days were only once-in-a-while planned affairs when necessary. I became more familiar with the new mall names that everybody liked to wear instead of Limited Too: American Eagle, Abercrombie, and Aeropostale. I observed my friend to understand how shopping as a teenage American girl was conducted: walk through the store, pick out clothes that look appealing, go in the dressing room to try them on, show them to your shopping partner, receive compliments and compliment your shopping partner's choice, then buy it. It was bizarre not shopping with my mom, who used to essentially pick my clothing for me, and buying clothes for fun was a strange concept—but I liked it. [. . .]

In the course of these changes, I felt myself drifting away from my old Chinese friends. I attempted to incorporate the new fun things I had learned into my time with the Chinese group. I tried to take them downtown to hang out, instead of spending time inside the house. They were bored by my desire to browse Urban Outfitters before the movie started, and were unenthused at the idea of stopping by the Cheesecake Factory after the movie to have some cheesecake and snacks and conversation—it was a waste of money. When we vacationed on a cruise together, I proposed we go to the teen dance party, but was rejected because nobody wanted to dance. I was growing increasingly bored at Chinese parties, where we mostly sat around and watched movies or talked about inane things like school and more school and school-related things. I now preferred spending time with my American friends. They were more fun, more spontaneous, more interesting. Eventually, I attended the Chinese parties less and less frequently until I stopped going altogether. I continued to indulge in more American things, going out more frequently, learning to apply makeup and paying more attention to my fashion style. When I started dating an American boy in late junior year, I felt like I had truly jumped off the deep end. [. . .]

While home had always been the more dominant place I spent my time, with the start of high school senior year and lots of American friends to hang out with every afternoon, I started skipping my mother's daily dinners and eating a lot of American food. I would leave the house and be out and about all day, returning home in the darkness when everyone in my house had gone to sleep. [. . .]

I think the most valuable thing my American friends gave me was American confidence and outspokenness, the belief in expressing and being true to yourself without caring what other people think about you—not worrying constantly about your "face." Once, I had tried to hide and pretend I didn't care about anything in an attempt to never be judged by anyone. People literally called me a robot. But I am not a robot, and I have since learned that it is okay to be more than a robot. I learned to not care so much about the judgments of others. I love and I feel and I think and I dream and I hate and I am proud of all of this—this is me, this is my identity.

10   Part of that identity, is, and forever will be, Chinese, and I don't want to forget that. Traditional Chinese values call for a balance, the yin and the yang. I am composed of two cultures—American and Chinese. It's been, and always will be, a struggle trying to juggle these two. I've spent so long trying to cultivate the American, my previously weaker side, but now it's time to embrace openly the other weakening

side too, to be true to this part of my self. This isn't my Amy Tan phase. This is who I am.

- -

Now, take a look at the following student texts, which were written in response to an assignment for an anthropology course. What kind of documents are these?

- -

EXAMPLE 2: Louisa Rodriguez, "Identity in Context"

Growing up in Guatemala, I never felt particularly Latina. Sure, we spoke Spanish at home and ate our share of beans and tortillas, but my parents also wanted me to leave Guatemala one day to go to America. I went to an "American" private school with courses taught in English, brought home clothes from Aeropostale and Abercrombie during our yearly trips to Miami, and was more interested in listening to Lady Gaga or Taylor Swift than the salsa and reggaeton music popular in Guatemala. But when I came to the United States last year for a high school exchange program, I suddenly found myself embracing my Latin culture. It wasn't just that my new classmates wanted me to practice Spanish with them or tell them about my country. It was that everything I'd been striving for in Guatemala—like dressing in American clothes and listening to American music—no longer made me different. Being Guatemalan made me different, and I liked that. I learned, like Claire Zhang did in her essay "Amy Tan Phase," that identity is selective. It all depends on the context. Zhang's essay suggests that identity isn't something we have, it is something we do in different situations.

While she was growing up, Zhang wanted to downplay her Chinese heritage and become more American. In grade school and high school, when she was surrounded by her family and friends from Chinese School, she desired to be more like her American classmates.

She studied American culture the way an anthropologist would. When a reference to a tv show or celebrity came up, she writes, "I would simply pretend I knew what everybody was talking about and then learn what I needed to in the privacy of my home, using the internet or television." As a child growing up in a Chinese family, she found American culture new and different. In this context, Zhang wanted to de-emphasize her Chinese culture, since she was exposed to it everyday, and learn more about the things her American classmates liked. I felt the same way as a kid growing up in Guatemala. I would pore over Seventeen magazines I bought in Miami, cutting out pictures of styles I could try or of my favorite singers and actors to put up in my room. Knowing about American culture was a way to stand out, a way to show that you were part of the "cool" group at school.

In college, Zhang began to miss her Chinese culture. Zhang writes that "Being away from home for the year also made me realize another thing—I *miss* Chinese-ness." Zhang never noticed many aspects of her Chinese culture because they were just part of her everyday life—the language she heard her mother speak, the television shows they watched, the foods they ate at home, and so on. Her food only stood out when her friends asked about unusual dishes in her refrigerator. Similarly, while I never really craved the refried black beans, plantains and tortillas that are a staple in Guatemalan cooking, when I'm faced with the endless array of pizza, pasta, barbecue, and Asian food "stations" in the dining hall, I start to crave the simple food we would eat at home.

If identity depends on the context, what does that mean for people who belong to two cultures? Zhang concludes that her identity is naturally split, like the yin and the yang of Chinese culture, and that the best solution is to find a balance between the two. If identity depends on the situation, that means making an effort to put yourself in both situations, because it is only within those situations that identity can take shape.

EXAMPLE 3: Russell Johnson, "Identity in a Material World"

When I read Claire Zhang's essay, "Amy Tan Phase," at first I could not relate. I grew up in the United States, and my family is plain, white, American. I have never felt a struggle between two ethnic cultures the way Zhang did. However, as I thought more about Zhang's essay, I realized that I could relate to her struggle between two different material cultures—one frugal and practical, the other frivolous and materialistic. Zhang's essay shows how American consumer culture provides much of the material we use to craft our "identities." The "materials" we wear, the things we consume—these are seen to be keys to American identity.

For Claire Zhang, being "American" meant shopping at certain stores, like Limited Too, or later, Aeropostale or American Eagle instead of J.C. Penney or Ross. It meant shopping for fun, too, not just for utility: "I observed my friend to understand how shopping as a teenage American girl was conducted: walk through the store, pick out clothes that look appealing, go in the dressing room to try them on, show them to your shopping partner, receive compliments and compliment your shopping partner's choice, then buy it." Zhang learned there was a protocol for shopping that other girls seemed to naturally understand. When I was growing up, I could not join the American culture Zhang describes, either. I was raised by a single father who worked two jobs to support my brother and I. Most of our clothes came from Walmart. Once or twice a year, like at the start of school, my dad would march us in and wait while we picked out a new pair of shoes, some jeans and a few shirts. Those had to last us for the school year. While guys do not care about fashion as much as girls, there were still certain things you had to have to fit in with the different social groups, like Hollister polo shirts or NBA jerseys. I could not afford either of those. This not only made me feel like I did not belong with the popular kids at school, but I've never thought about how it also makes me somewhat different from the image of the American kid.

It is not merely the quality of items one has, but the quantity that determines identity. Zhang describes how she also compared her possessions to those of her friends: "I marveled at the fact that my neighbor had a drawer full of at least 20 different swimsuits, when I only had two swimsuits, and how she had a room littered with Beanie Babies and Build-A-Bear bears, when I only had one Build-A-Bear bear that I got as a birthday present." Being American is about conspicuous consumption—owning more than you need, and being able to show it off to others. As young kids, we often use toys to form parts of our identity. There was the one kid in my elementary school who had collected every Transformer toy, or the one who had hundreds of video games in his own private game room to play them in. These kids seemed secure in knowing that the others wanted what they had. Their possessions gave them power—they could invite you to play with their toys, or they could exclude you from the group.

For Zhang to become American, she had to embrace the materialism of American culture. Buying things forms a big part of our economy and, increasingly, our identity. Does that make those of us who do not have these things less American? In a way, it does. If poor people were seen as truly American, then that would expose the lie of the American dream, in which everyone can be wealthy, everyone can buy as much stuff as they want. Not having things, or not having the right things, can mark you as not quite American.

USE THE TOOLKIT

Let's use the three genre toolkit questions to examine these texts.

What Is It?

You probably recognize these as examples of student essays that respond to a reading assignment, sometimes called reader response essays, reaction papers, or simply "response papers" or "response essays." (Here, we will call them "response essays.") And you have probably written this type of essay yourself.

Who Reads It?

Response essays may be read by your instructor, or by other students in a class. In some college courses, you might be asked to share your response essays as a way to start a group discussion. Or you might be asked to post them online and to comment on the responses posted by others in your class.

What's It For?

Response essays serve a few purposes. They help students to work through the ideas in a reading. They can lead to class discussions, or to longer writing assignments. For example, Russell might expand his ideas into a research paper (Chapter 11) exploring the history of materialism in American culture. Luisa might interview other students about how their identities change in different contexts, and then share her results in a report (Chapter 14).

Use the Rhetorical Situation

Response essays occur within a typical rhetorical situation. Your role in this rhetorical situation is that of student. The audience is usually your instructor, or maybe fellow classmates, and your purpose is usually to demonstrate to the instructor (or possibly your classmates) that you have read and engaged with the text. The timing of the document will likely be dictated by the course schedule, with a specific due date.

Using the tools in Chapter 1 and 2, then, we already know quite a bit about a response essay. But how would you go about writing one? Writing a good response essay requires more in-depth knowledge of this genre and how it works.

In this chapter, you will learn how to find out how a genre works so that you will be prepared to write it yourself. You'll dig deeper into this genre—its typical contents, style, and forms—and identify what kinds of choices you get to make as a writer of this genre.

We will use response essays as our example genre in this chapter, but the skills that you will learn in this chapter are applicable to *any* genre that you encounter. The process of learning to write a new genre can be broken down into three tasks:

1. Finding examples
2. Identifying conventions
3. Locating options

We will explore each of these steps in more detail.

B. Finding Examples

When you start to write a genre that is new to you, consider how you might locate examples from which to learn. For any unfamiliar writing task, looking at examples of the document you've been asked to write will give you a better sense of the options open to you, as well as the conventions for that genre.

To find examples, you can do one of two things: ask people you know, or look them up.

Ask People You Know

If you are asked to write a response essay in a class, the first thing to do is to ask your instructor for an example. You might also ask friends or classmates if they don't mind sharing theirs with you. For a classroom writing assignment, it is usually fair to ask friends who have taken the course already to look at their assignment to get a sense of how students have organized the genre in the past.

But, be sure to check with your professor first to be sure that you are not violating a course or college rule about plagiarism. Note, also, that under no circumstances should you copy a friend's assignment or use your friend's ideas or those from an online source without crediting them. Most colleges consider these actions to be academic dishonesty or plagiarism (Chapter 27).

In the case of the response essay, you'll need to fill in your own personal details and thoughts, anyway. But you can get a sense of how others have organized their information or written about their reactions to a text.

Look Them Up

The Internet is probably the best source for examples of genres. Try searching for the name of your genre and add the word "sample" or "example" to your search. Thus, you would type phrases like this into your search engine (such as Google): "response essay example" or "sample student response essay." In almost any case, you will be able to find plenty of hits. Your goal is not to find a template or formula for a response essay, but to learn more about the audience, purpose, and typical contents for this genre.

It is important to conduct your Internet search for samples in an organized fashion. As you search, figure out a way to keep track of your examples: (1) you can create a file on your computer to store digital files, (2) bookmark websites in your browser, (3) use electronic research tools (Chapter 24), or (4) print and save examples in a paper file. The genre examples will be useful as you are planning and drafting your own project, so you'll want to have them handy.

When looking at examples, it is important to remember that no one example represents the only way to write a type of document. It is more useful to compare a few different examples of a genre to see where they are similar and where they differ. This can help you to figure out which features of the genre seem relatively fixed, and which ones can be changed.

EXERCISE 3.1: Searching for Examples

We have included two examples of response essays in this chapter, but they were both written by students in the same college course. Try to locate more examples of response essays written for college courses. You might also locate instructions given to students about how to write this genre. Collect at least three examples to share with your classmates. Then, write down a list of observations from the materials you have collected.

C. Identifying Conventions

Once you have located examples of your genre, you can begin to identify common elements—or *conventions*—among them. If a feature recurs in many or most examples of a genre, you can consider it a convention of that genre—something readers will generally expect to see included. For instance, readers will expect to find a list of education and work experience in a résumé, because those are conventions of the résumé genre.

Take another look at the response essays at the beginning of this chapter. Let's explore the similarities that they share.

You might focus your analysis by considering the following:

- **Design:** What does the document look like? Does it include images? Special text or fonts? How are the contents arranged on the page?
- **Organization:** How are items organized in the document? Are there sections or headings? What goes in each section or part? What order do they go in?
- **Content:** What kinds of information are included in the document? What is the message or overall point? Is there a main claim or thesis (Chapter 18)? What kinds of evidence are included?
- **Style:** How is the document written? What kinds of vocabulary are used? What kinds of sentences? (Short or long sentences? Past/present/future tense verbs? Full sentences or bullet points? Statements or questions? Simple vocabulary or jargon?)

To make the task of identifying conventions easier to remember, use the acronym DOCS (Design, Organization, Content, Style).

Let's try the DOCS method to identify the conventions of the response essays provided previously.

Table 3.1 Sample DOCS Analysis

Genre	Response Essay Conventions
Design	Includes an original title and the student's name at the top; single or double-spaced; written as several paragraphs, not a single block of text; includes a works cited section
Organization	Has a definite introduction and thesis; paragraphs expand on thesis with examples drawn from the text and from personal experience; conclusion may sum up overall message or ideas gained from the text OR suggest questions to explore further.
Content	May include personal experiences and reflections/opinions, but also includes evidence from the text. Makes an argument about the text—tends to focus on a key factor or two—does not just list everything the writer noticed.
Style	Uses personal voice "I," but is still not too casual in tone. Uses academic vocabulary or terms ("metaphor," "tone," etc.).

The term "response essay" makes it seem like the genre involves casual writing, where you can simply jot down a range of ideas or opinions, as in a journal entry (Chapter 3). However, response essays actually use many of the features found in a formal academic essay. They have an introduction, body, and conclusion. They have a central thesis (Chapter 18), or main claim, that the writer supports using examples from the text and from their own experience.

The thesis usually involves more than a personal opinion or reaction. For example, neither Luisa nor Russell simply state that they like or dislike the reading, nor that they agree or disagree with the author. Instead, they each offer a thesis that is analytical and debatable.

Luisa's thesis is: "Zhang's essay suggests that identity isn't something we have, it is something we do in different situations."

Russell's thesis is: "Zhang's essay shows that today's consumer culture provides much of the material we use to craft our 'identities.'"

The thesis in each essay also does more than state the obvious. Each writer tries to say something new and interesting about the reading and what it means.

The writers also link their responses to key concepts and terms from the class in question. Luisa and Russell wrote these responses for an anthropology class focused on ethnicity and culture in America, so they tended to focus on a key concept they had been discussing in class: identity. If they were writing responses in a literature class, they might focus more on the style, imagery, or characters in the reading.

Finally, these response essays tend to be more formal and serious in tone than the term "reaction" or "response" might suggest. You might assume that a "response" could be written as a series of observations, almost like a journal entry (Chapter 2). However, a response essay is often more polished and organized than a journal entry or set of notes, since it will be read by an academic audience (your instructor or possibly your classmates).

You can use the DOCS technique to examine any genre you encounter as you plan how to write your own.

EXERCISE 3.2: Analyzing Genres   ?

Using the materials you collected for Exercise 3.1, fill out the DOCS chart in Table 3.2. Then, compare your results to Table 3.1. Do you notice different kinds of conventions in sample essays from different kinds of courses? Do instructors from different courses have different expectations for what a response essay should look like?

TABLE 3.2 BLANK DOCS ANALYSIS CHART

Genre
Design
Organization
Content
Style

Be prepared to share your results with your group or class.

D. Locating Options

Some genres are more flexible than others. As you investigate examples of your genre, consider how much leeway writers seem to have. Do all of your examples look pretty standardized, or do writers have different options?

In some cases you, as a writer, can even shift the conventions of a genre. For instance, you might create a video response essay to post on your blog—a newer twist on the genre of the response essay, which usually appears in print.

As you get to know the genre you are writing, consider your options (or resources), and your limitations (or constraints).

Resources

In most cases, you will have a number of resources open to you as you begin to write, even as you conform to conventions of a genre. These resources may be internal (part of the genre itself) or external (part of the situation in which you are writing).

For instance, a response essay may be presented in print, or online, or both. It may range from a few paragraphs (for a quick in-class assignment) to many pages in length (for a more formal assignment).

Your resources for a response essay also include the different kinds of information you can include, such as the kinds of ideas and information in the text you are responding to, and the kinds of personal connections you might draw to your own experiences. Both Luisa and Russell located resources in the text they read and in their own identities and cultures, which helped them to make sense of the reading.

Your resources might also include the amount of time you have available to write the response, the expected length of the response, and so on. Length might be seen as a limitation, but it can also be a resource—it is sometimes harder to confine your ideas to a single page than it is to write a two-page response essay.

Constraints

You will also face some constraints, or factors that limit the range of options you have. The genre itself may not provide as many options to writers. For instance, a response essay keeps its focus on the text or reading assignment in question. That means that your essay should not stray from that focus to a different topic. While you might compare the reading to another text you've read or to other ideas, it is usually not okay to change the focus entirely. For example, Russell had more to say about his own opinions on why materialism is bad for American culture, but he decided not to include them so he could focus his response on the reading.

Different genres will have different types of resources and constraints. A research paper (Chapter 11), for example, requires you to discover which bibliographic style to use (MLA or APA, etc.). A film review (Chapter 9) requires you to identify criteria (such as directing, acting, or cinematographic elements) and evaluate them.

External constraints can include time, materials, and format. For example, your response essay might have to be written and submitted within two days, and you might be required to submit it as a blog post for your class website.

Internal Resources or Constraints

- Design (font, spacing, layout, color, images, bibliographic style)
- Organization (headings and sub-headings, order of items, required sections)
- Content (level of detail, technicality, types of evidence)
- Style (grammar, formality, vocabulary)

External Resources or Constraints

- Time, deadlines
- Money
- Equipment & Materials (video cameras, color printers, ink, etc.)
- Length

By looking at more examples, you can determine how much leeway you have, or the kinds of choices you get to make about your own project.

Now, examine this essay by a student writer, published at Teen Ink, a website for young writers.

Foxxy

"The Way of a Cherokee"

I don't remember much before the time I lived in Shelby, Montana, with my grandparents—which is probably why I always think I spent the first five years of my life there when in truth it was really only two. Still, even those memories have been scattered with the mountain wind and aged over the years.

I remember the hill beside my grandparents' house. (Actually it was a doublewide trailer on a plot of 20 acres that my mom used to say "could be 50 if it was stretched and rolled out flat.") I remember a time before the land was planted with trees, before it was fenced, when it was wild mountain country. Mud piled at the base of the slope, forming a wide berth of bog that was a deathtrap to any human who walked through it.

When I was six and my youngest sister, Sierra, was four, we would sit on the floor at Grandpa's feet and listen as he weaved tales about the wild prairie deer that would come across the hill if one knew when to look. Sierra and I were young tribal warriors sitting before the imaginary fires and listening to dreams that danced around the room in the smoke. The wise and mighty chieftain sat before us—ancient and proud—his eyes gleaming with youth, his words entrapping us in the world of the springing deer.

We wanted to see them.

5   Sierra and I pulled on our boots. It had rained for the past week, and the birthing liquid of the land had impregnated the Mother; she was ready to start a new life. My boots were dusty black with vivid blue trim featuring the icons of my young life—Batman and Robin. The two Gotham City saviors took my breath away, and even to this day I admire their daring and capacity to care for the people of Gotham.

Together, we marched up the hill to catch a glimpse of the white-tailed deer Grandpa had told us about. We avoided the bog at the base and bounced with pent-up excitement as we climbed without a trail to follow. In our imaginations we could already see the fluffy flags of the does, the white spots of the fawns, the towering antlers of the bucks. They danced in our minds to the beat of a drum and the song of a flute without seeing us. If they saw us, these rare and shy creatures would fly away and we would be left with only a taste of what they were like.

For a long time we kept a silent vigil, picking a spot on the crest of the hill that overlooked miles upon miles of empty wasteland to some, dreamland to us. After a half hour, most children get bored and restless, but Sierra and I were different. The only movement we made for several hours was to sit down with our legs crossed—"crisscross applesauce" my kindergarten teacher would say, "the way of a Cherokee" my grandpa called it. We liked Grandpa's way better. Cherokee was in our blood; applesauce was not.

Several hours after we began our lookout, hunger settled in our bellies like a ravenous beast craving the heart of a buffalo. We had seen no deer, none of those splendid white-tailed folk we'd heard so much about. We wanted to wait until we saw one of those graceful beings dance past, but finally we could stand it no longer. Our starvation drew us to the house as a metal trap beckons to the red fox too curious for his own good.

Sierra and I glanced at each other and without words vowed to dine on a quick lunch and dash back to resume our watch. We stood and woke our sleeping muscles, stretching tired limbs until they were ready for use. I took a quick look around, drinking it all in. The hills, the plains, the cloudless Montana sky, my home, my land: I would belong nowhere else.

10   Although Sierra and I had avoided the bog going up, we trudged right through it on our way back. It lapped at our ankles, drank in the sweet nectar of our energy, chewed us up but wouldn't spit us out. We struggled and Sierra managed to break free, but I was trapped, my foot stuck hard and fast.

The bog made sick squishing noises as I tried to pull my boot out, but it was caught and the bog wouldn't let go. Sierra laughed before she sobered up enough to fetch Grandpa. We both knew the wise man could get me loose.

So I stood and waited patiently, pondering how to get myself out of the mud. I almost fell in the process, and I recaptured my balance to discover my foot hanging above the trapped boot, the sock dirty and foot tingling.

When Sierra finally appeared with Grandpa looking like an old cowboy with his gray Western hat, dusty brown boots, work-faded jeans, and red plaid shirt, I was just coming out of the bog. With that crooked smile of his, Grandpa traversed the bog, stepping lightly in certain spots and finding balance on the mud rather than in it. He bent slowly, took hold of my boot, twisted it left once, right once, and plucked it out of the mud like a ripe apple from a wild tree.

He was a cowboy. He was a chief. He was a Cherokee. Grandpa was a wise man.

Sierra and I are older now. Grandpa left us in 2003, but something about the "Spirit Dreams" CD by Thomas Walker brought the jolt of memory back—a memory of my grandpa's tales and the adventure Sierra and I went on to discover their truth.

By the way, deer really are rare and shy creatures, and they do dance past quickly if you know when to look.

Imagine that you are in the same anthropology class as Luisa and Russell. How would you write a response to Foxxy's essay? Your instructor has given you Luisa and Russell's examples in class, so you know something about the genre you are supposed to write. But you have to write about a different reading, and you have to be sure not to echo the kinds of claims Luisa and Russell made about culture and identity in their essays. In addition, the instructor wants you to post your response on a class blog.

You might fill out an analysis of your options and constraints as shown in Table 3.3.

Table 3.3 DOCS Analysis of Resources and Constraints for a Response Essay

	Resources	**Constraints**
Design	• Blog format allows for links. Can I include links to other readings or definitions? • Can I include pictures? What purpose would they serve?	• Must be under 2 pages long, or equivalent—short enough to read easily on screen. • Need to think about tags to add to my blog post so others can find it.
Organization	• How do I order different points/items? • Where does the main idea/most important one go? • How do I focus the reader on the key pieces of evidence I have?	• I have four main points, but only two pages—should I cut something?
Content	• How general/specific should my personal observations be? • How many examples should I give from the text?	• Can't fit more than a few examples into two pages, but need to provide detail. • Needs to say something new about the text—can't repeat what the teacher said or what is in the examples.
Style	• How will I describe my personal experiences—how informal or formal should I be about them? • Can I use a humorous tone, or would that be inappropriate? • What concepts from class can I use to show that I understand the text?	• Needs to be straightforward and pretty concise. • Needs to have lots of impact but in a short amount of space.

EXERCISE 3.3: Getting Started

Re-read the text "The Way of a Cherokee" and Luisa and Russell's response essays. Now, make a list of items you can use in your own response essay. You should list the following:

- Three or four possible examples from the text that you would like to use.
- Key concepts you might use. Is this essay about culture? Identity? Childhood? Education? Can you focus on the writing itself (style, imagery, characterizations)?
- Possible personal connections you can draw. Does Foxxy's experience growing up remind you of something that happened to you as a child?

GROUP ACTIVITY 3.1: Developing Theses

As a group, share your own observations from the reading "The Way of a Cherokee." In your group, come up with a list of possible thesis statements (Chapter 18) that could focus a response essay. Then, choose one or two that you think would be especially interesting to share with the class.

E. Conclusion

Reading this chapter taught you how to write a new genre by looking at examples, identifying conventions, and choosing strategies to use. You have learned how to consider issues of design, organization, content, and layout to help you compose your document.

At this stage, you have assembled three of the main "tools" for your genre toolkit.

In Chapter 1, you learned about the three genre toolkit questions you can use when you encounter a genre for the first time: "What is it?" "Who reads it?" and "What's it for?"

In Chapter 2, you learned how to assess your rhetorical situation when writing a genre.

In this chapter, you learned how to start writing a new genre by discovering how it works.

Now, whenever you are given a new writing task, you will be able to get started by asking questions, discovering situations, and examining the genre at hand. In the next chapter, we'll learn how to use the final part of the toolkit: developing a writing process.

Figure 3.1
The Genre Toolkit for Chapter 3

In Part 2, you will find more specific guidelines for many of the different genres you are likely to encounter in college and the workplace—but not all of them. There are hundreds and hundreds of different genres that you may encounter, and we cannot cover all of them in one textbook. However, by using your genre toolkit, you will develop the skills you need to write any new genre you find.

F. Chapter Project: Write a Response Essay

Write a response essay to the reading "The Way of a Cherokee." You might consider how the essay deals with themes of identity, childhood, and culture. Or, you might choose to focus on the techniques the writer uses to craft the essay: the language, characterizations, descriptions, tone, etc. Be sure to organize your essay around a main thesis (Chapter 18) and to provide support from the text and from your own personal experience.

Multimedia Option

Prepare a video response essay to "The Way of a Cherokee" that you could post on a class website. You'll have to do some online research to find samples of video response essays. Then, identify the conventions, resources, and constraints available to you. Lastly, consider what choices to make given the rhetorical situation.

Developing a Writing Process

In Chapters 1, 2, and 3, you learned how to examine a genre, a genre's rhetorical situation, and the features for a genre you plan to write. In this chapter, you will learn how to write a document in that genre by developing a writing process. Usually, writing a document is more complicated than just sitting down, opening up your word processor, and typing a complete document, start to finish. This chapter describes the range of activities involved in writing a document, activities you can use to develop your own personalized approach.

A. Discovering Your Writing Process

Think about the last time you had a writing task to do—whether for a classroom assignment or for a workplace, community, or personal goal. How did you approach it? Did you plan ahead of time, and then write? Or did you just sit down and get going? Did you revise what you wrote after finishing a complete draft, or edit each sentence as you went along?

Your writing process refers to the set of actions that you used to complete your project, from the time you began thinking about the project to the time you finished it.

People who study writing often divide the writing process into five actions, as shown in Figure 4.1.

You don't necessarily need to do all of these actions in this exact order. Most writers move between different writing actions at different stages of a project. They often return to earlier actions as they go along, moving between brainstorming, drafting, revising, and editing activities until the project is finished.

Even publishing your writing—sharing it with a wider audience—might not be the end of a writing project. For example, you might post a draft to your blog, get feedback from readers, and then revise and re-publish the draft.

Instead of thinking about your writing process as a series of steps, think of the actions in Figure 4.2 as building blocks you can move around.

In Part 3 of this book, you'll learn strategies to help you streamline your writing process. But, in this chapter, we provide a quick overview so you can get started on a project right away: writing a personal essay.

Keep in mind that there is no single "correct" writing process that you must follow. As you can see in Figure 4.3, different writers use different processes. Sometimes, a

Figure 4.1
The Writing Process

Figure 4.2
Writing Process as Building Blocks

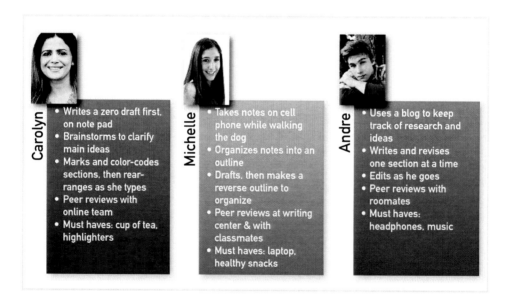

Carolyn
- Writes a zero draft first, on note pad
- Brainstorms to clarify main ideas
- Marks and color-codes sections, then rear-ranges as she types
- Peer reviews with online team
- Must haves: cup of tea, highlighters

Michelle
- Takes notes on cell phone while walking the dog
- Organizes notes into an outline
- Drafts, then makes a reverse outline to organize
- Peer reviews at writing center & with classmates
- Must haves: laptop, healthy snacks

Andre
- Uses a blog to keep track of research and ideas
- Writes and revises one section at a time
- Edits as he goes
- Peer reviews with roomates
- Must haves: headphones, music

Figure 4.3
Different Writers, Different Writing Processes

writer will vary her writing process depending on the situation or genre. Writing is often more like improvising than following a routine. Our focus here is on helping you develop some different strategies you can use to plan out a writing process.

EXERCISE 4.1: What Is Your Writing Process?

Take a look at Figure 4.3, which includes brief profiles of three different writers. Then, write a profile (Chapter 5) of your own writing process. What procedures and materials do you tend to use when you write? What are your "must have" items? Where do you like to write? Do you like to be around people when you work, or do you prefer to work alone?

GROUP ACTIVITY 4.1: Come up with a Group Process

With your writing group, share your typical writing processes or strategies. Then, make a list of strategies you can use as a group to accommodate everyone's preferred writing techniques for future group projects. Will you share your work in print or online? (Consider your instructor's preferences, too.) What kinds of electronic tools will you use to share and comment on documents? Will you meet outside of class at the library or a coffee shop? What tasks will you focus on when you have group time together? How will you handle absences from team members?

Share your plan with the rest of the class, and then use it to keep everyone on task for the rest of the course.

B. Composing a Personal Essay

Next, let's take a look at the genre we'll be discussing in this chapter: a personal essay. In particular, we focus here on the type of personal essay that investigates core values and beliefs, one that is written for a national project called This I Believe. Thousands of people have submitted their essays to This I Believe, and each month a few are chosen to be read on National Public Radio.

∙∙∙

EXAMPLE 1: Maisha, "Two Worlds, One Great Nation"

You may think it's simple to sum up an exact definition of what it means to be American, but it's quite difficult. Everyone has their own perception supported by a personal experience. I'm no different. My opinion changes from time to time, however there is one aspect that always remains the same. I believe that when you are allowed to be a part of multiple cultures, you are an American. What I mean by that is, yes, you belong to the American culture but you are not limited and have the freedom to join other cultures and create a whole new identity as you wish. I think that's what makes America more exceptional than other nations.

I am able to keep two different cultures that play a massive part of my life. I am American but I am also Bengali, since my parents are from Bangladesh. The Bengali culture is definitely more complicated to be a part of since I did not grow up in Bangladesh like my parents did. It is problematic for me to maintain my identity as a Bengali into my daily life as an American as well. At home, I may speak Bengali and dress in traditional clothes but once I'm out that door, I switch out of my Bengali self into my American self. However, I always somehow end up combining the two to find a definition of myself. That's the beauty. I have the choice to choose between the two but I also have the choice to mix both. I can contribute to both cultures and be able to really express who I am.

When I was younger, I was obsessed with fitting in. I wanted to be like my friends who had the image of a "true American," while I didn't. I didn't like to wear the traditional clothes from my country and I was embarrassed to bring in food of my culture for lunch. I didn't want to be Bengali. I wanted to be American. That was the time when I didn't know you had the freedom to be whoever you wanted. As I grew older and gained more knowledge and learned more about the world, I realized that no one was ever a "true American." My friends may have looked more American than me, but inside, I was just as American as they were. America is made up of all kinds of people with different races and sexes and that's why this nation is a home to people who don't feel like they don't belong. But they do. We all belong in this country because that's what the United States is all about. It's not about fitting in and trying to be American, it's about having the freedom to choose what you want.

So what is my belief about what it means to be American in simple words? To be able to be you.

EXAMPLE 2: Mark, "I Believe in the Senses"

I was born with four senses—the classic set of sight, touch, taste, and hearing. That's everything right? Well it took me a while growing up to realize that not everyone was missing the sense of smell, the one sense I was born without. Doctor's don't know why, I myself have no explanation; an early onslaught of MRI's and CATSCANS left us only guessing, and the response "wait are you serious? How is that possible?" has become almost as common in introductions as "Hi, my name is Mark." In reality though, it doesn't bother me, in fact I kind of enjoy having such a unique disorder. I have lived my whole life without it so I don't really know what I'm missing. Plus, it has caused me to consider the miracle of our senses—the beauty and wonder of such simple processes that facilitate every experience we will ever have. Our senses, which so often go unnoticed, deserve more credit, and though I only have four that is enough for me to recognize just how incredible they are.

The pleasure of taste: biting into one of my Dad's homemade biscuits. Impossibly fluffy, fragments of heaven that, when covered in the perfect amount of butter, have the power to pull me out of bed Sunday morning. It's sipping the frothy surface of a just-made mug of cocoa and feeling the glory of ideal temperatures and perfect chocolate proportions fall like world peace into my stomach. It's the wonder of tin-foil dinners on a campout, how the flavor in each bite brings the crackling of the fire, the bright stars, and solitude of being lost out in nature completely to life. I cherish taste.

The comfort of touch: sinking into a warm bathtub after a long, cold day and letting the water remind me I still have nerves (yes, I can admit I still take baths on occasion). It's hugging my Mom every day after high school and having her little arms that barely make it all the way around me dissolve every single problem for a split second. It's lying down in my soft bed when my eyes can no longer stay open and letting my blanket silence every concern about the past day while my pillow reassures me that all I need to do now is to rest. I cherish touch.

The joy of hearing: being swept away in the harmonies of a 4-minute musical masterpiece. It's the goose bumps I get from my favorite song, how the marriage of genius lyrics and heart-wrenching notes can subdue me completely for half a day. It's the tone of a familiar voice that lets me know I'm home; the relief of Friday's school bell that announces "finally, the weekend has come." It's the quiet, sacred sound of our Church choir that softly touches my spirit and connects me briefly with a higher Existence. I cherish hearing.

The beauty of sight: living my whole life in Texas and then waking up one morning to see the first snow of a Utah winter. It's getting inches from an original oil painting and seeing the geography of each brush stroke, realizing how every single line testifies of the artist's passion. It's making eye contact with the most beautiful girl I've ever seen—being stopped in my tracks to watch her walk by, forgetting about everything else momentarily to wonder how any one girl could look so flawless. I cherish sight. 5

For most people there would be another paragraph. But even though I'll never know what smelling is like, I know the greatness of the senses I do have and the fact that they make life everything I love. I believe in the senses.

USE THE TOOLKIT

Suppose you are encountering the personal essay genre for the first time. Let's use the three genre toolkit question from Chapter 1 to examine this new genre.

What Is It?

These are personal essays that appeared on the website for This I Believe, an organization that shares essays written by people of all ages and from all walks of life.

You'll notice that this type of essay draws on personal experience, that it uses the first-person voice ("I"), and that it does not rely on research or other kinds of "library sources." Each essay uses personal experience to send a message. In the first essay, Maisha draws on personal experience to highlight how important it is that America provides opportunities for individuals to integrate different cultural traditions and beliefs. The second essay has a simpler message, but uses descriptive language to really make that message—about the importance of human senses—come alive.

Who Reads It?

Anyone can visit the website for This I Believe and read these essays. Sometimes, the essays are read aloud on National Public Radio—the project began in the 1950s as a radio program—so radio listeners might also be included among the "readers" for these essays. Often, students are asked to write essays for This I Believe, so we can assume that the audience for these essays includes other students who are seeking to understand the genre itself. More broadly, personal essays similar to these may be published in magazines, or collected into books, as some of the This I Believe essays have been.

What's It For?

According to the organization's website, these essays are meant to encourage readers to share their beliefs and to learn about the beliefs of others, not to persuade readers to adopt the author's beliefs. Therefore, the purpose of a This I Believe essay is to prompt reflection on a topic, not necessarily to persuade the audience.

Use the Rhetorical Situation

The rhetorical situations that prompt personal essays can vary. You can often encounter personal essays in published books and magazines, but increasingly, people are sharing their personal stories on blogs and websites such as ThisIBelieve.org and StoryCorps.org. The essays may be actively solicited by publishers or organizations, or they may be prompted when writers feel they have something to share about their life experiences.

EXERCISE 4.2: Use the Genre Toolkit

Go to ThisIBelieve.org and find examples of two more essays that interest you. Using the DOCS method you learned in Chapter 3 (and shown below in Table 4.1), analyze the genre. List both the resources (or options) offered by the genre, and the constraints (or limitations) that seem to be present in the genre.

Table 4.1 Sample DOCS Analysis Chart

	Resources	**Constraints**
Design		
Organization		
Content		
Style		

What features do these personal essays seem to have in common? How much freedom do writers seem to have in this genre? Are there any constraints on this particular type of essay? Post your analysis to your course management system, or share with your writing group.

Now, let's consider how you would go about writing a personal essay for This I Believe.

C. Prewriting

A writing process usually involves prewriting, or the set of actions you do before you actually sit down to write. Prewriting actions help you to generate ideas, clarify points, or address problems you encounter. If you were writing a personal essay for This I Believe, you might start by listing things you believe in, and then jotting down notes for one or two ideas that you might write about.

You can employ a range of different techniques to help you come up with ideas. Some of them don't even involve putting pen to paper.

You can prewrite at any point in your writing process, not just when you are beginning. All of these techniques can help when you get stuck or feel like you have "writer's block" (see Figure 4.4).

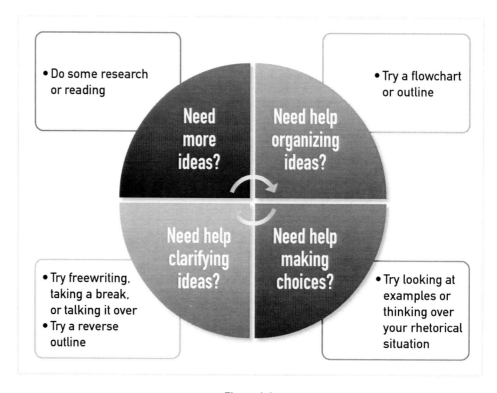

Figure 4.4
Prewriting Techniques for Writer's Block

You'll learn more about prewriting in Chapter 16, but for now, keep the following five ideas in mind.

1. Prewrite Whenever You Need Ideas or Get Stuck

As we noted earlier, there is no single "correct" writing process. This means that you don't necessarily need to start by prewriting. If you are ready to start drafting a paper, then go ahead and write. Prewriting works best when you are stuck—when you are suffering from "writer's block." Sometimes you need to clarify your ideas, or you need to organize different points you want to make.

If you find that you are stuck, you can sit down and try a few different techniques. If you are used to working on your computer, you might try writing with a pen and paper, or vice versa. Sometimes switching to a different medium can help you get out of a rut.

- Try freewriting whatever comes to mind for three minutes, without editing or erasing anything (Chapter 16).

- Try drawing a concept map or cluster chart of your paper (Chapter 16).
- Try outlining what you have written so far (called a "reverse-outline") (Chapter 20).

2. Prewrite by Reading or Doing Research

The preceding techniques tend to work when your problem relates to your own ideas—usually a problem with how to organize or clarify them. But if you don't have any ideas, it doesn't always help to wrack your brain. Instead, you might find new ideas by doing some reading and research.

Imagine you have to write an opinion paper about global warming. You could probably sit down and rattle off some of your own opinions or ideas, but you might soon get stuck, especially if you don't usually keep up on the latest discussions about global warming in science or politics.

Your best bet would be to read some recent articles about climate change. Chances are, you will disagree with some of what you read, or want to extend points others have made. Reading what others have said can often help you to discover new ideas of your own.

3. Prewrite by Thinking through Your Toolkit

The genre toolkit can also help you to brainstorm ideas. One of the best ways of coming up with ideas or solving a writing problem can be to think back over the rhetorical situation and genre for your writing task (Chapters 1 and 2). Take notes or write lists of points about your genre or rhetorical situation. Or, try using the DOCS prompts (design, organization, content, and style) to plan out your document (Chapter 3). As you write, you can return to the toolkit again and again.

Consider the case of the personal essay for This I Believe. You might develop ideas by browsing the website and thinking about what kinds of stories the organization might be looking for—stories that encourage others to think about core values and understand where other people are coming from. That gives you a clue about the kinds of things you can focus on in your essay. Has there been a time in your life when you have felt misunderstood, or when your core values have been challenged?

You might also find yourself stuck when you are not sure about the genre you are writing, or about a particular problem within a genre. Say you've started writing your personal essay, but you get stuck because you aren't sure how to conclude it. Taking a look back over your examples will give you a sense of how others have ended their essays. You might try out one of those strategies, or develop your own after seeing some of the possibilities.

4. Prewrite by Talking to Others

Sometimes the best thing you can do is talk to someone about your writing—with a classmate, a friend or family member, your dog, or even yourself (in a journal or in a voice memo). Talking over your ideas or your frustrations can often lead to new insights. For a This I Believe essay, you might ask a friend or family member to help you brainstorm some ideas drawn from experiences in your own life. Just remember to take notes so you don't forget what you've come up with.

5. Prewrite by Taking a Break

Sometimes, your brain just needs time to process ideas. Try doing something else: take a walk, do some laundry, get a coffee, or finish some errands. You may be surprised how often ideas come to when you are not thinking about a project. Some people take a notepad with them on walks and errands, or bring a cell phone with a voice memo or note-taking feature. That way, they can record ideas whenever they occur to them.

EXERCISE 4.3: Prewrite for your Personal Essay

To start, brainstorm some ideas for the kinds of core values you believe in.

1. Look at the list of themes on the This I Believe website to get you started: http://thisibelieve.org/themes/. Which of those themes seem interesting or important to you? What comes to mind when you think of those themes?
2. Choose three or four themes, and then think about what kinds of personal experiences or stories you could write about that would illustrate those themes. Which one seems to give you the best material to write about?
3. Next, choose one theme to explore in greater depth. Read some of the stories online that pertain to that theme. Make a list of conventions or choices that might be useful for you to try out, based on those examples.

Be prepared to share your brainstorming ideas in class or online, and to talk about which techniques you found most useful.

GROUP ACTIVITY 4.2: Values Inventory

With your group, brainstorm a list of "core values" that might drive a "This I Believe" essay. Then, discuss which of those values would seem most interesting to readers. Do any of those core values seem tired or clichéd? Can you come up with ideas that seem fresh and interesting? Try to find a core value for each team member to write about.

D. Drafting

Like prewriting, drafting can occur at many different stages of a writing project. You don't necessarily need to write an entire document in one sitting—especially if it is a long one. In fact, most authors alternate between prewriting, drafting, revising, and editing their work. You might write one section, then prewrite for another, then go back and revise the first one, then scrap it and rewrite it entirely.

You'll learn more about drafting techniques in Chapter 17. For now, consider the following strategies for drafting a document.

Set Goals

Drafting a writing project can seem overwhelming, especially if you are asked to write something that seems longer or more difficult than anything you've written before. Any time you sit down to write, try to set a manageable goal for yourself. Then, when you've met that goal, take a break—call a friend, go for a walk, or work on something else. Often, rewarding yourself after reaching a writing goal makes writing easier.

Your goal can be small—you might decide to write 200 words, or finish two paragraphs, or just to write for 15 minutes. Those small goals can add up to a lot of writing, especially if you write consistently.

Break It Up

In order to make the most of short writing sessions, it helps to break up writing projects into smaller sets of tasks. For example, you might decide to organize your This I Believe essay by including an opening anecdote, an explanation of the theme and how it applies to your life, an example drawn from your personal experience, and a conclusion. Each of those sections could be written separately. You might decide to write about a memory or experience first, then consider how you can link that experience to the overall message of your essay.

You do not necessarily need to write things in the order in which they'll appear in the final document. In fact, it often helps to start somewhere in the middle. If there's a section of a document that seems easiest to write, start with that. Then, you'll have some momentum going into the next section.

Go with the Flow

While setting small goals and breaking up long projects works much of the time, you'll occasionally find that you get a sudden burst of inspiration or energy. Take advantage of those moments. If you can, go with the flow and write for as long as you have that spark of energy.

Also, see if you can identify what helps you to feel inspired to write. Does doing research help? Brainstorming with friends? Focusing on something else? That way, you'll be able to develop your own strategies to help generate that spark.

Try Different Places and Different Writing Tools

A change of scenery can inspire you to write. If you've been stuck writing in your room, try going to the library or taking your laptop outside (if the weather's nice). Many students prefer to write in coffee shops populated by fellow students; others prefer the isolation of a library table or a quiet room. Find out what works for you.

Similarly, try writing with different tools. If you are used to composing on your computer, try a pen and paper, and vice-versa. Some writers even dictate their writing to a computer voice-recognition program or voice recorder because talking out loud helps them focus their ideas.

EXERCISE 4.4: Start Drafting your Personal Essay

Using the ideas that you have brainstormed, begin drafting your This I Believe essay.

As you draft, keep a time log of the different strategies you used—where did you write? What tasks did you do, when? How did you start? What seems to work best for you?

Be prepared to share your draft, and to discuss your drafting techniques, with your classmates.

E. Revising

There are two important things to understand when it comes to revising your writing.

First, revising is not the same as editing. Editing tends to be a later action in a writing process, one that focuses mainly on style and wording, and we will learn more about it in Section F of this chapter. Revising, on the other hand, is an in-depth reconsideration of your draft and its content, organization, and ideas.

Second, we equate revising with "seeking feedback" on your draft. The only way to revise successfully is to solicit useful feedback on your draft from competent readers. We do recognize, however, that there are many ways to seek feedback: from your peers (who might ask for your feedback in return), from your instructor, and, most importantly, *from yourself.*

Next, we will look at different ways to seek feedback and to revise your writing.

Seek Feedback from Others

The best way to get feedback from others is to ask someone to read your paper—a friend, classmate, co-worker, or professor. Many colleges offer writing centers where peer tutors are available to help you with any stage of the writing process, including revising.

The key to getting good feedback is to ask good questions. Don't just say, "Can you read my paper?" Instead, ask specific questions or point to specific parts you need help with. One good place to start figuring out how to ask specific questions is the assignment sheet for your writing assignment. Read your assignment sheet carefully: have you met all of your professor's expectations? (For some examples of good feedback-generating questions, see Chapter 22.)

Give Good Feedback

In most college writing classes, you'll be expected not only to seek feedback, but to give feedback to your classmates. No one likes to get a paper back from a peer workshop with just a few punctuation corrections and no substantive comments. Such poor feedback won't help the writer improve the document.

Thus, you need to learn to be a good critic as well as a good writer. Learn how to not only notice what is wrong, but also how to make suggestions for improvement.

As you read another student's draft, focus on the ideas, organization, and genre. Make suggestions to help the writer better suit the genre's conventions, make the organization clearer, or get her ideas across more clearly. Put yourself in the shoes of the intended audience. Would you find this document confusing? Convincing? Be sure to explain *why*.

Revise Your Own Work

One of the best ways to improve as a writer is to begin looking at your own writing with fresh eyes, as though you were seeing it for the first time. There are a few techniques that can make it easier to see your writing with fresh eyes:

First, it helps if you can take a break after writing and let your writing "rest" for a few days. When you return to your document to revise it, it will seem new to you and problems will be easier to spot.

Second, as you read over your work, slow down and think about (1) the rhetorical purpose for your work, (2) the genre you are writing, and (3) the audience's needs. Read through multiple times, each time taking only *one* of these challenges into account.

Third, read your document out loud. Reading out loud slows you down and forces you to consider every word on the page.

Change Things Around

Research shows that novice writers tend to revise mostly at the level of sentences, swapping out one word for another, or occasionally rewording a phrase that sounds awkward. These are good changes to make, but advanced writers tend to make larger revisions as well: scratching out whole sections, moving paragraphs around, adding new paragraphs, clarifying points, and so on.

As you are revising, ask yourself about the big picture of your document. Think about where you need to add or subtract ideas, provide more or less information, or define a term.

Key Considerations for Revision

As you revise, use the following items from your Genre Toolkit to analyze your own writing. You've already applied these considerations to examples of the genre you plan to write—now, do the same for yourself.

- Rhetorical Situation (Chapter 2)
  - Author's Role and Purpose: How do I come across to my readers? Is the document's purpose clear?
  - Audience's Needs: Does the document meet my audience's needs?
  - Document's Timing: Does this genre have good timing? Can I accomplish my writing by deadline?
- Genre: Does this look like the type of document it is meant to be? Use the DOCS method (Chapter 3).
  - Design & Layout: Is the layout and design typical of the genre? If not, should it be?
  - Organization: Does the organization suit the genre? Does the order of points or sections make sense?
  - Content: Is the type of content suitable for the genre? Should there be more examples, more evidence, more information?
  - Style: Is the style suitable for the genre? Are there sentences that are unclear, or too casual, or too formal?

EXERCISE 4.5: Revise your Own "This I Believe" Essay

Read over your essay draft. Using a highlighting tool, mark places where you might do the following:

1. Convey the rhetorical purpose for your work. Is the overall message or core value clear?
2. Emulate a convention of the genre you are writing. Are there places where you might emulate samples you've read? Where and why?
3. Modify a convention of the genre you are writing. Are there places where you might do something different from what you have seen? Where and why?
4. Meet the audience's needs or concerns. Is there anything readers might find confusing if they weren't there to experience the story you are relating? Is there anything you can do to make the story more vivid for readers?

GROUP ACTIVITY 4.3: Create Revision Questions for Your "This I Believe" Essay

1. Come up with a list of specific questions or criteria for revising your personal essay.
2. Exchange drafts with a classmate, along with revision questions to help provide good feedback.
3. Trade feedback with your classmate.
4. When you get your feedback, use it to write a revision plan, identifying at least four things you will change or improve when you revise.

F. Editing and Proofreading

At some point in the writing process, you will want to focus on the finer points of writing: word choice, sentence structure, grammar, and the like. You'll find more advice about sentence-level concerns in Chapter 22. For now, though, keep the following two principles in mind.

Plan Some Time for Editing

Leave yourself time to read over your work carefully before it is due. It is hard to catch simple errors or awkward-sounding sentences when it is four in the morning and your paper is due in five hours. Whenever possible, schedule time to read over your work when you are fresh and well rested.

Read Carefully

As you read over your work, try to slow down and focus on one thing at a time. You can try reading your paper out loud, or getting a friend to read it to you. That way, you will be less likely to skip over mistakes or funny-sounding sentences. Or, try reading with a pen or highlighter in hand, making a note whenever you notice something that needs work.

If you are reading on the screen, use your word processor's features to help you make notes. Most software programs provide tools that allow you to highlight text in different colors, add written or spoken comments, strike out words, and more. You can also use spelling- and grammar-check tools, although be careful to examine each change the program suggests carefully, as computerized tools do not always get it right.

Focus on whether your sentences sound right—do they say what you want them to say? Would they confuse a reader? If so, see if you can write things in a different way.

EXERCISE 4.6: Edit and Proofread Your "This I Believe" Essay

Edit and proofread your draft, marking your changes either on paper or on your screen. Save the edited version as a new document, then compare the edited version with your earlier version. Share your editing process with your group or post the edited version to the class discussion board.

G. Publishing

A common phrase among writers is: "Writing is never done. It's just due." You can spend hours and hours revising and tweaking your work, but in professional and academic contexts, at some point you will have to publish—"make public"—your writing.

For student writers, the writing process usually ends when an assignment is due in class. However, you may also be asked to submit your work for publication—to post it to a course website or blog, or submit it to an undergraduate journal or your student newspaper. In these cases, publishing involves a few more steps than simply printing out your essay and handing it to your professor.

Keep in mind that you should think about publishing as you work through the other actions in the writing process, not necessarily just at the end. How and where you publish your document can affect the choices you make throughout. For example, if you are publishing your writing as a blog post, you may want to include hyperlinks to other documents online. That's something you might consider as part of your brainstorming and drafting process.

Depending on what and where you are publishing, you may need to do the following:

- Change the formatting (fonts, spacing, layout) to meet the publisher's guidelines. For example, a letter to the editor for your student newspaper may be limited to 500 words, in which case you may need to edit your writing down to fit the space constraints (and possibly return to the drafting stage).
- Reconsider your audience (which may mean going back to the brainstorming phase). Perhaps you have written an essay, but want to turn it into a column for your student newspaper. This means shifting your genre and audience, so you will need to cycle back through your writing process to address those issues.
- Add additional parts to conform to a genre's conventions. An undergraduate journal might ask for an abstract or works cited list, or a short bio statement about you, or a cover letter.
- Address technical considerations or constraints. For example, you may need to submit your files in a specific electronic format or meet file size limits.

We'll address all of these issues in more detail in later chapters. For now, though, keep in mind that where and how you publish your work affects all of the decisions you make during your writing process.

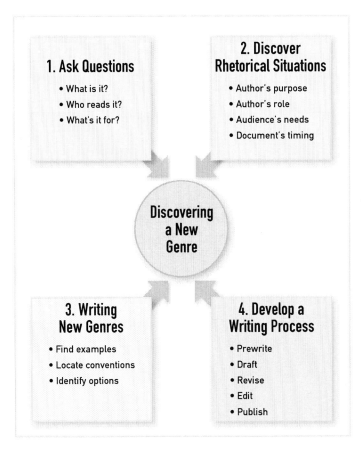

Figure 4.5
The Genre Toolkit for Chapter 4

H. Conclusion

In this chapter, you have learned how to generate a flexible writing process that you can adapt to the task at hand. Keep in mind that you can use different writing actions at any time: brainstorming, drafting, revising, editing, and publishing. You do not need to use the same writing process for every assignment you write. The point is to keep in mind that writing involves different kinds of activities, and that you can develop your own favorite approaches based on what works best for you.

At this stage, you have assembled all the tools you need for your Genre Toolkit.

In Chapter 1, you learned about the three genre discovery questions that you can use when you encounter a genre for the first time.

In Chapter 2, you learned how to discover your rhetorical situation when preparing to write a genre.

In Chapter 3, you learned how to start writing a genre by determining how it works.

Finally, in Chapter 4, you have learned the tools to help you plan your writing process.

In Part 2, you will find more specific techniques for many genres that you are likely to encounter.

I. Chapter Project: Write a Personal Essay

For this assignment, you will prepare a personal essay that focuses on your own core values. Consider values related to your education, career, personal life, and or family life. Prepare a narrative essay that could be submitted to This I Believe.

With your complete essay, hand in a cover letter (a kind of business letter, Chapter 12) that explains the writing process you used to prepare your essay. Did you try any new techniques? What strategies did you find most helpful? What do you think you need to work on in this course to improve your writing?

Multimedia Option

Create an audio version of your personal essay that you could submit to StoryCorps .org.

Group Option

Prepare an audio podcast in which each member contributes a personal story that addresses a common theme or topic. You might listen to podcasts of This American Life (ThisAmericanLife.org) for examples of this type of story. Your group should work together to practice, revise, and edit each story before you record them.

Profiles

A profile is a verbal portrait of a person, a group, a place, or a thing. Whereas a portrait, such as a painting or a photograph, can portray its subject with an image, a profile portrays its subject with words.

In college, you might be asked to write a profile in a variety of situations. In some cases, you will be asked to profile yourself. For instance, you might write an introduction to a portfolio of work you completed in a course. You might write a profile of a person or organization in your community for a course on social work, or of a patient with a particular mental disorder for a psychology course.

Profiles also appear in the workplace. For example, if you work for a consulting business, you might be asked to write a profile of the clients you have served. If you work for a non-profit organization, you might write a set of profiles describing the kinds of programs you offer. Journalists frequently write profile articles for magazines and newspapers. An obituary is even a profile of sorts.

In this chapter, you will learn how to write several kinds of profiles that you may encounter in your college career.

A. Profile Mini-Genre: Social Network Profile

Take a look at the following three profile pages from Facebook, the social networking site.

EXAMPLE 1: Social Network Profile of a Band

Facebook profile of a band.

EXAMPLE 2: Social Network Profile of a Company

Facebook profile of gaming company Nintendo.

EXAMPLE 3: Social Network Profile of a Nonprofit Organization

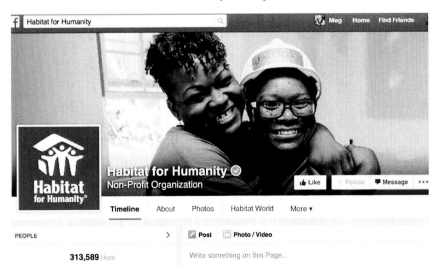

Facebook profile of nonprofit organization Habitat for Humanity.

Let's use the three genre toolkit questions from Chapter 1 to examine this genre.

What Is It?

These three profiles are short, digital snapshots or outlines of an individual, company, or group. Each profile includes photographs and text, including background information, a description, and/or links to further information.

Who Reads It?

Public Facebook profiles can be viewed by anyone with access to the Internet. In particular, users of Facebook tend to read this type of profile. Facebook readers want to learn more about the person or group whose profile they are reading.

What's It For?

Social network profiles, including profiles for Facebook, are meant to share information about a person or group. These profiles are for a band (The Most Loyal), a company (Nintendo), and a nonprofit organization (Habitat for Humanity). The Most Loyal's profile helps fans stay connected to them and their music; Nintendo's profile helps fans of their products stay up-to-date with the company and its offerings; Habitat for Humanity's profile shares information about the organization and even has a link for "Get Involved" to encourage participation by newcomers. A social network profile is thus a widely viewed, brief profile webpage that the individual or corporate author can use to present a "public face" to readers who want to learn more.

EXERCISE 5.1: Design Your Professional Social Network Profile

A social network profile helps create your online identity. You might already have a Facebook or Google+ profile or a profile on LinkedIn (a professional networking site).
    For this exercise, design a networking profile for yourself for Facebook, LinkedIn, or a similar site. If you already have a profile on these sites, then you are to revise your profile for a different audience, say, potential employers. Be sure to keep the following in mind:

- Be very careful when you select what to place online. Your online identity is hard to change. Even if you delete your profile from a social network site, it remains stored (or "cached") in various locations around the web, easily accessible for years.

- Select a profile photograph of yourself that you wouldn't mind being viewed by a wide audience, including your professor and future employers.
- Think about what qualities of yourself you want to emphasize. Do you have any special skills or experiences that you want to share with friends, family, and future employers?
- Sometimes it is useful to have your résumé (Chapter 12) next to you while you are writing your social network profile. Be sure that your résumé and your social network profile are consistent (such as your education and employment history).
- Once you have designed your profile, you may decide whether you want to publish it on Facebook, LinkedIn, Google+, or all three.

GROUP ACTIVITY 5.1: Design a Social Network Profile for Your Group

Often, collaborators will use a social network group profile to coordinate their projects together. For example, a planning committee for a high school reunion might create a page for the reunion committee to keep each other posted on the events they are planning. For this activity, create a Facebook group profile for your group.

- You will need to decide what sort of profile image best represents your group: a photograph of your group sitting together? An image of a mascot? Be sure to use an image that has a Creative Commons (cc) license and not one that is protected by copyright. For a good database of (cc) images, check out the Wikimedia Commons.
- You will also need to decide how to describe your group. Look at the preceding examples for Habitat for Humanity and Nintendo. What information would you like to share with a wide audience?

B. Portfolio

Similar to a social network profile or a résumé (Chapter 12), a portfolio is a profile of a person or group that showcases the subject's experience, talents, and/or creations. What makes a portfolio unique among profiles is that it contains samples of the subject's work—music (for a band), images (for a photographer), and clips (for a journalist).

Students often create portfolios to present a collection of work and other artifacts to demonstrate a learning process that has led to mastery of a subject.

Portfolios have traditionally existed in hard copy, but more and more portfolios are appearing in online form. Here are some examples of online portfolios.

EXAMPLE 1: Online Portfolio of a Band

Online portfolio of the band Minor Stars.

EXAMPLE 2: Online Portfolio of an Artist

Online portfolio of an artist.

EXAMPLE 3: Online Portfolio of a Poet

Andrea Selch

Home   Works   Events

Biography

Author photo by Diane Amato

Andrea Selch has an MFA from UNC-Greensboro, and a PhD from Duke University, where she taught creative writing from 1999 until 2003. Her dissertation was a history of poetry on commercial radio in the United States from 1922 until 1945. Her poems have been published in *Calyx, Equinox, The Greensboro Review, Oyster Boy Review, Luna, The MacGuffin,* and *Prairie Schooner.* Her poetry chapbook, *Succory,* was published by Carolina Wren Press in 2000. Her full-length collection of poetry, *Startling,* was runner-up in the 2003 Turning Point competition and was published by Turning Point Press in October, 2004. [*Startling* was re-issued by Cockeyed Press in 2009.] Her most recent small collection, *Boy Returning Water to the Sea: Koans for Kelly Fearing,* was published in 2009 by Cockeyed Press. She is the winner of 2008 Hippo Award from The Monti for her spoken story, "Replacement Child." In 2001, she joined the board of Carolina Wren Press and is now President and Executive Director. She lives in rural Hillsborough, North Carolina, with her partner and their two children.

All of Selch's books may be ordered through the Carolina Wren Press website or Amazon.

Selected Works

Poetry
Startling
" ...there is nothing very quiet about Andrea Selch."
                --Ron Silliman

Poetry Chapbook
Succory
Carolina Wren Press Poetry Series, #2 (2000).

Poetry/Art
Boy Returning Water to the Sea: Koans for Kelly Fearing
Poetry by Andrea Selch with illustrations by the late William Kelly Fearing.
Cockeyed Press, 2009

Quick Links
E-mail the author
Authors Guild
findauthors

Online portfolio of poet Andrea Selch.

USE THE TOOLKIT

Let's use the three genre toolkit questions from Chapter 1 to examine this genre.

What Is It?

A portfolio is an in-depth profile of a person or group that provides detailed information about its subject, along with a sampling of the subject's work. All of these example portfolios provide background information, examples, and images to educate the reader about the subjects of the portfolios. The first example is the online portfolio of the band Minor Stars; the second example is the online portfolio of artist M. Scott Myers; the third example is the online portfolio of poet Andrea Selch. The primary difference between an online portfolio and a social networking page is that the portfolio provides a sampling of the subject's work. For example, on the Minor Stars website you can listen to the band's music; on Myers's website you can view images of the artist's paintings. The home page of an online portfolio usually has a menu that allows readers to view samples of the subject's work, to read a biography about the subject, and to learn how to get in touch with the subject.

Who Reads It?

Anyone with Internet access can read these portfolios, because they are published on the world wide web; but, they tend to be read by people seeking detailed information about the subjects of the portfolios. Because there are many bands, artists, and professors who have portfolio websites, chances are people will come across these portfolios by searching for the specific figures in question. However, they may also stumble upon these portfolios while browsing. Portfolios can also be prepared in print form for a more limited audience. In many writing classes, students prepare final portfolios featuring their best work from the course, and the audience is typically their instructor.

What's It For?

These three portfolios serve their readers by providing detailed information about their subjects. The fans of a band can learn more about the band's members, view the band's show dates, and listen to samples of its music. Buyers interested in art can view paintings and purchase them on an artist's website. Writers and readers can learn more about an author and the author's work.

EXERCISE 5.2: Design a Mockup of an Online Portfolio

You might want to create a portfolio to showcase your experiences and talents online, for a few purposes. Some colleges encourage students to create portfolios as a graduation requirement and to showcase what they have learned from their coursework. Other students create portfolios as a job-seeking document, something employers will see if they search the job applicant's name online.

For this assignment, design a "mock-up" of your own online portfolio, or e-portfolio. A mock-up is a plan for your design and contents.

The following steps will help you to create your mock-up:

- Describe what kind of image you want to create for yourself. This will influence everything from the contents you put up to color choices. Is this a strictly professional site, or do you want to include a sense of who you are as a person?
- Indicate what pages you want to have in your portfolio. Some portfolios include samples of previous work—while artists might include samples of their music or art, you might include samples of your writing or other projects related to your major or interests.

- Sketch out a layout for your e-portfolio (either on paper, or using PowerPoint or desktop publishing software). Look at the menus on the home pages of the e-portfolios pictured previously. What would your menu look like? You might have pages called "home," "education," "work experience," "leadership experience," or what have you. You might find it useful to have your résumé (Chapter 12) on hand while you design your e-portfolio. You should also consider the visual design of your website (Chapter 29).
- What will your home page look like? Would you include a portrait of yourself? What text would you want to include on your home page?

MULTIMEDIA EXERCISE 5.1

After you write the text and sketch out a design for each page of your e-portfolio, design and publish your page online. There are many free services that host e-portfolios, such as Wordpress.com, or your university might offer free web space and tools for e-portfolios. Research free web hosting services that provide a web platform, and select one that you would like to use to host your e-portfolio. You might need to learn more about the platform by studying tutorials they provide. Once you feel comfortable using the platform, build your e-portfolio and launch it online.

C. Program Profile

A program profile is a profile of an entity like a government program, a research institute, or a university department. Profiles can be printed in booklet form (like the "viewbook" materials published by colleges), or they can exist online. Let's take a look at some examples of online program profiles.

EXAMPLE 1: Program Profile of a Scholarship

Program profile for a scholarship sponsored by the World Bank.

EXAMPLE 2: Program Profile of a Public Health Service

Program profile of a public health service.

EXAMPLE 3: **Program Profile of a College Major**

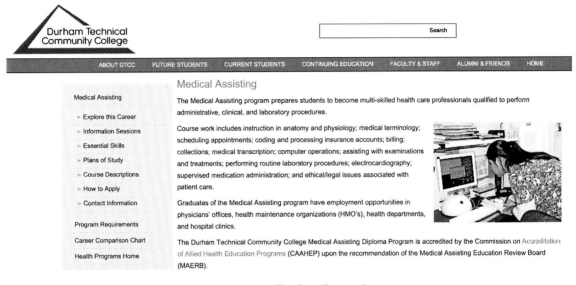

Program profile of a college major.

Let's use the three genre toolkit questions from Chapter 1 to examine this genre.

What Is It?

A profile of a program is related to an online portfolio, in that they both exist online and share information with a wide audience of readers about their subjects. But the nature of a program—an ongoing series of related activities and events that share a single goal—means that the program profile will need to meet different audience expectations than those met by an online portfolio. For example, the academic program in medical assisting (Example 3) has an ongoing series of courses and requirements that students and faculty will want to know about. Furthermore, the purpose of the program profile differs from a portfolio in that a portfolio showcases the subject's works, whereas a program profile does not.

Who Reads It?

Program profiles usually exist online, which means they can be read by anyone with an Internet connection. However, writers of program profiles probably have a more specific audience in mind when they design their profiles. For example, profiles of particular academic programs are meant primarily for people who are thinking of studying in those areas, while scholarship program profiles probably target people who would like to apply. In general, readers of program profiles are looking for detailed information about the programs profiled, and they have probably found the profile using a web search for that type of program.

What's It For?

Let's look at the examples. The profile of the Joint Japan/World Bank Graduate Scholars Program (Example 1) first gives a description of the program and then guides potential applicants through the process (and helps potential donors to the program learn more about the program). The profile of the child health care program (Example 2) describes the program and then gives links to contact information for those interested in participating. The profile of the Medical Assisting program at Durham Technical Community College (Example 3) describes the program and provides detailed information on the course of study for those interested in applying for the program. Thus, a program profile is a printed or online description of a program (which is an ongoing series of related activities and events that share a single goal) that provides detailed information for readers interested in the program.

EXERCISE 5.3: Write a Program Profile of a College Program

Imagine that you have been involved with a new, interdisciplinary educational program for your college that brings together students from at least two different departments to work on public service projects. For example, you might have a program that supports education majors and English majors who volunteer to teach English language skills to immigrant farm workers through a Farm Work Literacy Project.

- Your job is to design a profile of the program. You can use the example of the Farm Worker Literacy Project just described, or you can come up with a program of your own.
- Think about the kind of information that you will need to provide on the website for the program.
- Think about the two very different audiences you will need to address: students interested in participating, and donors interested in supporting the program with money.

EXAMPLE 3: Profile Article of an Organization

Stephanie Gottschlich

The New Recruits: Students Answer the Call for Next Generation of Air Force Scientists

Justin Estepp describes himself as "just a bench engineer." But with a small army of student research assistants at his side in the Air Force Research Laboratory's 711th Human Performance Wing complex at Wright-Patterson Air Force Base, Estepp is grinding out game-changing research at the intersection of engineering, neuroscience, and psychology that the United States Air Force views as a new frontier for achieving military superiority.

"We hear people say 'mind reading' a lot, but that's not it exactly," Estepp says, describing his research in monitoring cognitive state. "It's a three-legged stool of applied or behavioral neuroscience: figuring out what technologies best monitor the physiology of a human, such as eye-tracking and EEG; how we can relate that physiology to their cognitive state; and then how we can augment a human's performance based on that cognitive state."

Estepp—who earned a bachelor's degree in biomedical engineering from Wright State in 2006 and is finishing his master's degree in the same field—is an associate research biomedical engineer in the wing's Human Effectiveness Directorate, Warfighter Interface Division. He is among more than a half-dozen, up-and-coming Wright State grads managing research programs inside the fence in that directorate, researching how technology can enhance a warfighter's performance in the sky, in space, or in cyberspace. Wright State grads are doing everything from researching how UAVs can fly by voice command, to evaluating new, noninvasive techniques to stimulate the brain to improve attention span, to optimizing displays so that pilots or airmen can better interpret images, among other areas.

The Air Force Research Laboratory, headquartered at WPAFB, manages the Air Force's science and technology program, a $2 billion research juggernaut employing about 9,600 people. Its eight directorates emphasize a particular area of research, and for Human Effectiveness, the key word is "human." It focuses on integrating biological and cognitive technologies to boost a warfighter's performance in instances such as operating multiple unmanned aerial vehicles, or overcoming fatigue and loss of concentration while looking at computer screens.

In designer jeans and eyeglasses and Doc Marten boots, his blazer draped across a chair, Estepp belongs to a sophisticated, postmodern generation of engineers and scientists who will move up the ranks in their various directorates to lead the Air Force research agenda in the decades to come.   5

Out of concern for a shortage of scientists and engineers, AFRL has been cultivating a cadre of young technical talent to work in government labs instead of the private sector, so that when 40 percent of its workforce retires over the next two decades, the military maintains its technological superiority.

For engineers and human factors psychologists, AFRL is an opportunity to make breakthrough discoveries in fields such as unmanned aerial vehicles, modeling and simulation, sensors, cyberspace, intelligence and reconnaissance, and human performance.

Chris Meier, a Wright State student who hopes to continue working for AFRL after completing his master's degree in biomedical engineering in 2014, is one of four Wright State engineering students working with Estepp as research assistants. "The private sector probably couldn't touch the kinds of experiences we get here, from day one," Meier said, who admits the initial attraction is in getting to play with technology's latest toys.

But for a lot of students, the base is an intimidating black box. "I really had no idea research goes on at the base until I heard about it through classmates," said Sabrina Metzger, a senior in biomedical engineering. Through contact with other Wright State students, and through faculty, Metzger found the research assistant positions in the Human Effectiveness directorate. "Once you get here, you realize it's more laid-back than you think, and you have a lot of autonomy," she says.

10   Estepp knows the value of these internships: like a lot of young professionals working at WPAFB, the Dayton native stayed in the area because of an interesting internship at the base that kept him here.

After graduating from Fairborn High School, Estepp joined the inaugural class of AFRL's Wright Scholar Research Assistant Program in 2002, the summer before his freshman year at Wright State. The program enables high school juniors and seniors to work with AFRL researchers for 10 to 12 weeks on projects including testing materials, tracking data, creating databases, charting data, and computer modeling and programming. That introduction to AFRL led to engineering internships that kept him working in the lab all the way through completion of his master's degree. In 2008, he joined AFRL as a full-time engineer.

When Estepp's lab needs student research assistants, he often taps Wright State because it offers the only biomedical engineering program in the region. From providing continuing education toward advanced degrees, to collaborations with faculty, to networking with other researchers, Wright State is "well positioned to facilitate a lot of collaborations" that would benefit the technical researchers in AFRL.

"There are a lot of us who will at some point work on advanced degrees, and Wright State is perfect for that," because of its proximity and interdisciplinary programs. "And we have access to its students, just down the street. All in all, the university is a great resource."

USE THE TOOLKIT

Let's use the three genre toolkit questions from Chapter 1 to examine this genre.

What Is It?

These profile articles are documents that present text and images describing a person (in the articles on Lucas Threefoot and Lanie Wright) or group (in the article on the Air Force Research Laboratory at Wright State). All three appear in magazines that have content posted online. They tend to include quotations from the individuals in question, provide descriptions of their accomplishments and background, and, in the cases of the Air Force Research Laboratory, connect those accomplishments to the support of the university or state. Profile articles may also appear in newspapers. A lengthier profile might turn into a biography, which is essentially a book-length profile that provides greater detail and depth.

Who Reads It?

These magazines are available online, so anyone with an Internet connection could view them. However, in all three cases the magazine addresses a particular community. The Lucas Threefoot profile appears in *1859*, a magazine that features news and profiles of interest to readers living in Oregon (or potentially those living elsewhere who want to maintain a personal connection to the state). The Air Force Research Laboratory and Lanie Ward articles appear in campus magazines, which highlight news, people, and events at a university or college—so readers might include parents, students, faculty, staff, alumni, and donors.

In general, readers of profiles are interested in learning more about the person, place, group, or event that is being profiled. Sometimes readers are conducting research and specifically search for articles about a subject. Sometimes readers simply discover a profile article that looks interesting to them and spontaneously decide to read it.

What's It For?

Profile articles describe their subjects in ways that are both entertaining and informative. Sometimes profile articles praise their subjects; sometimes they criticize their subjects; sometimes they remain neutral or objective.

In these examples, the articles take a complimentary tone, praising the individuals or groups. This is especially likely in the campus magazine profiles, which serve to advertise a college, its programs, students, and faculty to the audience (especially alumni and donors). Thus, the profiles not only inform, but also guide the reader's opinion on the subjects of the profiles.

Profiles can also present familiar subjects in a new light—that is, an article might take a new angle on a subject, or even criticize its subject. Magazines that profile political leaders, such as *Rolling Stone* or *The Economist*, often take a more critical tone.

Thus, we can see that profile articles are primarily texts—but they can feature photographs or other kinds of supporting media—that inform readers about a person, group, event, or place. Profiles can guide readers' opinions about the subjects of the profiles by striking a tone of praise or criticism.

EXERCISE 5.4: Plan a Profile

Think of a person, group, event, or place that you might want to write a profile article about. Think about how you might begin to research and write your profile by answering the following questions:

1. Do you have access to the subject of your profile? For example, is the person someone you might be able to interview, or is the person hard to reach or deceased?
2. How will you gain information about the subject of your profile? Can you visit the event? Can you do library or Internet research?

3. How long will your profile be?
4. What is the intended audience of your profile? Do you want to publish it in the campus newspaper? Put in on the Internet, say, on a blog?
5. What sort of tone do you want to take toward your subject? Is there a particular *angle* that you want to take that makes your profile special or unique?

E. Strategies for Profiles

Imagine you've been assigned to write a profile article about a member of your community. Let's look at a profile written by a student. This profile was published on the school paper's website. After reading this article, we will learn some strategies for how to write profiles.

Sarah Creek
March 10, 2014
Journalism 305: Science Writing

Profile of an Engineering Professor: Dr. Grace Yang

Dr. Grace Yang's interest in power systems began when she first learned about hybrid electric vehicles (HEV) as a college student in China. She soon decided to go to graduate school to learn more about designing power systems for HEVs, earning a Master's and a PhD at the Massachusetts Institute of Technology. Today, Dr. Yang is an assistant professor at Greenview State University, where she is part of the Center for Sustainable Energy Systems (CSES). Dr. Yang works with a team of researchers invested in designing a green energy infrastructure, or "smart grid."

Dr. Yang spends some of her time designing and testing components, but spends just as much time writing—at least fifty percent of her time, by her estimate. As a junior faculty member, Dr. Yang writes grant proposals to fund her research projects, prepares conference presentations and posters, and writes research articles. She also serves as guest editor for a journal, so she is responsible for assigning others in her field to peer review papers considered for publication. In addition, she writes reports for government agencies or outside agencies who want to track progress on research they have funded.

"Not many students realize that writing is especially important for science and engineering professionals," Yang stated. "But good writing will help you to advance in your career."

Oral communication is also important in Dr. Yang's job. She estimates that 20 percent of her time involves some form of oral communication, which could mean meeting with faculty, students, or industry representatives, giving presentations at conferences, talking over ideas with colleagues.

Prewriting (Content)

When Sarah sat down to write a profile of Dr. Yang, she began by asking herself the questions that you did in Exercise 5.4. These questions are useful when brainstorming a profile (Chapters 15 and 16).

1. Do you have access to the subject of your profile? For example, is the person someone you might be able to interview, or is the person hard to reach or deceased?

In this case, Sarah did have access to the subject: she sent a professional email to the professor and requested an interview. The professor kindly agreed. They had lunch together and Sarah asked her questions, which she had prepared in advance (Chapter 24).

2. How will you gain information about the subject of your profile? Can you visit the event? Can you do library or Internet research?

Sarah not only interviewed the professor, but she researched the professor online. Professors at universities often have online profiles or portfolios that provide basic background information about the professor's education, publications, and research and teaching interests. *Before* she interviewed Professor Yang, Sarah read her profile on the university's website. Reading the profile helped Sarah brainstorm some questions for the interview.

3. How long will your profile be?

Sarah knew that her profile would need to be relatively short in order to be published on the school paper's website. She kept this intended length in mind when she set out to write her profile.

4. What is the intended audience of your profile? Do you want to publish it in the campus newspaper? Post it online to a blog?

Sarah already had a planned venue where she would publish her profile article. Sometimes, though, you might write a profile as a classroom assignment. In that case, be sure to follow your professor's instructions carefully.

5. What sort of tone do you want to take toward your subject? Is there a particular *angle* that you want to take that makes your profile special or unique?

In this article, Sarah takes a unique angle when writing about this scientist. Rather than focusing on the professor's scientific research, she focuses on her *writing*. Often, non-scientists do not realize that scientists do a lot of writing—rather, they imagine that scientists work in a lab with machines or chemicals. This article presents Professor Yang *as a writer*, not just a scientist, which makes Sarah's perspective unique and interesting.

Drafting (Organizing)

To draft her article, Sarah started by reviewing the notes she took from her research and her interview with Professor Yang.

You might also consider a few different ways of organizing your profile:

- You might use a narrative style, telling a story about your subject. You could either include yourself in the narrative (a more personal approach), or tell your story as an outside observer.
- You might use a descriptive style, which focuses more on characteristics of your subject or elements of his or her life.

After reviewing her notes, Sarah decided to blend a narrative and descriptive organization, beginning by telling how Professor Yang started her career as a researcher in green technology, and then describing her day-to-day life as a professor.

Next, you might consider how many details to include and where to include them. For a person, you might consider:

- Physical attributes
- Personality characteristics

- Qualifications (education, job experience, etc.)
- Accomplishments (books written, art produced, etc.)
- Quotations from or about that person
- Anecdotes about that person
- History or background

You could adapt those categories if you are writing about a place, program, or some other subject. For example, for a profile of your town you might mention famous people who lived there or historic events that occurred there, or you might interview people to get quotations about that place.

Revising (Style)

Once you have a draft, focus on making your profile accessible and interesting for your audience. Sarah used the term "smart grid" to help readers connect what they might have already heard about green technology. You might also consider the following ideas:

- Terms you may need to explain or define for your reader.
- Adding "local color"—specific names of places, people, dialect, or customs.
- Figurative language, such as metaphors, similes, and the like (Chapter 21).

In her peer workshop, Sarah received suggestions from her group that helped her to adopt the neutral zone of a journalist. Had she written for another audience, such as the university's alumni magazine, she might have used a more celebratory tone. Sarah might have described Dr. Yang's tendency to dress casually in jeans, or her obsession with whitewater rafting, in order to portray a youthful, adventurous professoriate. Readers of an alumni magazine tend to be potential donors or supporters of the university, and in this case Sarah might want to encourage readers to support the university's research efforts.

Editing (Design)

You might consult examples of the type of profile you are writing to determine how to finalize your profile to suit the conventions of that genre or publication. Some profiles may include plenty of pictures, especially ones that appear online; others may include none at all. You can also pay attention to formatting—should your profile have headings and sub-headings? Should it appear in columns?

You might also consider how to refer to the sources you used for your writing. For a newspaper or magazine, you probably would not use formal citation styles such as MLA. Instead, you'd use informal citation, or possibly hyperlinks (for a digital version), to lead readers to other sources.

Finally, you might consider the limitations imposed by your genre or publication. In this case, Sarah has a strict word limit for her article, so she condensed the article to fit the parameters of her assignment.

Troubleshooting

Here are some common challenges that students face when writing profiles.

I can't find a good subject for my profile   Start by thinking about who (or what) will be easy to access. Angelina Jolie might make a good profile subject, but she might not be easy to contact (unless you have a personal connection). More local figures can be interesting to read and write about, and you may be surprised that they are often willing to speak to students. You might search for people who direct organizations on campus or in your community, people who do certain kinds of work (such as farmers, or directors of a homeless shelter), or people who have unique histories (you might find senior citizens especially interesting for this reason). The same goes for places or companies—Google might be more difficult than a local software company; the Taj Mahal (while interesting) might be less accessible than a local landmark. Look online for lists of people and places in your community, such as lists of tourist sites for your town, lists of municipal government representatives, or lists of local volunteer organizations.

I can't conduct an interview with my subject   Some people may be difficult to pin down for an interview—they may be very busy, or they may not want to be interviewed. Sometimes, your subject is deceased. In that case, you can try interviewing people who know/knew your subject—co-workers, family members, friends, and the like. Imagine you want to profile the president of your university. Chances are this person would be hard to reach, but since he or she is a major figure in your community, you would probably find plenty of other people who would have something to contribute. You can also do more research about your person—try searching for your subject online or in library databases.

You can use the same approach for an historical subject or someone who has passed away. Depending on how long ago they lived, you may still find people who can tell you about your subject. If the person lived long ago, you will need to use historical documents to tell you about them. Local figures can be good for historical profiles, because your local library or college may have archival materials you can use (such as personal letters or diaries).

My subject won't answer my questions in an interview   First, be sure that you have worded your interview questions so that they do not require simple yes/no answers. If your interview is already over, you might call or email your person and see if they mind answering a few follow-up questions. Then, you can reword your questions to see whether they can offer more details.

Example Question:	Do you find working with students interesting?
Revised Question:	What do you find most rewarding about working with students?
Follow-up Question:	When we spoke, you mentioned that you enjoyed working on undergraduate research projects with students. Can you tell me more about the kinds of projects you have worked on with some of your students?

Sometimes, people may find certain questions uncomfortable—too revealing or personal, say. In this case, you might note which questions seemed to evoke this reaction. A good interviewer will try to rephrase these questions or to ask follow-up questions to evoke a good response, but you might also consider why your subject might have found that question difficult to answer. You might mention this in your article, if you think it would interest readers or shed light on your subject.

I can't find a unique angle to take on my subject   You might need to conduct more brainstorming—even if you already have a draft—to help you determine your angle. One good technique might be to ask people what they already think of the person. Can your profile offer a new perspective? (Sarah thought it might be interesting to focus on Prof. Yang's writing, since scientists are typically portrayed as engaged in laboratory research.) You can also search for other profiles of your subject, to see if you can offer a fresh perspective. If someone is usually profiled as a professional, you might offer insight into their personal life or interests, for example.

F. Chapter Project: Write a Profile Article

Imagine you have been asked to write a profile article for a campus student magazine. Choose one of the following options:

- Profile a member of the community in which your campus is located.
- Profile a member of the faculty whose research focuses on your future profession or career field.
- Profile a place on campus or in the campus community.

You can review the profiles and advice in this chapter to help you. To recap, though, you should:

- Research your subject (using interviews, secondary sources, or both)
- Find an interesting angle
- Choose an organizational strategy (such as narrative or descriptive)
- Select interesting details
- Develop a style appropriate to the topic and genre

Group Option: Create a Profile Series

Imagine you have been asked to write a series of profiles for a campus magazine. You might profile students, instructors, majors or programs, or even places on campus. You will each write a profile to go in the magazine.

As a group, you will need to decide on:

- A focus or theme (what subjects will you choose to profile?)— you might all profile student athletes, or programs that are contributing to social problems, or places where students gather on campus.

- An appropriate format and design for your publication (such as visual elements, fonts and headings, length, etc.).
- A style guide for your publication (what kind of tone should the writers take? How formal should the writing be?).

You will be responsible for reviewing and editing the profiles, together, so that they make up a cohesive group for your publication.

Multimedia Option: Create a Profile Video

Create a video profile of a person or place in your community that will appear on a local website (your campus newspaper, say, or a community newspaper). In addition to the considerations just listed, you might consider:

- What kinds of footage should I shoot? (Interviews with people? Where should the interview be set? Should I include still or moving scenes of places and people?)
- What other elements can I add? (Text? Subtitles? Transitions between elements?)
- What kinds of audio material should I have? (Will I have music? Voiceover narration? etc.)
- What should the pacing of the video be? (Do I want lots of short shots or clips, or longer ones?)

Inquiries

An inquiry is an informal investigation into or a record of anything you encounter in the world. Examples of inquiries are wide ranging, and include a food journal, an exercise diary, a sleep diary, a baby diary, a gardening planner, and many others. Once the data gathered in an inquiry takes on a more formal shape, it can become a report (Chapter 14), an analysis (Chapter 8), even a proposal (Chapter 13).

In the classroom, an inquiry can be used as prewriting for other, more formal genres. For example, class notes taken by a student can form the groundwork for a research paper later in a semester. Reading notes on an assigned reading can later become part of a book review for a class assignment.

In a professional setting, observation notes taken by an ethnographer might later be used to write a field report about a culture. A journalist takes reading notes when conducting research and later uses those notes to write a news report (Chapter 14).

In this chapter, you will learn about a variety of written inquiries that you might encounter in an academic setting.

A. Inquiry Mini-Genre: Student Class Notes

Class notes are a type of inquiry students use to investigate what they are learning.

EXAMPLE 1: Student Notes from an English Class

Josephine Perry: St. Augustine on Love
English 316: 2/18/14

AD 354–430
Bishop of Hippo (now in Algeria). Born in Algeria (then part of Roman Empire).
Studied rhetoric in Carthage, during which time he lived a hedonistic lifestyle (girls girls girls);
taught rhetoric in Carthage for 9 years, then in Rome, then in Milan.
Love life: had a son with a woman in Carthage; dumped her to get engaged; dumped his young bride as well as another concubine.

Later wrote: "By love I mean the impulse of one's mind to enjoy God on his own account and to enjoy oneself and one's neighbor on account of God, and by lust I mean the impulse of one's mind to enjoy oneself and one's neighbor and any corporeal thing not on account of God."

AD 386—religious conversion; gives up teaching rhetoric, swears off marriage, becomes a priest. Moved back to Africa & became a famous preacher. Goal was to convert people in Hippo to Christianity.

Lisa asked a good question: What relationship did Augustine's mistreatment of women have with his decision to convert and become a priest? Did he feel guilty?

EXAMPLE 2: Student Notes from an Engineering Class

Patrick Lam's notes for a Component Based Software Engineering course.

EXAMPLE 3: Student Notes from a Psychology Class

Class: Psych 209   Date: October 2, 2014
Chapter/Topic: Chapter 1   Page: 4 of

Notice that I left this blank. I don't fill it in until I am finished with the chapter.

Lecture Notes Oct 2/5	Questions	Textbook Notes
D. Measurement - looking for some certain things. Example: student who is weighed on scale.	Monitor in Psychology (Magazine)	3. Possible limits of "free choices." B. Science makes systematic observations

1. Reliability: consistency of a measure.
2. Validity: does a measure truly assess quality that it is claimed to measure? Truthfulness of a measure.

I titled this section "Questions," but I often write other misc. things that I want to remember here. I think of it as a multi-purpose column

3. Accuracy: Agreement with a known standard (process of calibration).
└ Focus remains with these two because the 3rd will often be disputed.

E. Testable Questions -
- Can hypothesis/claim be falsified at least in principle (Notion of Falsifiability) by Carl

I didn't hear the last name of someone the professor mentioned during lecture so I left a blank space. If I think the name is important I can fill it in later if its mentioned or I know what to ask the prof later on.

F. Public Reporting: Many places they can publish.
- Peer Reviewed journals (most esteemed).
- Sci are proud and want to get it out
- way you establish reputation
- We have to be aware of knowledge in order to

Psychological Science (Peer Reviewed journal)

When I take a break from reading, I like to leave a note to remind me where I left off.

• Scientists systematic observations include:
a. precise definitions of phenomena being observed
b. reliable + valid measuring tools that yield useful + interpretable data.
c. generally accepted methodologies
d. System of logic for drawing conclusion and fitting those into general theories.

C. Science Produces Public Knowledge.
• An objective observation isn't someone who is completely objective (like Peirce thought). It just means something that can be verified by more than 1 observer.
- Done through replication: where someone redoes another's study and gets same results.
• Replication can only be done if they know precisely what was done. This is done by rules that are found in Publication Manual of APA.

8-13 • Introspection: a form of precise self report.
- The problem w/ introspect is that its subjective and not verifiable.
- John B. Watson concluded that something can only be "scientific" if its directly observable and can be verified

Jenna Shrewsbury's notes for a psychology course. She annotated her own notes to demonstrate her study process.

USE THE TOOLKIT

Let's use the three genre toolkit questions from Chapter 1 to examine this genre.

What Is It?

These class notes were all written by college students. You'll see that most students list the course title and date at the top of each page. Possibly, the students wrote that information before class began, in order to keep notes organized.

The notes are not always written in complete sentences. Some are funny asides that the author wrote to herself to help her remember important points (e.g., "girls, girls, girls" in Josephine's English class notes in Example 1).

The students have written down notes from what the professor said in class as well as notes from class discussion. Josephine, in Example 1, wrote down a question that another student asked that she found important. In this way, the student has engaged in discussion by listening closely to what others are saying. Jenna, in Example 3, has included a column for questions that she might need later on when she is working on a paper.

You'll see that each student has developed his or her own note-taking system. Josephine, in Example 1, takes notes on her computer, while Patrick in Example 2 and Jenna in Example 3 feature handwritten notes. Jenna, in Example 3, has developed a template that she prints out and uses for all of her classes.

Who Reads It?

Each student wrote these notes primarily for his or her own use. They need to take good notes because these notes are important to their grades. For example, one student might use his notes later in the semester to prepare an essay for the course, while another might use her notes to study for a final exam.

Sometimes, though, students share their class notes with each other—for example, to help a student who missed class get caught up.

What's It For?

Class notes help a student learn the material. By taking notes, the student summarizes, in her own words, the readings, lectures, and class discussions of a course. Putting course material in one's own words is essential to this type of inquiry—and all inquiries—because using one's own words forces a writer to formulate her own ideas about a subject. Later in the semester, these ideas might become the content of an essay, a presentation, or an exam answer.

EXERCISE 7.1: Evaluate Your Class Notes

Review your class notes for two of your classes last week: one class you really enjoy, and one class that you enjoy a little less.

Compare these notes. Write your answers to the following questions:

- Do you write more notes in the class you enjoy, or more in the class you don't enjoy? Why do you think that is?
- Would someone else be able to read your class notes and understand them? Does this hold true for both classes? Why or why not?

- Do you have a system for note-taking? What is it? If not, should you develop one?
- Do you write down ideas that you come up with when you take notes? Do you write down ideas that come from other students? Why or why not?

GROUP ACTIVITY 7.1: Exchange and Evaluate Class Notes

In your small group, trade your class notes with each other. Read your classmate's notes. Write your answers to the following questions, and be prepared to share your answers with your classmates.

- Can you understand what your classmate has written? Why or why not?
- Would these notes be helpful to you if you needed them in a crunch? Why or why not?
- Does the note-taker write down ideas that he or she has come up with? Does he write down ideas that come from other students? Why do you think he or she did/didn't do these things?

B. Blog Entry

Blogs are an online collections of writings, sketches, images, and other media that the authors have written (or gathered) to reflect on their lives, on events that have occurred, on media, or on their thoughts or dreams.

EXAMPLE 1: Blog Entry for a Mass Communications Class

Disappointment: *Rizzoli & Isles*

By Brandy

As a fan of Tess Gerritsen's books, when I learned TNT was giving Gerritsen's central characters a show of their own, I was excited, and set my dvr accordingly. Then, I set about waiting to see who had been cast in the titular roles. Don't ask, it never really occurs to me that I could, you know, use the internet to find out stuff like that in advance. It was obvious from the first commercials I saw that whatever TNT's *Rizzoli & Isles* was going to be, it wasn't going to be too much like the books. For about 7 books I'd imagined Rizzoli, as she is described, with a mop of unruly dark curls, and as good looking, but in an unconventional way; Dr. Isles was, as she is often described, the queen of the dead, a little goth, with red lipstick and straight black hair cut in a bob with straight bangs—which is, as it turns out, how Ms. Gerritsen looks (well, not exactly goth, but you get the idea). While there was never any doubt in my mind these women would be beautiful in their own ways, um . . . Angie Harmon and Sasha Anderson were not exactly the faces that leapt into my mind as I read these books. . . .

Like I said, although I'd initially hoped for something a little different, this review isn't about comparing the television show to the books. The characters, stories, and tone of each is distinct enough that a real comparison is impossible. The books are detective fiction, pure and simple. The television show walks the genre lines between serious police procedural and comedy. It is almost as if the producers really wanted an hour long comedy, and knew stretching a sit com that long would grow tedious, so they decided to incorporate a police procedural to bump up the story. I've never seen an episode, so I could be wrong, but *Rizzoli & Isles* makes me think it is like a female Nash Bridges.

It might surprise you, but the light nature of the show is not really what bothers me. A lot of police procedurals err in the opposite way, taking themselves too seriously. What bothers me about *Rizzoli & Isles* is that the light tone is achieved at the expense of the title characters. At every turn the show undermines the power of two strong women working together, and becoming friends by making every second conversation between the two about getting, or having, a relationship, every third conversation about the case—as if their jobs are an afterthought, and the remaining conversations about clothes and shoes. There has to be some sort of heterosexual romance for at least one of the women in nearly every episode because the writers are working overtime to ensure that it is clear Rizzoli & Isles are not lesbians. (Well, except for those episodes where they pretend to be lesbians—you know, for laughs.) As a viewer it is impossible to take either Rizzoli or Isles seriously because at every turn we are reminded that Rizzoli can't get a man because she is not feminine enough, and that despite looking like a fashion plate Isles can't function socially because she is just too smart.

EXAMPLE 2: Blog Entry for a Sociology of Gender Class

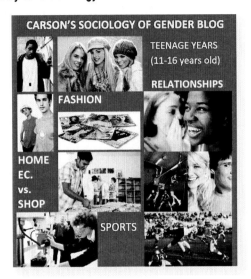

A visual blog by Carson McDonald.

EXAMPLE 3: Blog Entry for a Political Science Class

Straw-Man Fallacy and the "Anti-Antiterror Left"
By Lucia Gonzalez Hernandez

In a column titled "The 'Al-Qaeda Seven': The Anti-Antiterror Left and Legal Standards," the editorial staff at the *Wall Street Journal* agreed that the insinuations made by Lynn Cheney and her colleagues at Keep America Safe about the seven Justice Department lawyers who defended Guantanamo Bay terror suspects were "unfortunate." (Essentially, in dubbing the lawyers the "Al-Qaeda Seven," Lynn Cheney implied that these attorneys, who worked *pro bono* to provide representation guaranteed by our Constitution, worked on behalf of Al-Qaeda.)

But the WSJ also criticized many on the left who they find hypocritical: "Many liberals seem to believe that while it was a war crime to agree with [former VP] Dick Cheney's antiterror methods, it is somehow a lawyer's patriotic duty to defend terrorists. This is the mindset that these columns describe as that of the anti-antiterror left."

When I first read this phrase, "the anti-antiterror left," it struck me as the typical hawk-right hyperbole used to create a straw-man. The straw-man fallacy is a favorite of those who participate in political discourse, both in the media and in Washington (or Raleigh, for that matter). The fallacy works like this: you exaggerate (through overstatement, for example) the position of your opponents in order to make their positions easier to refute. Hawks on the right have often criticized pro-peace Americans as weak or unamerican.

For example, Lynn Cheney's KAS writes in its mission statement: "Amidst the great challenges to America's security and prosperity, the current administration too often seems uncertain, wishful, irresolute, and unwilling to stand up for America, our allies and our interests." For KAS, then, the Obama administration won't "stand up for America"—an exaggeration used for persuasive effect.

5   So: labeling folks who think Gitmo should close and that former VP Cheney's prewar tactics were misleading as "the anti-antiterror left" first appeared to me as a straw-man fallacy, ripe with hyperbole.

But then I thought about it. What does the term "antiterror" mean? It seems to refer to a set of principles, such as those espoused by former VP Cheney and his daughter, such as rendition, waterboarding, and the like. Had the WSJ used the term "pro-terror," they would have committed the straw-man fallacy, and probably many other fallacies as well. But they did not.

I wonder, should those on the left who disagree with the Cheneys, the WSJ, and KAS, disagree with the label of "anti-antiterror"? Perhaps, rather than disagreeing, their strongest rhetorical move would be to claim the label as their own.

USE THE TOOLKIT

Let's use the three genre toolkit questions from Chapter 1 to examine this genre.

What Is It?

All three of these blog entries have a few things in common. They gather together ideas in an informal fashion. They reflect upon events in the author's life: a television show watched, the experience of being a teen, an article read in a newspaper. The verbal blog entries include phrases such as "I wonder," "I'd hoped," and "I thought," indicating the reflective nature of a blog. All three demonstrate how the blog entry is a form of inquiry: each explores a topic, using words, images, and hyperlinks to investigate and record ideas. Brandy's blog entry about the television show *Rizzoli & Isles*, for example, is less formal than a review essay (Chapter 9), but it still explores the strengths and weaknesses of the show. Indeed, Brandy might build upon the blog entry later in the semester to write a review essay of contemporary television shows.

Who Reads It?

Blogs can be very private, written only for the eyes of the author. These blog entries, and most blogs written for school or published online, are meant to be shared with others. For example, Lucia wrote her blog entry, Example 3, in response to a prompt from her political science teacher to write about a current event. While blog entries remain reflective and informal, they are written in a fashion that is easy for others to understand.

What's It For?

Carson put together his visual blog entry, Example 2, in preparation for writing a paper on gender differences. Brandy wrote her blog post, Example 1, because her professor asked her to reflect on a new television show. All of these blog entries are meant to influence readers' opinions on current cultural events. Blog entries, then, can be written with a more formal project in mind, or for their own sakes, that is, for reflection and generating ideas.

EXERCISE 7.2: Keep a Blog for One Week

For one week, write every day as though you were writing for a blog. Write for a minimum of ten minutes each session. Each session, pick a topic to write about. You can pick a topic from one of your classes (brainstorm for an assignment, for example), or from a book you've read, or a television show or movie you've watched.

MULTIMEDIA EXERCISE 7.1: Create a Visual Blog Entry

Pick one of the following topics. Using PowerPoint or similar software, create a visual blog. You can download pictures from the Internet and insert text to reflect upon the images. You can even record audio (an "audio PowerPoint") to accompany your visual blog entry.

- Friendship
- Romance and love
- Adventure
- Travel
- The environment

C. Reading Notes

Reading notes are reflective pieces written in response to texts. Students write reading notes to prepare for classes, for exams, or for writing papers about books. They are an informal version of reading response essays (Chapter 3). Reading notes are a kind of inquiry because they record the reader's informal investigation of a text.

EXAMPLE 1: Reading Notes for a Rhetoric Course

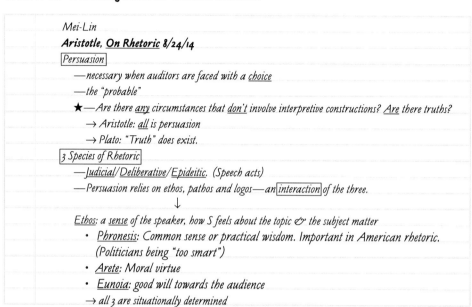

Mei-Lin

Aristotle, <u>On Rhetoric</u> 8/24/14

Persuasion

—*necessary when auditors are faced with a <u>choice</u>*

—*the "probable"*

★—*Are there <u>any</u> circumstances that <u>don't</u> involve interpretive constructions? <u>Are</u> there truths?*

→ *Aristotle: <u>all</u> is persuasion*

→ *Plato: "Truth" does exist.*

3 Species of Rhetoric

—<u>Judicial/Deliberative/Epideitic</u>. *(Speech acts)*

—*Persuasion relies on ethos, pathos and logos—an* interaction *of the three.*

↓

<u>Ethos</u>: a <u>sense</u> of the speaker, how S feels about the topic & the subject matter

• *<u>Phronesis</u>: Common sense or practical wisdom. Important in American rhetoric. (Politicians being "too smart")*

• *<u>Arete</u>: Moral virtue*

• *<u>Eunoia</u>: good will towards the audience*

→ *all 3 are situationally determined*

EXAMPLE 2: Reading Notes for a Research Paper

Terrence B.

Notes on Pamela Lewis Reading

Pamela Lewis, "Behind the Glass Wall: Barriers that Incarcerated Parents Face Regarding the Care, Custody and Control of their Children" (2004)

Lewis's arguments:
• Lewis suggests that visitation is a legal right.
• Legal barriers and prison rules unjustly prevent visitation.
• Limited access to legal services makes hearings problematic for incarcerated parents.
• Legal services often given only when parental rights are being terminated.

My thoughts:
• In what ways can visitation be construed as a "legal right"? Under the U.S. Constitution? At the state level? Is it a fundamental right under the Due Process Clause?

- If felons can be stripped of their fundamental right to vote, can they also be stripped of their right to parent? Draw an analogy with voting and the movement to restore the franchise to felons?
- If parenting is a fundamental right, should there also be a right to counsel in situations where parental visitation is challenged?

EXAMPLE 3: **Reading Notes for a Literature Course**

Michael M.
Elizabeth Barrett Browning Response: "The Cry of the Children"

I am interested in discussing the types of accusations EBB makes in "The Cry of the Children." This is not a mere woe-and-pity poem meant to demonstrate the plight of the helpless. She makes accusations and threats, that are both gendered and political.

In the first stanza, Browning writes, "Do ye hear the children weeping, O my brothers / Ere the sorrow comes with years? / They are leaning their young heads against their mothers / And *that* cannot stop their tears." Here she makes what appears to be an emotional appeal to her fellow countrymen, her "brothers." She emphasizes the children's misery by showing that even their mothers' care does not bring them solace. Although these may appear to be gender-neutral, in particular the invocation of "brothers," I argue that she makes a specific accusation towards men, and men in power—government, industry—to do something. The mothers, in contrast, are helpless to help their own children. Browning repeats the call to "brothers" in line 9.

The call for help is also directed at the nation as a whole, but even this is a gendered call and accusation. At the end of the first stanza she refers to "the country of the free" (12), but later, at the end of the second stanza, she refers to Britain ironically as "our happy Fatherland" (24). The nation, and its political powers, are the father-figure of this poem, in contrast with the helpless mother-figures.

The children living in poverty, laboring in mines and workhouses, wish for death as an escape from misery. Their lives spent in the dark mines and factories contrast with the sunshine and vegetation outside. In stanza five, Browning writes, "Sing out, children, as the little thrushes do; / Pluck you handfuls of the meadow cowslips pretty." In response, the children compare this natural beauty with "the weeds anear the mine" and reject the speaker's offer of comfort in natural beauty: "Leave us quiet in the dark of the coal-shadows." The natural world, often associated with the feminine, contrasts starkly in the masculine world of industry.

USE THE TOOLKIT

Let's use the three genre toolkit questions from Chapter 1 to examine this genre.

What Is It?

All three examples of reading notes just presented discuss a particular text in detail. Mei-Lin, in Example 1, examines *Rhetoric* by Aristotle; Terrence, in Example 2, examines a legal article by Pamela Lewis; Michael, in Example 3, examines "Cry of the Children" by Elizabeth Barrett Browning. Terrence's research paper is examined in greater detail in Part 3 of this book.

All three students note the name of the text and the name of the author. Mei-Lin's notes on Aristotle resemble an outline of the ideas in Aristotle's text. Terrence's notes are more of a quick summary of the arguments of the article and his reflections on those arguments. Michael's notes on Browning are highly reflective and resemble a journal entry (Chapter 2). Thus, reading notes and journal entries can overlap as genres.

Who Reads It?

Reading notes are typically written for the note-taker to read. Sometimes, though, a note-taker will share the notes with classmates or a teacher.

What's It For?

By recording the reader's informal investigation of a text, reading notes accomplish many things. First, they help the note-taker better understand and recall the reading material. Second, reading notes can be the beginning stages of research, helping the note-taker assemble research material in preparation of writing an outline or a paper (Chapter 24).

EXERCISE 7.3: Write Reading Notes

Look through your school newspaper (either the print version or the online version) and select a short article or opinion piece to read. Once you have finished reading, write some reading notes by answering the questions below:

- Who is the author? What can you learn about the author from the article? How does the author's identity affect your feelings toward the text?
- What do you believe is the main purpose of the article? Find a quotation from the article that supports your belief.

- In what ways does the author accomplish this main purpose? By giving examples? By conducting research and sharing it with readers?
- How does this text make you feel? Angry? Hopeful? Why?

GROUP ACTIVITY 7.2

Look through your school newspaper (either the print version or the online version) and select a short article or opinion piece to read. Once everyone in your group has finished reading the piece, discuss how you would answer the questions in Exercise 7.3. How would these questions help each of you better understand the text that you have read?

D. Observation Notes

Observation notes are notes taken by writers to record events that they have witnessed. Like they do with reading notes, writers record observation notes to prepare for classes, for exams, or for writing papers about what they have witnessed.

EXAMPLE 1: Observation Notes for an Anthropology Assignment

Name of Observer: Zachary Fitzgerald
Location: Campus Courtyard
Date: April 18, 2014
Time: 12:30 p.m.–1:00 p.m.

Observations of the Campus Courtyard

I observed student interactions at the Campus Courtyard, a popular outdoor "hangout" spot located between the library and the student union. The courtyard is a shady, rectangular area paved in brick, with built in benches. It is surrounded by trees and azalea bushes (which were in full bloom). There is a large, round fountain in the center.

At the start of the observation period, there were two main groups of students who were hanging out in the courtyard: a group of skateboarders surrounding the fountain, and a group of students clustered in the southwest corner. Other students walked through the courtyard on their way to the Student Union, the library, or classes, but I focused on those who were sitting or standing in the courtyard for most of the observation period (thirty minutes).

The skateboarding group consisted of three male and two female students. There were three skateboards between them. One of the male students was showing a female student a trick, and then encouraging her to practice it. The remaining two males were standing with the other female, talking. Occasionally, they would take one of the skateboards and do a lap around the paved area. The students were dressed in similar styles: tight jeans (usually black), t-shirts, and sneakers.

The students in the southwest corner included four women and two men. At the start of the observation period, one of the women was speaking, glancing at a notebook, and gesturing frequently. After she spoke, the other students cheered and applauded briefly. Then, a few students seemed to offer comments. Next, a male student began to speak—also referring to a notebook. The group proceeded to go around the circle, with each student speaking and the rest listening and applauding, followed by a short period in which different students spoke. Some of the students had food with them—one was eating an apple, another a sandwich.

Reflections:

The skateboarding group and "speaking" groups both seem to represent different sub-cultures found on our campus. The skateboarding group shared a style of dress, common interest, and set of bodily habits. As we have been learning in class, these are some of the components sociologists study when they study culture. The "speaking" group's sub-culture was less obvious, but my interpretation was that perhaps they were practicing for the upcoming campus poetry slam. The students seemed to share a particular style of emphatic, rhythmic speaking, and a particular way of responding to each poem with encouragement. My observation supports the idea that sub-cultures exist on a college campus, and that they share certain, observable traits (dress, style of speech, interests, etc.).

EXAMPLE 2: Observation Notes for an Education Course

Student-Observer: Belinda W.
Student-Teacher: Sierra M.
11th Grade English, 9:00am Friday
May 7, 2014

Peer Classroom Observations: Sierra M.

1. Students were all on time, and many were early.
   Conclusion: They were obviously excited for the class and ready to begin.
2. The one student that was late apologized directly to Sierra after class and explained that he was held up for a class related errand.
   Conclusion: It was clear he respected her and the rest of the class.
3. The banter and conversation at the beginning of class was not that much different than the conversation during class.

Conclusion: The atmosphere was extremely comfortable. The students weren't intimidated by the dynamic of class and so felt comfortable to share their ideas.

4. The students did not talk over one another but almost all of them spoke.

Conclusion: They all seemed extremely respectful of one another and of Sierra, and they were invested in the group discussion.

5. They were all leaning forward over their desks.

Conclusion: All were engaged and wanted to be there.

6. Most of them did not raise their hands before they spoke.

Conclusion: The classroom dynamic resembled a conversation rather than Sierra wielding the power and directing discussion. The conversation also never dove off topic into an unproductive tangent.

7. Several students would refer to the previous student when they spoke, either disagreeing or agreeing with them.

Acknowledging that the dialogue was with the students and not necessarily with Sierra, they engaged respectfully with each other. It was very exciting to see students conversing with each other in such a positive way.

8. When one student was searching for the answer to a question posed the others chimed in to help him.

Conclusion: The students seemed to have solidarity with each other and Sierra.

9. Students would praise other students.

Conclusion: Sierra built a supportive atmosphere in the classroom.

10. Students stayed on topic the entire time.

Conclusion: Although Sierra was not necessarily directing discussion per se, the students understood that they were there to discuss language and rhetoric. Although the topic varied from song lyrics to advertisements to a short story they related it all to language and rhetoric.

11. The students disagreed with one another.

Conclusion: Students felt comfortable enough to engage and take opposing stances to the topics under discussion and allowed that one was not right or better than another.

12. The students were taking pictures with a camera that Sierra had brought in since this was the last class period that they had.

Conclusion: At first I thought this would be very distracting but it was actually a great way for the students to express themselves. Again, they were respectful with it and it turned out to be a bonding experience instead of a disruption.

13. The students participated in group discussion for the majority of the class period stemming from individual student's presentations on songs or advertisements.

Conclusion: Again, while there were several students that clearly felt more comfortable talking than others, I didn't notice any of them acting like they felt shut down. This was also a great way for students to have the center of attention if they wanted it while not losing the positive momentum of the group discussion.

14. They moved quickly from each student presentation to the next.

Conclusion: Once the conversation began to slow down about each topic, Sierra would suggest a new presenter. This had the effect of moving the class forward without shutting any one off too quickly or exhausting the conversation past productivity. It also allowed several students to have a few moments to speak about what they had brought in and many were clearly excited to share their song or advertisement with the rest of the class.

Final Thoughts: I was most surprised at the insightful comments that these students were making. They seemed far beyond the 11th Grade level, and I think that stemmed from the expectation of the class. Sierra expects a lot from the students, and they gladly rise to the occasion and beyond. I also found it to be an incredibly positive environment even while students were disagreeing with each other and bringing up controversial political subjects. I appreciated Sierra's frank conversation with her students. Her interaction with them was as respectful as her interaction with her peers, and, as a result, she has a class full of students that respect her back. I also appreciated Sierra's bold move to draw the attention to herself as a feminist at one point to make a point about audience. I think students could benefit from more interaction like this.

End: 9:50am

EXAMPLE 3: Observation Notes for a Chemistry Course

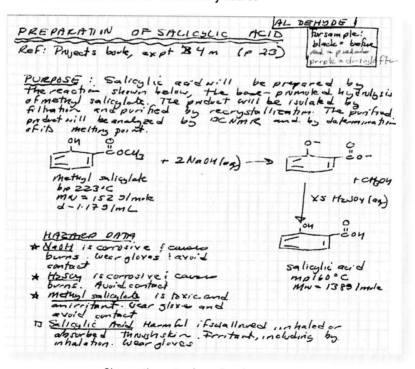

Observation notes for a chemistry course.

USE THE TOOLKIT

Let's use the three genre toolkit questions from Chapter 1 to examine this genre.

What Is It?

Like reading notes, observation notes are informal investigations—only they are investigations of *events* the writer has witnessed, rather than investigations of texts. The preceding examples provide observations of three different events or locations: students hanging out at a campus location, an English class meeting, and a scientific experiment. All three documents share similar qualities: (1) they are informal in tone and presentation; (2) they all have a title of some sort at the top, recording when and where the observations took place; and (3) they all record the author's investigations as they took place, usually in a chronological fashion.

Who Reads It?

Often, observation notes are only meant to be read by their author. Sometimes, though, students share their observation notes with their teacher or group mates. Zachary's observations were written as a sociology assignment. Belinda's student-teacher observation notes were written for her professor in her education course. Lab notes would be shared with a lab partner.

What's It For?

Students who write observation notes often must prepare a more formal project, such as a paper or a lab report, using the field notes as a primary source of data (Chapter 23). In Example 2, Belinda's notes serve two purposes: to provide feedback to a fellow student-teacher, Sierra, and to show Belinda's own knowledge about teaching to Belinda's professor.

EXERCISE 7.4: Conduct a Field Observation

Choose a location on or near your college campus. Plan to spend one hour observing a particular facet of social interactions at that location. For example, you might observe how often students are on their cell phones while ordering at the coffee shop, or whether or not people wipe off the gym equipment after using it. Take notes during your observation, and then write a one-page summary of your observations.

E. Strategies for Inquiries

Review Belinda's classroom observation of Sierra's student-teaching (Example 2). Imagine that you have been asked to write observation notes in a similar fashion, with a list of observations and then a list of conclusions to follow. This "double-entry" strategy is a great way to structure observation notes if you haven't been given a structure by your instructor. You can write your observations first, then reflect upon them later. Let's go step-by-step through this writing process.

Prewriting (Content)

When writing field notes, you will either be assigned a group or location to observe, or your instructor will allow you to choose what to observe.

If you are allowed to choose the group or location that you will observe, be sure to choose with care. You will be examining it very closely and spending a lot of time with the subject. You can select a location that is familiar to you, such as the student gym, but if you do, try to observe a specific action that you haven't noticed before. You can also select a location that is unfamiliar to you; in this case, try to record as much detail as possible about the people and the locale.

Check with your instructor to ensure that you are following best practices for informing your subjects about your observation and that you are not violating anyone's privacy or intruding on private space.

In Belinda's case, she was assigned a specific group to observe: Sierra's high school classroom. Belinda knew that she could not name any student names in her observation notes because naming names would violate the students' privacy.

Drafting (Organizing)

Be sure to put a heading at the beginning of your field notes. In the heading, identify the location or group of people that you observed. Record the date and time as well. Provide as many details as feasible about the observations in your heading.

Provide a title for your observations. Belinda titled her field notes "Peer Classroom Observations: Sierra M." This title informed readers about exactly what is contained in the field notes. (Example 3, the lab notes, is titled "Preparation of Salicylic Acid," another accurate and helpful title.)

Belinda initially took her field notes by hand. She drew a line down the center of a piece of notebook paper. She wrote observations on the left side of the line, and she wrote her conclusions based on those observations on the right side of the line. This kind of note-taking is called "double-entry" note-taking. Table 7.1 is an excerpt of her original notes.

Table 7.1 Belinda's Double-Entry Notes

OBSERVATIONS	CONCLUSIONS
Students were all on time, many early	Excited for class to begin
The one student that was late apologized directly to Sierra after class and explained that he was held up for a class-related errand	Respect
The banter and conversation at the beginning of class was not that much different than the conversation during class	Comfortable, not intimidated, relaxed dynamic

Revising (Style)

Although field notes are informal in style, if someone besides the note-taker will be reading them, they must be revised carefully. Be sure to use complete sentences in your revision, even if you wrote your original notes in fragments.

Belinda revised her double-entry notes into an organized list of observations. After each observation, she wrote a conclusion. She labeled her conclusions with the word "conclusion" so that her professor would understand the structure of her notes. She typed her notes neatly on her computer rather than turning them in handwritten.

Editing (Design)

Your heading and your time notations should be easy to read. You can type them in boldface or underline them if your notes are hand-written. These headings and notations are the structural bones of your observation notes.

Belinda's notes have two time markers: the start time and the end time of the class period. Because a class period is already well structured, the time markers are not as crucial. If you are observing a less structured event, such as a party or a similar informal gathering, time markers help your reader understand how much time has passed between each of your observations.

Troubleshooting

Here are some common challenges that students face when writing inquiries.

What if people want to talk to me?   Although your role is more of an observer than a participant, if someone wants to talk to you, record that conversation as part of your field notes. If your teacher agrees, you should explain what you are doing there and ask them if it's OK with that person for you to observe and take notes.

What if I can't think of an interesting place to observe?   Every potential location can be an interesting place to observe—you are responsible for making the observation interesting. Even if you are in a familiar place, like a coffee shop, start paying close attention to all of the people there. What are they doing, exactly? What kinds of conversations are going on? Eavesdrop a little bit. Stand by the counter and really watch what the baristas are doing back there. What sorts of jobs do the workers do? Why? When examined closely, even your regular coffee shop can appear as a whole new world.

You should discuss with your instructor whether you should get the permission of the baristas or the manager to stand there and observe. You don't want to get in the way or cause other inconvenience!

F. Chapter Project: Write Observation Notes

Conduct a field observation of a location on your campus to evaluate how well campus resources are utilized by students. Any location on campus is open to your observation. For example, you might observe how often students stopped to pay attention to the artwork on display in the Student Union, or how many students used a video game room in the Student Union over the course of an hour.

Spend one hour at the location, keeping track of how many people come and go, recording what they do and whatever else you notice. (What kinds of games were played in the video room? Were there more men or women?) Revise your notes and type them up so that you can share them with the student affairs office.

Group Option: Comparative Field Observations

As a group, conduct the field observation requested by the student affairs representative in the Chapter Project (Section F of the chapter). Each group member should record his or her own field notes at a different time of day.

Once the observations have been gathered, compare your field notes to those of the other observers in your group. How similar are these notes? How different?

As a group, compile your notes into one "master" version that you can share with your student affairs representative.

Multimedia Option: Presentation of Findings

Put together a presentation, such as a PowerPoint, presenting your findings (Chapter 29). Be prepared to deliver a talk on your findings (Chapter 30).

Analyses

An analysis is a document that helps readers to interpret information. The goal of an analysis is to break down complex information into its components. For example, during a football game you might see an expert analyzing a play in slow motion, showing the blocking, the quarterback's motion, the receivers' routes, and so on. They might then offer an interpretation of why that play was effective (or not).

In college, analyses are common assignments. You are probably familiar with some types of analyses already, such as a literary analysis. In humanities courses, analysis is often used to interpret texts—a short story, a work of art, or a speech, for example. In other courses, though, you may be asked to analyze information, such as the latest trends in consumer preferences for a business class (a market analysis) or common themes in a series of interviews you conducted for a sociology class (a content analysis). In a film class, you might write a scene analysis. In each case, the goal is to take something complex (a data set, a series of transcribed interviews, a film) and break it into simpler terms by identifying common features or patterns.

In the workplace, you may be asked to write an analysis for a number of reasons. If you work for a library, you might be asked to analyze the needs of community members (community analysis). If you work for a retail company, you might be asked to analyze demographic information about customers (customer analysis). An engineer might analyze the energy efficiency of a building (building analysis). Business consultants analyze the performance and goals for companies using a SWOT analysis, which stands for "strengths, weaknesses, opportunities, and threats." In the health sciences, lab technicians perform various kinds of analyses, such as a blood type analysis or an analysis of an x-ray or image. In all of these cases, the writer's goal is to process complex information for the audience, using key concepts or patterns to make that information manageable.

In this chapter, you will learn to write several kinds of analyses. We will focus on the types of analyses you will be most likely to encounter in college humanities courses, but keep in mind that the genre toolkit can help you to discover other kinds of analyses that you may encounter in the future.

A. Analysis Mini-Genre: Keyword Analysis

Take a look at the following images.

EXAMPLE 1: Keyword Analysis of a Speech

President Barack Obama's speech announcing the death of Osama bin Laden.

EXAMPLE 2: Keyword Analysis of a Court Opinion

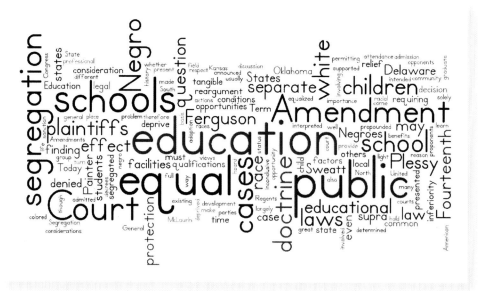

Brown v. Board of Education, U.S. Supreme Court, handed down in 1954.

EXAMPLE 3: Keyword Analysis of a Government Document

The Declaration of Independence, drafted by Thomas Jefferson, delivered July 4, 1776.

USE THE TOOLKIT

Let's use the three genre toolkit questions from Chapter 1 to examine this genre.

What Is It?

All of these images provide fodder for a kind of analysis, called a *keyword analysis,* in which a long text is broken down by the words it contains most often, or its keywords. The size of the words in a word or tag "cloud" indicates their frequency in a text—the bigger the word, the more often it is used. You may have seen similar kinds of keywords analyses—often called *word clouds* or *tag clouds*—on blogs and websites. Sometimes, bloggers will post a keyword analysis showing the categories they post about most often.

The keyword analysis examples shown here were made using a service called Wordle (http://www.wordle.net), which allows users to make these images and post them in a public web gallery.

As the reader, you can then examine the keyword analysis and *interpret* what it means. The keyword analysis shown in Example 1 analyzes President Obama's May 2011 speech announcing the killing of Osama bin Laden. Example 2 analyzes the Supreme Court opinion for *Brown v. Board of Education,* the 1954 decision that led to desegregation of American schools. Example 3 analyzes the text of the Declaration of Independence from Britain of the American Colonies. In each case, the most common words tell you something about the text. For example, the word "children" figures prominently in Example 2, which you might interpret to mean that the Supreme Court justified their decision in part by appealing to the audience's concern for children.

Who Reads It?

Keyword analyses are usually read by visitors to websites, where they may be posted, or by scholars who study language and rhetoric. For example, a scholar hoping to analyze the language used in the Declaration of Independence might include a keyword analysis in a research paper (Chapter 11).

What's It For?

Keyword analyses can give you a sense of what a text is about. They provide a visual tool to help you interpret the text, giving insight into its main themes and ideas. For instance, in Example 3, you might notice that the word "powers" figures prominently. Why is this the case? You might look at instances of the word "powers" to determine why the word is so central to the Declaration of Independence.

Or, in Example 1, you might consider why the words "country" and "people" appear more prominently in the speech than such words as "justice" and "security." What effects do these kinds of words have on an audience? If you wanted to say more about Obama's speech, you might write a longer analysis using some of the tools of rhetoric. In fact, you could write a rhetorical analysis, an analysis genre that you will learn about later in this chapter.

EXERCISE 8.1: Do a Keyword Analysis

Choose a speech or text that you find interesting. You might go to AmericanRhetoric .com for a long list of famous speeches. Then, use a keyword analysis tool, such as Wordle (http://www.wordle.net) or TagCloud (http://www.tagcloud.com), to do your own keyword analysis.

Next, write a paragraph or two in which you interpret your findings. What words were used most often in your sample? What might that say about the rhetorical situation for the speech—its effect on an audience, how it reflects the speaker, or what it has to do with the timing for the speech? Did the frequency of certain words—or their infrequency—surprise you? Did you find what you expected? (See Chapter 2 for more on rhetorical situations.)

GROUP ACTIVITY 8.2: Group Scene Analysis

As a group, do Exercise 8.3. Have each member of your group select a different scene from the same literary work and write an analysis of how it functions in the film. Imagine that you are also contributing to a special issue of a journal on the film you have chosen. As a group, write the introduction to that special issue, highlighting the main themes or commonalities you uncovered in your individual analyses.

MULTIMEDIA EXERCISE 8.3: Video Scene Analysis

Do Exercise 8.3, but prepare a video presentation for your scene analysis. Imagine that your analysis will be submitted to a web-based undergraduate literary journal for a special issue on adaptations of literature for the screen.

To get ideas, you can search for examples of student scene analyses on YouTube. You can use still shots and clips from your films, voiceovers, and text to explain how your scene functions.

D. Rhetorical Analysis

A rhetorical analysis can take as its object a film or work of literature, and it can consider many of the same elements. However, the central goal of a rhetorical analysis is to account for the effect of a work on readers or viewers. Rhetorical analysis can be applied to a variety of texts and even objects: speeches, editorials, articles, books, websites, and even works of art.

EXAMPLE 1: Rhetorical Analysis of a Government Document

Cody M. Poplin
English 102i

Rhetorical Strategies and Effectiveness
in the Declaration of Independence

It is a document enshrined in America's foundation. It speaks of liberty, pursuing

dreams, and the annihilation of an oppressive government. It accomplished every goal conceived for it and is still studied today because of its historical impact. The Declaration of Independence is more than a letter from one vehement aristocrat to a King; it is what it was meant to be, a rallying cry of the soul and a standard for freedom. Through its resolute tone and formal style, the writers of the Declaration forged a rhetorical piece with various strategies, and ultimately changed the shape of the world.

Historians accredit the transcription of the Declaration to Thomas Jefferson. The future president of the United States held a powerful position in the Virginia House of Burgesses, and he was influential in the crafting of American ideals of Republicanism and the expansion of this new Nation. But to credit the entire document to one man would not do it justice. Fifty-six men signed the Declaration that affirmed war with Great Britain was inevitable and obligatory. While every one of them played a commanding role in the formation of the document, one must believe that Jefferson spoke for more voices than those of a few men when he penned, "We hold these truths to be self-evident, that all men are created equal."

Jefferson proclaimed without fear that King George III, the named audience of the text, must suffer the consequences of his tyrannical actions. He enumerates the "usurpations" of the British Crown, such as taxation without consent, and the amassing of troops in the Colonies. The document begins by stating that decent respect for the "Law of Natures God" calls the revolutionaries to "declare [that] which impel them to separation." This statement conjures up ideas of a greater cause than merely human desires that should be granted, and this theme is carried throughout the manuscript as justification for the Colonist's actions. Another intended audience of the Declaration of Independence was the citizens of America themselves. The intrepid assertions would cause one to rise to bravery and rally to join one's fellow compatriots.

Jefferson's primary goal, and that of the signers of the Declaration, was to bind themselves to their resolution, list out the grievances of the people, and inspire others to fight. These goals were accomplished through listing of facts, persuasive wording, expounding on the offenses of the monarchy, and claiming that the revolution was of a higher calling. By employing a variety of rhetorical strategies, the writers of the Declaration of Independence created the first document that was truly for the people, by the people.

EXAMPLE 2: Rhetorical Analysis of a Novel

Kelly's Blog
Kairos, Violence, and *The Hunger Games*
Posted by Kelly Simpson

In an interview, Suzanne Collins, author of the bestselling book series *The Hunger Games,* shares what prompted her to write about a dystopian society in which children compete in televised war games:

> there is so much programming, and I worry that we're all getting a little desensitized to the images on our televisions. If you're watching a sitcom, that's fine. But if there's a real-life tragedy unfolding, you should not be thinking of yourself as an audience member. Because those are real people on the screen, and they're not going away when the commercials start to roll.

Collins herself suggests that *The Hunger Games* is more than a novel—it is an argument. The book seeks to persuade readers that our media culture inappropriately glamorizes violence and desensitizes us to the human costs of war. That argument gains force through the timing, or *kairos,* of the book and the cultural events from the 2000s that made it relevant to readers.

The timing of *The Hunger Games* helps to explain why it can be read as an argument against media violence. The book was published in 2008, seven years after the United States declared war in Afghanistan, and five years after the Iraq War began. Both wars were prominently featured on television, with live footage being broadcast around the world. However, until 2009 the United States had a ban on portraying images of fallen soldiers from that war, so viewers did not generally see the human toll of those wars. Images of dead soldiers or citizens in Afghanistan and Iraq were seldom shown, either.

At the same time, American viewers were inundated with a variety of reality television shows that seemed to celebrate violence, from Ultimate Fighting Championships (a no-holds-barred style of fighting with few rules) to reality shows such as *Jackass* and *The Real World*, which featured various forms of drunken debauchery and violence.

Concerns were raised about violence in music and other media after the 1999 Columbine massacre and a string of other school shootings throughout the following decade. In 2001, the United States Surgeon General released a report on youth violence, citing the Columbine massacre as its exigence, and in 2003, the American Psychological Association released a major report citing media exposure to violence as a key cause of aggressive behavior in youths. Youth violence was a major topic of discussion in the years leading up to the novel's release.

Thus, after a decade of war, reality television, and real life violence, the topic of children, war, and violence was timely, or kairotic, in 2008, when *The Hunger Games* was issued. 5

EXAMPLE 3: Rhetorical Analysis of a Public Controversy

Carlos Fernandez-Smith
English 112
October 31, 2013

Appraising *The Help*: *Ethos* and *Logos* in Critical Accounts

In 2011, the film *The Help* was released to great fanfare. An adaptation of the bestselling book by Kathryn Stockett, the film version boasted a star-studded cast, including Emma Stone, Viola Davis, Octavia Spencer, Bryce Dallas Howard, Jessica Chastain, and Cicely Tyson, and it generated buzz early in the award season, later garnering four Academy Award nominations. Yet, not everyone was enamored with the film, which tells the story of a young white woman in the segregated Mississippi of the early 1960s, a woman who sets out to tell the stories of the black women who served as maids in white women's homes.

While praised by some as an insightful portrayal of the struggles black women faced, others heavily criticized the film. In their assessments of the film, critics relied on the rhetorical appeals of *logos* (or logic) and *ethos* (or credibility). In fact, I argue that the combination of these two appeals is what made these criticisms persuasive.

Critics of the film tended to employ three main logical arguments: that the film was historically inaccurate, that it relied on threadbare racial stereotypes and stock characters, and that it misrepresented African American speech patterns. Perhaps the most prominent critics of the film's historical accuracy were members of the Association of Black Women Historians (ABWH). They issued a public statement about the film in 2011, arguing that it included many historical inaccuracies. For instance, members of the association claimed that the film overlooks historical evidence showing that many African American domestic workers were subjected to sexual harassment, exploitation and physical abuse at the hands of their employers. The ABWH states further that the film ignores the context of the Civil Rights movement in Mississippi, aside from a nod to the assassination of Medgar Evers in 1963. The film does not portray how Mississippi residents organized demonstrations in protest of his death, showing instead street scenes of "utter chaos and disorganized confusion." Indeed, Roxane Gay notes in her article that the film portrays the main African American characters, the maids, as oblivious to or uninterested in Civil Rights, even though the Civil Rights movement would have been in full bloom at the time the film is set. These claims rely on logos, or an appeal to the reader's sense of logic. By citing historical facts, the writers hope to shift readers' opinions about the film.

As many film scholars have noted, contemporary movies continue to offer limited roles to African Americans. Often, these roles depend upon stereotypes, such as the "magical negro," which sociologist Matthew W. Hughey describes as a "stock character that often appears as a lower class, uneducated black person" who helps to "save and transform disheveled, uncultured, lost, or broken whites . . . into competent, successful, and content people" (544). Critics argued that, in *The Help,* the main African American characters are "magical negroes," inspiring the white protagonist to complete her book about "the help." In an article in *The Rumpus,* author Roxane Gay notes that *The Help* contains "not one but twelve or thirteen magical negroes who use their mystical negritude to make the world a better place by sharing their stories of servitude and helping Eugenia 'Skeeter' Phelan grow out of her awkwardness and insecurity." By casting the characters in *The Help* as stereotypes, Gay makes a logical argument: in short, the film should be considered negatively because it traffics in stereotypes, and stereotypes are bad.

Critics also protested the use of another stock character, the Mammy, who is perhaps best exemplified by the character played by Hattie McDaniel in the film adaptation of *Gone With the Wind*. Until the 1960s, the Mammy character was one of the only ones African American actresses could hope to play. As scholar of African and Afro-American Studies Charlene Regester writes, such roles meant that African American female characters would remain "an indistinct figure, a shadow, in a film's background" (3), even if some actresses, like McDaniel, were able to "reform" the stereotypical role into one of power and agency (161). In the case of *The Help*, the Association of Black Women Historians noted that the Mammy character "allowed mainstream America to ignore the systemic racism that bound black women to back-breaking, low paying jobs" by representing domestic servants as "asexual, loyal, and contented caretakers of whites." For the ABWH, these roles did not provide actresses such as Octavia Butler or Viola Davis (who played two of the main roles) with an opportunity to reform the stereotyped roles. Although they are describing characters here, these claims are fundamentally part of the writers' use of logos: they make claims and support them by reasons. In this case, the writers use examples to support their claim that the characters in the film represent racial stereotypes.

In addition, both Gay and the ABWH members criticized the language used by the characters in the film. Gay argued that "The over-exaggerated dialect spoken by the maids evokes cowed black folk shuffling through their miserable lives singing Negro spirituals," while the ABWH argued that the dialect made a regional linguistic variation into a "child-like, over-exaggerated 'black' dialect." It is notable that both critics use the term "over-exaggerated." In doing so, they portray the film not only as inaccurate, but also suggest that the inaccuracy was intentional, molding the characters into stock caricatures rather than granting them a more realistic (and perhaps less comforting) role.

All of these logical claims work, in great part, because the writers of these critiques possess external ethos. The ABWH's members are all professors of history at major universities in the United States. Their statement appears on the ABWH home page, which includes the logo of the organization, and is signed by five of its members. Each member lists their affiliation with a university and the ABWH organization. The statement also starts off by invoking the title of the organization in the first line. In this way, the statement establishes the ethos of its authors, and we are to trust their arguments in part because they are made by scholars who have studied African American history extensively. This makes their claims that the film is historically and culturally inaccurate more compelling.

Likewise, Gay's article relies on different forms of external ethos. The end of the article includes a short biographical statement, which tells us that Gay is herself an accomplished author, who has published stories in *Salon, Brevity, Ninth Letter,* and other literary magazines, and a co-editor of a literary magazine, *PANK.* Yet, Gay also generates ethos within the text by identifying herself as an African American woman, by relating her own personal responses to the film, and by referring to her own views, as a writer, about the challenges of writing "across race." For instance, Gay begins her article by describing how reading and viewing representations of African American history can be "painful," "frustrating and infuriating," since such representations make her realize that, if born at a different time, "I too could have been picking cotton or raising a white woman's babies for less than minimum wage or enduring any number of intolerable circumstances far beyond my control." By invoking her own identity, Gay builds credibility. Her own racial background matters because she is discussing a film that purports to represent her history. Later, by detailing her own struggles as a writer to "get it right" when writing about another ethnic group, she builds credibility by portraying herself as fair minded and at least somewhat sympathetic to the creators of *The Help.*

Thus, critics of *The Help* tend to rely primarily on logical claims, or *logos,* but the success of those claims depends in great part on their ethos, both internal and external. Their criticisms likely hold sway with readers who trust that, as credible, informed speakers, the ABWH and Gay have viewpoints that should be valued. Despite the criticism lobbed by Gay, the ABWH, and others, though, *The Help* went on to box office success and at least some critical acclaim. Does this mean that critics were unsuccessful in their rhetoric? By raising these important issues, the ABHW and Gay were successful, at least, in creating awareness among some viewers that the film should be viewed critically.

Works Cited

Gay, Roxane. "The Solace of Preparing Fried Foods and Other Quaint Remembrances from 1960s Mississippi: Thoughts on *The Help*." *The Rumpus.* August 17, 2011. Web. October 23, 2013.

Hughey, Matthew W. "Cinethetic Racism: White Redemption and Black Stereotypes in 'Magical Negro' Films." *Social Problems* 56.3 (2009): 543–77. Print.

Jones, Ida El, Daina Ramey Berry, Tiffany M. Gill, Kali Nicole Gross, and Janice Sumler-Edmond. "An Open Statement to the Fans of *The Help*." Association of Black Women Historians. Web. October 21, 2013.

Regester, Charlene B. *African American Actresses: The Struggle for Visibility, 1900–1960.* Bloomington, IN: Indiana University Press, 2010. Print.

USE THE TOOLKIT

Let's use the three genre toolkit questions from Chapter 1 to examine this genre.

What Is It?

Like a literary or scene analysis, a rhetorical analysis identifies key concepts or features of its chosen text and then gives examples and interprets those examples. The rhetorical analyses presented here take different texts as their focus. Example 1 uses a government document, the Declaration of Independence. Example 2 focuses on a novel, *The Hunger Games,* and Example 3 focuses on opinion pieces (Chapter 10) written about a film, *The Help.* Unlike a literary or scene analysis, these rhetorical analyses focus not only on the quality of the texts, but how they are used to persuade an audience. In order to persuade, a text (or film) needs to make an argument and try to convince readers to accept it.

Notice that each writer chooses a different set of rhetorical tools for analysis. In Example 1, Cody focuses on tone and style. In Example 2, Kelly focuses on the timing of *The Hunger Games* (Chapter 2). In Example 3, Carlos focuses on the rhetorical appeals to logic (*logos*) and credibility (*ethos*) (Chapter 18).

If you are writing a rhetorical analysis, you might choose to focus on rhetorical concepts such as those listed in Box 8.3. In fact, you might consider some of the same concepts you are learning to think about in your own writing.

Who Reads It?

A rhetorical analysis may be written by students in a writing or rhetoric class, but it is also modeled after the kind of writing that rhetoric scholars produce. You may also see a rhetorical analysis in a news blog, magazine, or website. Kelly posted her rhetorical analysis of *The Hunger Games* on her course blog. Increasingly, experts use rhetorical analysis to explain the effectiveness of key speeches, such as the president's State of the Union address.

What's It For?

The goal of a rhetorical analysis is to explain how a text affects readers—why it persuades them, and what kinds of arguments it makes. In Example 1, Cody considers why style choices in the Declaration of Independence would have appealed to audiences in the 1770s. In Example 3, Carlos tries to account for why some readers found criticisms of *The Help* persuasive—even though the film went on to great success. Thus, the point of a rhetorical analysis is not simply to list out rhetorical features of a text, but to interpret them in terms of how they might affect readers.

Once again, you can use these three questions to guide your rhetorical analysis:

- What is it? (Identify the rhetorical strategy)
- How does it work in the text? (Exemplify)
- Why does it matter? How would it affect readers? (Interpret)

Box 8.3   Tools for Rhetorical Analysis

- *Ethos* (credibility) (Chapter 18) personal character.
- *Pathos* (emotions and values) (Chapter 18)
- *Logos* (reason and logic) (Chapter 18)
- Style (Chapter 21)

- Arrangement (organization) (Chapter 20)
- Delivery (presentation) (Chapter 29)
- Rhetorical figures (metaphor, simile, antithesis, etc.) (Chapter 21)
- Audience (Chapter 1)
- Timing (*kairos*) (Chapter 2)
- Purpose (Chapter 1)
- Genre (Chapter 1)
- Argument or claim (Chapter 18)
- Evidence (Chapter 18)
- Rhetorical situation (Chapter 2)

EXERCISE 8.4: Plan a Rhetorical Analysis

Step 1. Identify a current controversy. For example, identify something that is happening on your campus or something that is in the news.

Step 2. Compile a list of sources that pertain to this controversy. Check the editorial page of the newspaper or search online for blogs or other sources.

Step 3. As you read or listen to these sources, see if you notice patterns in the arguments that people are making about this controversy. Do the arguments tend to center around *timing* ("This isn't the right time to act.")? Do the arguments tend to center around appeals to *ethics* ("We should act because it is the right or moral thing to do.")? Use the Tools for Rhetorical Analysis (see Box 8.3) to help you identify five common rhetorical strategies in the texts surrounding your selected controversy.

Step 4. Compile a list of rhetorical strategies and the examples of each strategy that you have located in your texts.

E. Strategies for Analyses

Imagine you have been asked to write an analysis that will help people to understand a text, film, speech, or controversy. We'll take as our example a project one student, Carlos, worked on: a rhetorical analysis of the controversy surrounding the film *The Help*. Let's see how Carlos got started.

Prewriting (Content)

Carlos began by collecting his sources, for empirical research (Chapter 24), or primary sources. This included opinion articles from online newspapers and magazines, an official statement by the Association of Black Women Historians (ABWH), and database sources (Chapter 24), such as a scholarly article about stereotypes in film.

Carlos read each of his sources, making notes on his observations. For example, here is how he marked up the statement by the ABWH.

EXAMPLE: **An Open Statement to the Fans of *The Help* (excerpt)**

On behalf of the Association of Black Women Historians (ABWH), this statement provides historical context to address widespread stereotyping presented in both the film and novel version of *The Help*. The book has sold over three million copies, and heavy promotion of the movie will ensure its success at the box office. Despite efforts to market the book and the film as a progressive story of triumph over racial injustice, *The Help* distorts, ignores, and trivializes the experiences of black domestic workers. We are specifically concerned about the representations of black life and the lack of attention given to sexual harassment and civil rights activism.

During the 1960s, the era covered in *The Help*, legal segregation and economic inequalities limited black women's employment opportunities. Up to 90 per cent of working black women in the South labored as domestic servants in white homes. *The Help*'s representation of these women is a disappointing resurrection of Mammy—a mythical stereotype of black women who were compelled, either by slavery or segregation, to serve white families. Portrayed as asexual, loyal, and contented caretakers of whites, the caricature of Mammy allowed mainstream America to ignore the systemic racism that bound black women to back-breaking, low paying jobs where employers routinely exploited them. The popularity of this most recent iteration is troubling because it reveals a contemporary nostalgia for the days when a black woman could only hope to clean the White House rather than reside in it.

This is the main claim of the Statement.

Logos / facts: This paragraph provides one reason to support the main claim, that the film glorifies domestic servants using the Mammy figure.

Both versions of *The Help* also misrepresent African American speech and culture. Set in the South, the appropriate regional accent gives way to a child-like, over-exaggerated "*black*" dialect. In the film, for example, the primary character, Aibileen, reassures a young white child that, "You is smat, you is kind, you is important." In the book, black women refer to the Lord as the "Law," an irreverent depiction of black vernacular. For centuries, black women and men have drawn strength from their community institutions. The black family, in particular provided support and the validation of personhood necessary to stand against adversity. We do not recognize the black community described in *The Help* where most of the black male characters are depicted as drunkards, abusive, or absent. Such distorted images are misleading and do not represent the historical realities of black masculinity and manhood.

Furthermore, African American domestic workers often suffered sexual harassment as well as physical and verbal abuse in the homes of white employers. For example, a recently discovered letter written by Civil Rights activist Rosa Parks indicates that she, like many black domestic workers, lived under the threat and sometimes reality of sexual assault. The film, on the other hand, makes light of black women's fears and vulnerabilities turning them into moments of comic relief.

Similarly, the film is woefully silent on the rich and vibrant history of black Civil 5
Rights activists in Mississippi. Granted, the assassination of Medgar Evers, the first Mississippi based field secretary of the NAACP, gets some attention. However, Evers'

assassination sends Jackson's black community frantically scurrying into the streets in utter chaos and disorganized confusion—a far cry from the courage demonstrated by the black men and women who continued his fight. Portraying the most dangerous racists in 1960s Mississippi as a group of attractive, well dressed, society women, while ignoring the reign of terror perpetuated by the Ku Klux Klan and the White Citizens Council, limits racial injustice to individual acts of meanness.

We respect the stellar performances of the African American actresses in this film. Indeed, this statement is in no way a criticism of their talent. It is, however, an attempt to provide context for this popular rendition of black life in the Jim Crow South. In the end, *The Help* is not a story about the millions of hardworking and dignified black women who labored in white homes to support their families and communities. Rather, it is the coming-of-age story of a white protagonist, who uses myths about the lives of black women to make sense of her own. The Association of Black Women Historians finds it unacceptable for either this book or this film to strip black women's lives of historical accuracy for the sake of entertainment. . . .

When brainstorming for an analysis, first focus your attention on the text, like Carlos does. Your ideas should come from carefully reading or observing your object—whether it is a literary text, a speech, image, or film. You should read or examine your object several times, making notes about what seems interesting or significant to you.

Use tools for rhetorical analysis to guide you. As Carlos read his text, he focused first on the logic, or *logos,* of the piece, and then on *ethos* (Chapter 18).

Make notes on the text itself—often, highlighting and marking up a text can help you to deepen your analysis. You can do the same for an image or shot from a film—use digital tools to circle or mark key elements.

As you take notes, consider which of the key concepts or questions stands out for you, as a reader or analyst of your key object. Usually, an analysis focuses on a small set of concepts available, not all of them. If you simply run through every possible concept (say, *ethos, pathos, logos,* timing, and style for a rhetorical analysis), then your essay might end up rather disjointed—more like a list of observations than a coherent interpretation.

In his notes on the ABWH statement, Carlos seems to have noted the presence of *logos* and *ethos* several times. This became the focus of his essay.

Developing a Claim

Once you have noticed patterns in your notes, you might begin to formulate a key claim or thesis.

Take a look at the examples in this chapter. What kinds of claims do authors make?

If you think back to the purpose of an analysis—to explain how something works—that should tell you about the kinds of claims that are expected. An analysis is not like a review (Chapter 9), which evaluates whether something is good or bad. While you might mention which particular elements of your text are effective or ineffective, your primary focus is on explaining *why* this is the case, using the tools and concepts of the field you are studying (such as literature, film, or rhetoric).

Carlos tried out a few different claims, or thesis statements, based on his subject:

- Critics of the film *The Help* were persuasive largely because of their *ethos.*
- Criticisms made of the film *The Help* draws on the *ethos* of the writers as well as logical arguments; readers might trust the logical arguments because of the *ethos* of the writers.

Carlos decided that the second option would give him a more interesting angle for his analysis, because he could discuss the strategies used in the statement and also write about how they are connected.

You might also formulate a thesis that responds to what others have said about your object of analysis (Chapter 18). Perhaps you have read other analyses of your object that tend to overlook a key factor or offer an interpretation with which you disagree. For instance, Carlos saw that some bloggers and online magazines recast criticisms as "slamming" the movie or as "blasting" the film. These viewpoints, Carlos might argue, make the statement seem more like a rant or tirade, not the kind of measured response he interprets in their language.

Of course, you might also develop or modify your claim after you have begun drafting your essay and organizing your notes.

Drafting (Organizing)

When you are ready to draft your analysis, you can, of course, use any of the drafting strategies you find useful (Chapter 17). There is no one, correct way to draft an analysis. However, writers of analyses tend to use some of the following strategies:

- **Begin with your evidence.** You might start by grouping together the evidence you'd like to use for your analysis: quotations or passages (in a text) or key images (for a film). Then, consider how you might order those pieces of evidence. Do they fit into any patterns or groups? Writers often organize their evidence first, and then write the parts that introduce that evidence and interpret it. Carlos began by jotting down the main logical claims that he found in criticisms of *The Help* and then writing a section explaining how those claims worked. He then did the same for a section on *ethos,* showing how each source drew upon the credibility of its author.
- **Provide information your audience will need before they can get to the analysis.** Does your audience have the background information needed to go straight to the analysis? Or do they need to know something before they get started? For a work of literature or a film, the reader might need to know the overall plot before they can focus on the analysis. For a rhetorical analysis, your reader might need historical context: where was a speech given, or when was a text published? Your answers to these questions will help you draft

material for the first part of your analysis. Carlos began his analysis by briefly describing the film—when it came out, how it was received, and what it was about—before introducing the controversy he would analyze.

- **Frame your analysis in terms of popular or critical reception.** For this particular genre, you might consider introducing and/or concluding your analysis with a discussion or summation of scholarly or popular interpretations of your subject. For instance, Carlos started by discussing the critical reception of *The Help* by popular media critics, but he might have also begun by summarizing what scholars have said about the portrayal of domestic servants in film.

Revising (Style)

Keep in mind the following style tips when revising your analysis.

Use Appropriate Terminology.
Once you have a draft, focus on using the language of the discipline in question. For example, for a literary analysis (see Box 8.1), you should draw on terms related to literature, including the key concepts you may have discussed in class. Similarly, for a film analysis (see Box 8.2) you should employ terminology related to film. Pay attention to the terms your instructor uses in class, and try to work those into your essay. Carlos not only used the terms *logos* and *ethos* (Chapter 18), which he had learned in class, but also distinguished between "external" and "internal" *ethos,* to refer to *ethos* already possessed by the writer and to *ethos* generated within a text, respectively.

Introduce and Interpret Quotations.
You should also consider what language you use to introduce and interpret quotations and examples. If you look at the sample papers included in this chapter, you will see that writers often introduce quotations using phrases such as the following:

- "Christopher provides a detailed description of the police cell, noting that . . . " (Morris)
- "Gay argued that . . . " (Carlos)

You'll see they also follow quotations with sentences such as these:

- "This shows his anxiety about Jack's arrival." (Kerri)
- "By invoking her own identity, Gay builds credibility." (Carlos)

Each quotation is introduced and then interpreted. You should never insert a quote or example without framing it with your own language in this way.

Use Descriptive Language.
Keep in mind that your reader may not have read the text (or seen the film) you are talking about. Accordingly, you should use descriptive language where necessary (Chapter 19) to help the reader understand or picture

what you are discussing. Notice how Kerri refers to the "drab parking lot, cloudy gray sky, and pale buildings" in the scene she analyzes from *Brokeback Mountain*.

Editing (Design)

As you edit and format your paper, keep in mind the formatting your audience expects. For a formal scholarly paper, you'll use citations and follow the paper format of a particular citation style. Because he was writing his paper for an English class, Carlos used MLA style (Chapter 28).

For an online format (such as a blog post or online article) you can use hyperlinks, embed video, and use highlighting or different colors for emphasis.

Troubleshooting

Here are some common challenges that students face when writing analyses.

I can't come up with a thesis. Generating a thesis or claim for an analysis can be quite difficult, especially if you think of your essay merely as an exercise or assignment written for the teacher. Instead, think about how you can respond to what others might think about your subject, or what others have said about it. Then, you have an occasion to make an argument. Do some critics find that your favorite film is shallow or fluffy, but you think it actually has depth? Can you argue that those who focus on the style of your author overlook how she uses logical appeals? Do some research to get a sense of what others have said, and remember to correctly quote, paraphrase, summarize, and cite their arguments (Chapter 28).

I can't find any . . . (*pathos*, imagery, etc.). Sometimes, students go down the list of concepts available for analysis as though it were a scavenger hunt and are then surprised when they come up empty-handed. "Why is there no symbolism in this paragraph?" they wonder. "Why is there nothing remarkable about the camera angles in this scene?"

Not every concept will be relevant to your analysis in every case. If a certain concept does not seem to apply to your object, that is fine. In fact, the lack of a concept may in itself be noteworthy. Why might a filmmaker choose to use a single, static camera angle for a scene? Why might a speaker avoid making overly emotional appeals? You might be able to come up with an interesting interpretation to explain why this is the case.

My analysis is boring. Your goal as an analyst of a literary, rhetorical, or artistic text is to identify something interesting about it—something other people have not noticed. The most obvious observations are not always the most interesting. In Carlos's case, simply noting the presence of *ethos* and *logos* seemed less interesting than considering how these rhetorical appeals interacted. Focusing his attention in this way gave Carlos an interesting angle on his topic.

When you review your own notes, you might look for elements that seem surprising to you—for example, unexpected for the genre or rhetorical situation, or unusual for the author in question. You might also do some secondary research about your subject—the speaker or author, the rhetorical situation, timing, and so on—in order to develop a deeper understanding of how the text you're analyzing functions.

F. Chapter Project: Write a Rhetorical Analysis

Write a rhetorical analysis of a current controversy. Your task is to compose an analysis of one or more key texts involved in that controversy. To do so, you must undertake the following steps:

- Identify an object of analysis.
- Identify rhetorical concepts you will use for your analysis.
- Find examples to support your analysis.
- Interpret the significance of your findings for the controversy you are addressing.

If you get stuck, read over the section on *Strategies for Rhetorical Analysis.*

Group Option: Prepare a Networked Rhetorical Analysis

As a group, follow the assignment guidelines for the Chapter Project. Each member of your group will work on a different object of analysis networked to the same controversy. For example, if you wanted to analyze the controversy surrounding climate change (and what to do about it), you could each choose a key text—a speech by the president, a statement by scientists, an opinion piece by a politician, and so on. Then, you would each prepare an analysis of your text(s).

Collect your analyses together. As a group, write an introduction to your rhetorical analyses that identifies the key issues at stake in your controversy and provides an overview of the rhetorical strategies it entails. Make sure that your introduction also shows how the texts you analyze relate as a network.

Multimedia Option: Prepare a Digital Rhetorical Analysis

Complete the Chapter Project, but instead of preparing a traditional print document, compose your rhetorical analysis in an alternate format: a video analysis, screencast, podcast, or website. You should consider which media formats will allow you to provide evidence and interpretation of your object. (For example, a video format is a natural fit for a rhetorical analysis of a speech or film, but might not lend itself as well to the analysis of a text; a podcast might be a good fit for an analysis of a speech.)

MULTIMEDIA EXERCISE 9.3: Write an Online Book Review

After you have written your book review, share it on a website such as Google Books, Amazon.com, GoodReads.com, or Barnes & Noble's website, sites where the public can post reviews of books.

D. Website Review

A website review describes, assesses, and makes recommendations for improving a website.

EXAMPLE 1: Website Review for an Online Forum

Forum: Redesign Critiques
Posted by Megan M.

Hello,
Sorry for the delay in releasing this post. I just didn't see it for some reason.

I wouldn't have realized that button did something until you pointed it out. You could try making it bigger or making it animate a little bit, like a pulse action.

There are a few things that I find disorienting about this site. The first is that you're advertising complete IT solutions but you seem to be mainly offering web design and development. I don't know, maybe it's just me, but I would think it would be easier to target the clients you're looking for by emphasizing web development instead (thinking of SEO). Or maybe this is just a regional terminology thing too—to me "IT solutions" means more hardware, networking, servers, things like that.

5   The other thing I find disorienting is that the words in the logo don't match the words in the domain (pdgroup.co vs. Prima DG in the logo). Even writing out the full company name in the logo might be better. What DG stands for might not be immediately obvious either.

Also, I find the font size used for the body area to be very small and hard to read. The descriptions of the services you offer are very, very, brief and quite vague. I would expect to see more there, including samples of previous work.

I hope that helps. Overall the site looks really good. I like the drawing, it gives a lot of character and uniqueness to the site. And I think it gives the impression that there are 6 people busy working away on my project.

EXAMPLE 2: **Website Review for a Computer Course (excerpt)**

Hester Cho
Engl 318: Composition and Multimedia Design

Healthcare.gov: Website Review

Since its launch in 2013, Healthcare.gov has proven controversial. Designed by a Canadian firm, the website immediately experienced functionality problems due to coding errors and bugs. However, less attention has been paid to the visual design, usability and layout of the site. Viewing the website from this perspective reveals additional problems; namely, a failure to consider users' needs and to simplify content.

Navigation

The landing page for Healthcare.gov provides three main options: "See plans before I apply," "Apply now for health coverage," and "See if I can get lower costs." These options appear in colorful circles on the center of the screen. However, the user can also click on additional options using a navigation bar at the top of the screen: "Learn" (with secondary headings for "individuals and families," "Small Businesses," and "All Topics"); "Get Insurance" (which leads to a different page, the Healthcare Marketplace); and Log In. The items on the navigation bar represent different types of actions—one provides additional information, another leads to a separate site, and a third leads to a log in page. Thus, the page suffers from an unclear hierarchy. Should one click on the circles or the navigation bar? The two navigation options compete with one another and may end up confusing the user.

Aesthetics

The site uses a color scheme of blue, orange, and white. On the main page, two of the circles are a darker shade of blue on a lighter blue background, and one circle is orange. The text is white. Each circle features an icon to help distinguish it further. The orange "Apply Now" circle is slightly larger than the other two. Overall, the front page is neat and visually appealing.

Accessibility

The lack of a clear hierarchical navigation scheme would make this website difficult for someone to navigate using a text reader or other assistive technologies. In addition, the three main circles are images, not text, so they might also prose problems for those users. In addition, the design may not provide enough contrast for users with visual impairments: the white text on a blue background, and the lighter blue circles on a darker blue background may pose problems. It is, however, possible to navigate the site using only a keyboard, so that is a plus.

Summary

Overall, Healthcare.gov suffers from design flaws that may compound the problems users have been having with the site's functionality. The unclear navigation scheme may dissuade users from signing up for healthcare, and may make use for people with disabilities especially problematic. This is especially disheartening since, presumably, people with disabilities might represent a large part of the audience for the site—people who lack health insurance and/or have been denied coverage before. Given the site's important role in enacting part of the Affordable Care Act, it is unfortunate that greater care was not taken in its design.

EXAMPLE 3: Website Review for a Composition Course

Jonas Webber
English 101

Website Review of Ravelry.com

Overview

Ravelry.com is a social networking site for knitters and crocheters. It contains a database of

patterns and other tools to help crafters.

Appearance

The home page features the Ravelry logo: a red ball of yarn with the site name. There is

also a tagline, "Where my stitches at?" which is a trendy play on words and gives the site

a youthful flair. Down the left, main column is the Ravelry blog, with the latest news and

updates about the site. Down the right column are widgets, such as a search window and a

short help menu.

User Interface

The site is easy to navigate. Across the top of every page is the same menu, no matter what

page you're on. The first option is "My Notebook," which is like a Ravelry member's "Face-

book" page. (Ravelry members are called "Ravelers.")

The fonts are easy to read and the pages are laid out in a predictable fashion. Because the

site echoes other social networking sites, people who are familiar with social networks will

understand how this site works. For example, you can add other Ravelers as "friends" and

keep up-to-date on knitting topics in the forums.

Product/Service Enticement

The service this site offers is fortunately free. But even if it weren't free, as an avid knitter

I'd be willing to pay a nominal subscription fee, like ten dollars a year, for access to the site.

Suggestions for Improvement

The main flaw of Ravelry is that when you get a message on the site, the site is incapable of

emailing you a notification. Therefore, if you get a message but don't check your Ravelry

inbox all the time, you might not get the message in a timely fashion. Integrating external

notification would make Ravelry a better site.

Final Thoughts and Rating

On a scale of 100 points, Ravelry.com earns 95, because of the lack of external notification.

Otherwise, I highly recommend this site to knitters and crocheters.

USE THE TOOLKIT

Let's use the three genre toolkit questions from Chapter 1 to examine this genre.

What Is It?
A website review is a document that describes and evaluates the strengths and weaknesses of a website and makes recommendations for improvement, if any improvements are needed. These reviews usually feature several criteria, such as appearance, interface (how well the website interacts with users), and functionality (how well the website performs the task it is meant to perform). In Example 1, the reviewer pointed out many aspects of the website's appearance that could be improved on: a button's appearance, a confusing logo, and a font size that was "very small and hard to read."

Who Reads It?
Website reviews are often read by website owners or developers. Sometimes website owners commission reviews of their sites so that they can improve them. Teachers

also assign students to write website reviews as part of class assignments, as in Examples 2 and 3.

What's It For?

Website developers and owners read reviews in order to learn how to improve their websites. For this reason, getting reviews from a variety of types of users is valuable. Website reviews can also help web designers, even student web designers, figure out what a good website looks like, so that they can design good websites in the future. In fact, only a few months after Jonas wrote his review of Ravelry .com shown in Example 3, the website added the feature that he suggested (email notification of messages received). Other reviewers of the website had made similar observations, and the web developers listened to those reviews and improved the site.

EXERCISE 9.4: Compare Three Websites

Pick three websites that sell similar products (for example, Nike, Adidas, and Asics; or Amazon, Barnes & Noble, and Kobo).

Using Table 9.1, the Website Comparison Chart, compare the strengths and weaknesses of the three websites. You don't need to write complete sentences.

Table 9.1 Website Comparison Chart

QUESTION	1.	2.	3.
Do you understand what the site is about?			
Is it easy to use? Can you find what you're looking for?			
Is the content strong?			
Do you understand what the text is saying? Do you notice any spelling or grammar mistakes?			
If this site is offering a product or service, would you sign up or buy it?			
Is the site attractive to you?			

GROUP ACTIVITY 9.1: Test and Review a Website

As a group, select an e-commerce website to test and review, such as Amazon.com or BestBuy.com. Separately, attempt to navigate the site, testing as many features as you can. Keep notes on how easy or difficult it is to use the website. Use the chart in Table 9.1 to help you keep notes, if you wish.

Come together and compare your experiences. Were there certain parts of the site that were easier to navigate than others? Did more experienced computer users have an easier time with certain aspects of the website, or was the site accessible to users of all computer skill levels? After you have compared notes, as a group fill out the chart in Table 9.1, taking into account everyone's experiences on the site.

E. Strategies for Reviews

Suppose you've been asked to write a website review, similar to Jonas's review in Example 3, on behalf of an academic department at your school. You would begin by familiarizing yourself with the department's website: read all the content, check to be sure all links work, and assess the quality and usefulness of both its content and its design using the criteria for website reviews.

To learn more about strategies for writing website reviews, we'll look at how Jonas composed his review of Ravelry.com.

Prewriting (Content)

Jonas used the following questions to get started with his review. He answered each question for Ravelry.com using the chart in Table 9.2. He didn't worry about writing in a formal fashion on this chart. He just took notes as he navigated the site.

Table 9.2 Website Review Prewriting Chart

Website Review Questions	Ravelry.com
Do you understand what the site is about?	Yes. The site is very straightforward about its purpose as a social networking and resource site for knitters and crocheters.
Is the site easy to use? Can you find what you're looking for?	The site is very easy to use and intuitive, at least for a basic user. I haven't tried to add patterns or serve as an "editor," but as a basic user, the projects page, the pattern search, and the forums are a breeze.

Is the content strong?	The content is user generated: users add patterns to the pattern database and yarns to the yarn database. I was surprised to find that the online knitting community was so strong and computer-savvy. The staff of volunteer editors keeps the databases accurate and up-to-date. The content is thus very impressive, and probably the best reason to join.
Do you understand what the text is saying? Do you notice any spelling or grammar mistakes?	Considering how much of the site is user-generated there are rarely any errors in the formal pattern or yarn pages. There are errors in the forums, of course, but those are informal areas of the site and no one expects them to be well written.
If this site is offering a service, would you sign up for it?	I'm not a knitter or crocheter, so Ravelry isn't for me. I surveyed some of my friends, though, to see if they would be interested in joining. Amazingly, all of my friends who do knitting or crocheting are already members! I was so surprised because I had never heard of Ravelry before signing up for this project.
Is the site attractive to you?	The visual design of the site is one of its strongest points. Their logo is a cartoon drawing of the company owner's Boston Terrier and a ball of yarn. The colors are saturated (not pastel or country-fied). This site definitely appeals to the younger, hipper knitter—which I didn't really know existed until I did this project.
What's the number one weakness?	I asked my friends, and they all said the same thing: They wish the website would email them when they received a PM (private message). After using the site for a while, I can see how it would be annoying to not know when someone sent you a message.

Drafting (Organizing)

Once you have brainstormed your review, you can begin to turn your answers to those questions into a document that you can share with others. Turn your notes into complete sentences. Be sure that you've included enough detail to help your reader understand what you are describing. Don't forget to evaluate the strengths and weaknesses of the site, and to make suggestions for improvement.

Jonas's chart, as you can see, contains a lot of what would become his final website review. The more prewriting you can do, the easier your drafting will be.

Revising (Style)

Because your review will be read by website designers, your review must be written in a straightforward and easily understood fashion. Consider using short sentences. Prefer the active voice. If your review will be read by the website owner, you can even use a tone of command, especially when making suggestions (e.g., "To increase readability, you should consider changing the font color from gray to black.").

Editing (Design)

Make your review easy to read by using headings to separate material into chunks. Jonas used useful headings to break up the sections of his review: "overview," "appearance," "user interface," "product/service enticement," "suggestions for improvement," and "final thoughts and rating." Craft headings that make sense for your review.

Troubleshooting

Here are some common challenges that students face when writing reviews.

What if I don't know anything about website design?   You don't need to know anything about design to write a strong website review. Some computer users are more experienced than others, but websites must serve users of all different computer skill levels. As a non-expert, you'll be in a better position to evaluate how well a website works for the average user. Focus on your own experience, and what would have made your experience better.

What if I can't find anything that needs improvement?   If you can't find any aspect of the website that needs improvement, then you can praise the website designers for doing a great job. Be specific about what the website does well. For example, "This interface makes it easy for users to find information about courses. The search engine works well. I searched for three courses and was able to find information for all of them." Knowing what works is just as useful as knowing what needs improvement. When web designers need to add new features in the future, they'll be sure to add features that are similar to the effective ones they've created in the past.

Argumentative Genres

Argumentative genres are genres that aim to persuade. Writers of arguments use logic, evidence, emotions, and other means of persuasion to encourage an audience to agree with a claim or thesis. While the term "argument," in everyday use, describes a quarrel, here we use it not as a negative term, but to describe any genre in which the main goal is persuasion.

In college, you may be asked to compose arguments in any number of courses. Argumentative genres you may encounter in college include an editorial, letter to the editor, persuasive essay, persuasive speech, or the like. For example, in a history class you might be asked to take a position in a class debate on the causes of the Civil War. In a biology class, you might be asked to compose a persuasive essay arguing for or against stem cell research. In other situations, an argumentative genre might be hidden in the prompt for a traditional essay or "paper." For example, in an education class, you might be asked to write a paper that argues for or against instituting same-sex education in your state. To identify argumentative genres in a writing prompt, look out for words like "defend," "take a stance," "argue," "persuade," "take a position," and so on. In some cases, though, you will encounter arguments in other genres as well. For example, a film review (Chapter 9) might seek to persuade readers whether to go see a movie, and you are often asked to develop a claim or argument to support academic writing. (For more on argument as a strategy that crosses genres, see Chapter 18.)

In the workplace, arguments appear in a variety of settings. The most familiar examples of workplace arguments might be the "opening arguments" and "closing arguments" lawyers present in trials. These arguments are not quarrels, but attempts to persuade the jury to support one side of the case. In business, you may be asked to design a sales pitch to present to potential clients or investors. Journalists compose editorials and opinion pieces. Even the sermons composed by clergy members can be considered arguments, since they seek to persuade members of a religious group to abide by that group's doctrine.

In this chapter, you will learn how to compose a range of argumentative genres, genres whose main purpose is to persuade an audience. However, arguments tend to appear in other genres, as well—a recommendation report (Chapter 14) argues for a particular course of action, and a rhetorical analysis (Chapter 8) argues for a particular interpretation of a text. For this reason, you may also consult Chapter 18 on argumentative strategies that work in any genre.

A. Argumentative Mini-Genre: Print Advertisement

Perhaps the most common argumentative genre that you encounter in everyday life is an advertisement. Take a look at the following advertisements. Using the three genre toolkit questions, see if you can identify how this genre works.

EXAMPLE 1: Army Advertisement from 1985

Army recruiting poster from 1985.

EXAMPLE 2: **Army Advertisement from 2000**

Army recruiting poster from 2000.

USE THE TOOLKIT

Let's use the three genre toolkit questions from Chapter 1 to examine this genre.

What Is It?

These are advertisements for the U.S. Army. They appeared in print magazines in the United States over the last four decades. All of these advertisements have the same underlying claim: you should consider joining the Army. (For more on making claims, see Chapter 18.)

Army recruiting poster from 2010.

Who Reads It?

While anyone might encounter an advertisement such as these in a magazine, chances are the Army's marketing firm had a more particular audience in mind when they designed these ads. Their primary audience probably includes those who are most likely to consider joining the army—typically, young men and women who are looking for a career path.

However, each of these advertisements makes different assumptions about who the army is seeking to recruit. Example 2 addresses an audience who is considering college, and makes the argument that joining the army will help to defray college costs. Notice that the ad addresses the reader directly, using the second person ("you"). Those "you" statements help to construct a reader as someone who fits the image the Army Reserve is trying to create.

In comparison, how does Example 1 appeal to—or construct—an audience? You might notice that the ad features an image of a person. Considering that the army has traditionally been composed of men, it is notable that the person pictured is a woman. Why was the army trying to recruit more women to join? Why would focusing on an individual person, rather than the kind of image shown in the second ad, help to persuade women to join?

Finally, the last image does not include images of things or people, but a simple word, "STRONG," spelled out with the first letters of the names of six key battles in American history. It might be less obvious who is intended to read this ad, but we might surmise that the audience is expected to know about these battles, and to identify with them as part of a tradition. According to the Army itself, this campaign was developed "to specifically address the interests and motivations of those considering a career in the U.S. military," and was included mainly in media targeting young adults.

What's It For?

The Army advertises mainly to recruit soldiers. The needs for Army recruitment change over time. In the 1980s, when the first of these advertisements was published, the United States was not engaged in any major wars, although it maintained military outposts and engaged in various operations around the world. Accordingly, the goal at that point might have been to recruit members to join the reserves, who would train on weekends but would probably not be deployed abroad. This changed in the 2000s, when the wars in Iraq and Afghanistan drew soldiers not just from the full-time Army, but also from the Reserves. The third advertisement comes from this period, when the United States needed individuals who would be willing to serve in those wars. You can see that the Army tried two different strategies to persuade readers to join—first appealing to individual pride and purpose in the "Army of One" campaign, and then trying appeals to patriotism and history in the "Army Strong" campaign. These are examples of appeals to emotions and values, or *pathos* (Chapter 18).

EXERCISE 10.1: Create an Advertisement

Choose a product you use often or with which you are familiar. Then, imagine that you work for an ad agency that is designing a new campaign for that product. The company hopes to attract a new audience to their product—one that has not traditionally been targeted in their advertising.

Write an email (Chapter 12) to your manager explaining who the new target audience should be, and how you think an advertisement can appeal to that audience.

MULTIMEDIA EXERCISE 10.1: Design a Social Media Campaign

Choose a product you use often or are familiar with. Then, imagine that you work for an ad agency that is designing a new campaign for that product. The company hopes to use social media to create interest in their product. Design a social media campaign to generate "buzz" about your product. Submit an email (Chapter 12) to your manager explaining what audience you tried to appeal to with your advertisement, and what choices you made to attract that audience.

B. Column, Op-Ed, or Letter to the Editor

Advertisements are argument genres that usually share a single, fundamental argument: to recruit people. In the Army case, the goal is to enlist new recruits, but also, perhaps, to recruit other Americans as supporters of the Army. Other organizations and corporations may use advertising to "recruit" viewers or readers in other ways—as consumers of a product or service, or as believers in the image the company is trying to create for itself.

However, advertisements are not the only genres that "recruit" an audience. If you want to get people to agree with an idea, support a proposal, vote for or against something, or take a specific action, you might also write a more extended piece, such as an opinion column, op-ed, or letter to the editor. All three are genres that appear in newspapers and magazines, and all three seek to recruit readers to support an argument.

EXAMPLE 1: Opinion Column for a Student Newspaper

Nate Rushing

UF's Meatless Mondays Are Ridiculous

"Mmm, tofu."

That will soon be a more common phrase thanks to Meatless Monday and several other well-intentioned organizations. From now on there will be more vegan options in UF's feeding troughs.

Of course, we can only hope that soon UF will cease to see any point in keeping meat on the menu on Mondays.

I mean, sure, vegan food sucks, but there's countless benefits to counterbalance this fact, right?

First, meat is unhealthy. It's full of fat and other animal byproducts and bacteria. No chance of mad cow without the cow, right? Sure, salmonella can be spread through peanut butter, but it's meat that is the real problem, right? And, sure, you 5 can easily purchase super-lean cuts of both pork and beef, but that would require personal responsibility and discernment. And sure, we get vitamin B-12 almost exclusively through meat, and, more specifically, the bacteria in meat, but let's cling to that easy view of all bacteria being harmful.

Second, meat is unnecessary. What do we need meat for, anyway? Yes, it contains B-12, which, unless we take multivitamins or eat feces, we won't get without meat, but what's one essential vitamin? And yes, meat has complete proteins that contain all the essential amino acids all in one place, but hey, it's probably more efficient to spend time, money and effort getting together all the essential amino acids piecemeal. Yeah, I'm almost positive it makes sense to figure out exactly what plants contain—which of the twenty essential amino acids—and make sure that you eat enough of them on a regular enough basis to ensure you won't be malnourished.

Third, meat is inefficient. Surely the huge carbon meatprint I hear about is avoidable. It makes sense that, if cows eat corn to produce the meat we take from them, we can just cut the middleman and eat the corn ourselves. Never mind the fact that a huge portion of their diet is grass. Maybe grass is the next cilantro. Or we could just take the farmland that's currently being used for livestock and grow corn on it, right? This is a perfect solution, disregarding the immense amount of development and unnatural measures it would take to convert current livestock land to crop land, rendering the trade-off basically pointless.

For all these reasons and others, it's more than apparent that Meatless Monday has the right idea. My question is, why aren't we going to fully meatless Monday? Or meatless UF, for that matter. If meat really is this bad and pointless, why are we allowing this scourge on our campus at all?

Shouldn't we be looking out for our students, protecting them from the bad choices they may make?

10   Sure, we want college students to feel like they're adults, but we can't really trust them to make the right decisions—even the most basic ones like what to eat.

So, to the Meatless Monday folks, I say: Press on, fight the good fight for making other people's decisions for them under the assumption that the average layman doesn't have the time or wherewithal to truly know what's best for himself or herself.

I mean, really, where would we be if we let people truly exercise personal freedom? Nowhere good, that's for sure.

EXAMPLE 2: Letter to the Editor of a Student Newspaper

Dear Editor:

In response to your article "Meatless Mondays Marches to the Tune of Trayless Fridays" (20 Apr. 2011), I would like to compliment Kalamazoo College for joining the exciting campaign that is introducing thousands of students to vegetarian cuisine. Demand for meatless options on college campuses is growing every day, and students across the country are adopting Meatless Mondays as a result. A recent study by ARAMARK, a leading food-service provider, concluded that one in four college students are actively seeking out vegan options when they sit down to eat.

In fact, United Nations scientists have determined that raising chickens, pigs, and other animals for slaughter generates about 40 percent more greenhouse gasses than all the cars, SUVs, trucks, and planes in the world *combined*. Most students are also horrified to discover that chickens have their beaks cut off when they're only days old and that cows and pigs are often skinned and dismembered while still conscious. If these kinds of abuses were inflicted upon cats or dogs, it would result in felony cruelty-to-animals charges. Yet these practices are standard in an industry that refuses to make even the most basic improvements in the way that animals are treated.

Luckily, not only is going vegetarian the single greatest action you can take for animals and the environment, it's also the best choice that you can make for your health. Both the U.S. Department of Agriculture (USDA) and the American Dietetic Association have endorsed vegetarian diets. Don't forget that people can get all the protein that they need from nuts, seeds, yeast, grains, beans, and other legumes. Going vegetarian has never been easier or tastier, with so many delicious and cruelty-free dishes, such as vegan barbecue riblets and vegan pizza. For more information, visit peta2.com to request a free vegetarian/vegan starter kit.

Sincerely,
Amelia Jensen, College Campaigns Assistant

EXAMPLE 3: Op-Ed for a Student Newspaper

Rini Sampath

Insults against Disabled People Must Be Eradicated

In 2004, when 17-year-old Adam Holland cheerfully smiled for a photograph in his art class, he had no idea that the image would later re-surface as a popular meme.

Perhaps you've even seen it. No, it's not the iconic Bad Luck Brian or Scumbag Steve images that provide some giggles at the expense of another individual's dignity.

It's actually worse. And sickeningly offensive.

With one look at this recent meme, it's clear that Holland's physical features and cognitive ability are distinct from others. That's because Adam Holland has Down syndrome.

According to ABC News, a radio station in Florida re-purposed the original photograph of Holland at the Vanderbilt Kennedy Center into one in which he clutches a sign reading "Retarded News." This photo was used as promotion for its "Retarded News" segment, where talk jockeys would discuss odd news. 5

After learning of the photo's usage, Holland's family filed a lawsuit earlier this week against Cox Media, the owner of the Tampa, Fla., radio station WHPT-FM.

Unfortunately, this is not the first time a mentally disabled person has been mocked on the Internet. A quick Google search reveals that the Internet hosts a plethora of other tasteless graphics. This demonstrates a terrible epidemic in our nation—an epidemic of insensitivity toward the entire disabled community.

This isn't an isolated incident. It's actually a daily occurrence. For one, people constantly pepper everything from film dialogues to daily conversations with insulting uses of the word "retarded" to mean stupid or unintelligent. Even T-shirts and bumper stickers bare various forms of the word.

The Holland family might very well lose its battle in the courts since tort liability has protected the perpetrators of similar defamatory actions in the past. The Hollands' request of $18 million in compensatory and punitive damages might even seem unreasonable.

10   Yet, this hefty punishment could deter others from denigrating helpless individuals such as Adam Holland in the future.

Though the outcome of the actual case is unclear, this does not mean the Holland cause should lose in the eyes of the average American. Even if the law does not side in his favor, we ought to help him.

In fact, every individual can support Holland and stand up for the millions of others in the disabled community by eliminating the word "retard" from daily usage.

"When [it is] used as a synonym for 'dumb' or 'stupid' by people without disabilities, it only reinforces painful stereotypes of people with intellectual disabilities being less valued members of humanity," notes The Joseph P. Kennedy Jr. Foundation, a foundation created to help those with intellectual disabilities.

The first step to eradicating insensitivity toward disabled persons is to recognize the existence of these harmful words in our vernacular. Freedom of speech, after all, does not entitle any person to degrade another group of individuals.

15   Surely, disposing this word from common usage might seem unreasonable. To some, political correctness is a last priority when their lives are inundated by other concerns.

But this isn't just about political correctness. This is about being human. Every time someone uses this word, it trivializes the integrity of the disabled community. To create a world accepting of people from all walks of life, this change to word choice must occur.

In the end, able-bodied people can only say so much about the use of the word "retard."

But hearing it from someone who experiences mental disability? Now that creates an impact.

"I'm a 30-year-old man with Down syndrome who has struggled with the public's perception that an intellectual disability means that I am dumb and shallow," wrote Special Olympics athlete John Franklin Stephens. "Being compared to people like me should be considered a badge of honor. No one overcomes more than we do and still loves life so much."

Let's use the three genre toolkit questions from Chapter 1 to examine this genre.

What Is It?

A column, op-ed, or letter to the editor is a short, persuasive genre that appears in the opinion section of an online or print newspaper, in which the author argues a position about a current event or issue. Nate and Rini wrote columns or op-eds (also called "opinion pieces"), while Amelia wrote a letter to the editor.

Do you see any other differences between the two types of opinion pieces? You'll notice that Amelia begins her letter by referring to another piece of writing that had already appeared in the same newspaper, and that her text is slightly shorter than Nate's. We might conclude that a letter to the editor is usually a sort of response or follow-up to a longer news item, often a longer editorial or article. Most newspapers will print several letters to the editor in a single issue, and since space is at a premium, they tend to be short and concise. While online news sites don't need to worry as much about space, they still tend to encourage readers to respond in short, concise ways, often in short comments readers can post on an opinion column.

Who Reads It?

The audience for an op-ed or letter to the editor is partly determined by the newspaper in which it appears. College newspapers, for instance, tend to appeal mainly to students (who write the articles, too), but are also read by faculty, college alumni, and even members of the surrounding town or community.

Yet a more specific audience is also invoked by the writing itself. Take another look at Nate's editorial. Who do you think he is speaking to, specifically, among those who are readers of the University of Florida's college newspaper? You'll notice that Nate refers a couple of times to "students" or "college students," but he also uses the third person plural "we." While anyone could find Nate's column online, then, it seems that he is addressing students at his college. Meanwhile, Rini invokes a broader audience in her piece, which addresses an issue not confined to the college she attends, but one of larger scope: the importance of avoiding language that denigrates people with disabilities.

What's It For?

Just as the Army posters were trying to recruit people to join the military, these documents are trying to recruit people to support a particular position or argument. They use a variety of strategies to do so—providing reasons to support the claim, elaborating on those reasons with facts and other forms of evidence. (Turn to Chapter 18 for more on the structure of logical arguments.)

Let's take a closer look at the structure of Amelia's argument.

What is Amelia's main claim? You'll see that she does not quite state it explicitly, but that she supports Meatless Mondays and wants readers to do so as well. So, we might translate her claim as "You should support Meatless Mondays" or "Meatless Mondays are a good thing."

What reasons does she give? The first reason she provides is that Meatless Mondays are already garnering support from students, many of whom choose vegetarian and vegan meals. The second reason is that eating animals contributes to environmental problems, and the third is that eating animals often entails cruel and inhumane practices. Finally, Amelia states that eating a vegetarian diet is beneficial to your health.

Amelia, Nate, and Rini also appeal to the readers' emotions and values (Chapter 18), by choosing specific language and vocabulary to set the right tone (Chapter 21). For example, Rini chooses terms such as "mocked," "tasteless," and "offensive" to describe how Adam Holland was portrayed, terms that evoke the audience's sympathy for Adam and dislike for the radio station that used his picture.

 ## EXERCISE 10.2: Join a Debate

Read the opinion section of your local newspaper, and identify a current issue or debate you find intriguing. Write a letter to the editor in response to an article or editorial. Note that you do not necessarily have to argue "for" or "against" the issue—you may also extend what others have said, provide a different angle on the debate, or argue for a "middle ground" between two extremes.

 ## GROUP ACTIVITY 10.1: Letters to the Editor

As a group, choose a recent op-ed column in your local newspaper. Then, as individuals, write a letter to the editor in response to that column. Next, compare your responses by answering the following questions:

1. What claims did each of you make?
2. What reasons did you use to support your arguments?
3. Do any arguments seem to be supported by weak evidence? How can you make those weak arguments stronger?

(See Chapter 18 for more on the structure of arguments.)

GROUP ACTIVITY 10.2: Launch a Political Campaign

While we often focus solely on the candidates in an election, it actually takes a team to get someone into office. Most campaigns include a number of advisors and other team members. For this assignment, your group will act as a campaign team. First, decide who will act as the political candidate for your group. Then, as a team, develop an overall message: How will you portray your candidate's *ethos*, and how will you appeal to the values of your student electorate?

Next, choose a role and task for each group member from those listed here:

- Candidate: deliver a 4-minute campaign speech
- Speechwriter: write and coach candidate on speech
- Public relations consultant: prepare a press release announcing the speech
- Graphic designer: prepare a political campaign poster for your candidate
- Social network consultant: design a web campaign using social media tools

As a group, you will introduce your campaign to the class in a 15-minute oral presentation.

D. Satire

So far, we have examined arguments that work in visual, written, and oral genres, and we have examined a number of strategies writers use in those genres, including logic (claims, reasons, and evidence), appeals to the emotions and values, arrangement (or organization), and style. While these genres share a focus on persuading an audience, they have different conventions, in part because each one appears in a different type of rhetorical situation. Different kinds of argument genres appear in magazines, in newspapers, and at political rallies.

We turn now to another genre of argument, one that uses irony as its main rhetorical device. If you watch late night television shows, such as *The Daily Show with Jon Stewart*, you are probably familiar with this genre: satire.

EXAMPLE 1: Satire for a Student Newspaper

Pia DiGiulio

Uncontrolled Study Orgies Break Out in Gender-Neutral Dorm

The University Administration and certain parent groups have shown appropriate concern about the proposed, so-called "gender-neutral" housing situation that would allow male and female university students to live in the same dorm rooms.

Indeed, as the term "gender-neutral housing" is actually a euphemism that hides the dangers inherent in such living arrangements, I will not deign to use the term in this article. Rather, I will call a spade a spade and use the term "boy-girl sexy-time housing."

And it's not like I don't have evidence to back up my coinage. One dorm on campus has been experimenting (now *there's* an appropriate term!) with boy-girl sexy-time housing for a full semester now, and the results are in. There are orgies happening everywhere in Garner Hall. This evidence should be adequate to squash this proposed housing plan for good.

Specifically, there have been documented, wanton, uncontrolled, study orgies breaking out at all times of the day and night in Garner Hall. According to my sources, alcohol may or may not have played a role in these study orgies. Susan Day, a resident of Garner who asked me not to use her middle name out of concern for her privacy, bore witness to this travesty: "The orgies were everywhere you turned, in every room. Students had books strewn all over their rooms. Pens of every color, and notebooks—these fancy composition books from places like France and Japan. And they were *writing* in them. Shudder."

Dan Merkel, a senior and a Resident Advisor in Garner, fears for the safety of his 5 residents now that the boy-girl sexy-time housing plan is in effect: "They just can't control themselves. They're too young to know any better. Adults have to use their judgment to protect these students from themselves. I worry that they're just not going to get enough sleep because of all this studying. I worry what these intense conversations are going to do to their still-developing bodies. I just can't stop worrying. Someone needs to step in."

There you have it, readers. Under the best of circumstances, students can barely think for themselves. And now that they live in boy-girl sexy-time housing, they clearly can't think at all. Administrators, parents—it's up to you to do what you can to put a stop to the debauchery of boy-girl sexy-time housing.

(Author's Note: If you do write in to oppose the housing proposal, be sure to refer to the proposal as "Gender-Neutral Housing" to ensure that the Administration knows what you are talking about.)

EXAMPLE 2: Satire Pamphlet (excerpt)

Jonathan Swift

A Modest Proposal: For preventing the children of poor people in Ireland, from being a burden on their parents or country, and for making them beneficial to the publick.
First published: 1729

It is a melancholy object to those, who walk through this great town, or travel in the country, when they see the streets, the roads and cabbin-doors crowded with beggars of the female sex, followed by three, four, or six children, all in rags, and importuning every passenger for an alms. These mothers instead of being able to work for their honest livelihood, are forced to employ all their time in stroling to beg sustenance for their helpless infants who, as they grow up, either turn thieves for want of work, or leave their dear native country, to fight for the Pretender in Spain, or sell themselves to the Barbadoes.

I think it is agreed by all parties, that this prodigious number of children in the arms, or on the backs, or at the heels of their mothers, and frequently of their fathers, is in the present deplorable state of the kingdom, a very great additional grievance; and therefore whoever could find out a fair, cheap and easy method of making these children sound and useful members of the common-wealth, would deserve so well of the publick, as to have his statue set up for a preserver of the nation.

But my intention is very far from being confined to provide only for the children of professed beggars: it is of a much greater extent, and shall take in the whole number of infants at a certain age, who are born of parents in effect as little able to support them, as those who demand our charity in the streets.

As to my own part, having turned my thoughts for many years, upon this important subject, and maturely weighed the several schemes of our projectors, I have always found them grossly mistaken in their computation. It is true, a child just dropt from its dam, may be supported by her milk, for a solar year, with little other nourishment: at most not above the value of two shillings, which the mother may certainly get, or the value in scraps, by her lawful occupation of begging; and it is exactly at one year old that I propose to provide for them in such a manner, as, instead of being a charge upon their parents, or the parish, or wanting food and raiment for the rest of their lives, they shall, on the contrary, contribute to the feeding, and partly to the cloathing of many thousands.

5   There is likewise another great advantage in my scheme, that it will prevent those voluntary abortions, and that horrid practice of women murdering their bastard children, alas! too frequent among us, sacrificing the poor innocent babes, I doubt, more to avoid the expence than the shame, which would move tears and pity in the most savage and inhuman breast.

The number of souls in this kingdom being usually reckoned one million and a half, of these I calculate there may be about two hundred thousand couple whose wives are breeders; from which number I subtract thirty thousand couple, who are able to maintain their own children, (although I apprehend there cannot be so many, under the present distresses of the kingdom) but this being granted, there will remain an hundred and seventy thousand breeders. I again subtract fifty thousand, for those women who miscarry, or whose children die by accident or disease within the year. There only remain an hundred and twenty thousand children of poor parents annually born. The question therefore is, How this number shall be reared, and provided for? which, as I have already said, under the present situation of affairs, is utterly impossible by all the methods hitherto proposed. For we can neither employ them in handicraft or agriculture; we neither build houses, (I mean in the country) nor cultivate land: they can very seldom pick up a livelihood by stealing till they arrive at six years old; except where they are of towardly parts, although I confess they learn the rudiments much earlier; during which time they can however be properly looked upon only as probationers: As I have been informed by a principal gentleman in the county of Cavan, who protested to me, that he never knew above one or two instances under the age of six, even in a part of the kingdom so renowned for the quickest proficiency in that art.

I am assured by our merchants, that a boy or a girl before twelve years old, is no saleable commodity, and even when they come to this age, they will not yield above three pounds, or three pounds and half a crown at most, on the exchange; which cannot turn to account either to the parents or kingdom, the charge of nutriments and rags having been at least four times that value.

I shall now therefore humbly propose my own thoughts, which I hope will not be liable to the least objection.

I have been assured by a very knowing American of my acquaintance in London, that a young healthy child well nursed, is, at a year old, a most delicious nourishing and wholesome food, whether stewed, roasted, baked, or boiled; and I make no doubt that it will equally serve in a fricasie, or a ragoust.

I do therefore humbly offer it to publick consideration, that of the hundred and twenty thousand children, already computed, twenty thousand may be reserved for breed, whereof only one fourth part to be males; which is more than we allow to sheep, black cattle, or swine, and my reason is, that these children are seldom the fruits of marriage, a circumstance not much regarded by our savages, therefore, one male will be sufficient to serve four females. That the remaining hundred thousand may, at a year old, be offered in sale to the persons of quality and fortune, through the kingdom, always advising the mother to let them suck plentifully in the last month, so as to render them plump, and fat for a good table. A child will make two dishes at an entertainment for friends, and when the family dines alone, the fore or hind quarter will make a reasonable dish, and seasoned with a little pepper or salt, will be very good boiled on the fourth day, especially in winter.

I have reckoned upon a medium, that a child just born will weigh 12 pounds, and in a solar year, if tolerably nursed, encreaseth to 28 pounds.

I grant this food will be somewhat dear, and therefore very proper for landlords, who, as they have already devoured most of the parents, seem to have the best title to the children.

Infant's flesh will be in season throughout the year, but more plentiful in March, and a little before and after; for we are told by a grave author, an eminent French physician, that fish being a prolifick dyet, there are more children born in Roman Catholick countries about nine months after Lent, the markets will be more glutted than usual, because the number of Popish infants, is at least three to one in this kingdom, and therefore it will have one other collateral advantage, by lessening the number of Papists among us.

I have already computed the charge of nursing a beggar's child (in which list I reckon all cottagers, labourers, and four-fifths of the farmers) to be about two shillings per annum, rags included; and I believe no gentleman would repine to give ten shillings for the carcass of a good fat child, which, as I have said, will make four dishes of excellent nutritive meat, when he hath only some particular friend, or his own family to dine with him. Thus the squire will learn to be a good landlord, and grow popular among his tenants, the mother will have eight shillings neat profit, and be fit for work till she produces another child.

15   Those who are more thrifty (as I must confess the times require) may flea the carcass; the skin of which, artificially dressed, will make admirable gloves for ladies,
and summer boots for fine gentlemen.

As to our City of Dublin, shambles may be appointed for this purpose, in the most
convenient parts of it, and butchers we may be assured will not be wanting; although
I rather recommend buying the children alive, and dressing them hot from the knife,
as we do roasting pigs.

A very worthy person, a true lover of his country, and whose virtues I highly es-
teem, was lately pleased, in discoursing on this matter, to offer a refinement upon
my scheme. He said, that many gentlemen of this kingdom, having of late destroyed
their deer, he conceived that the want of venison might be well supply'd by the bodies of young lads and maidens, not exceeding fourteen years of age, nor under twelve;
so great a number of both sexes in every country being now ready to starve for want
of work and service: And these to be disposed of by their parents if alive, or otherwise by their nearest relations. But with due deference to so excellent a friend, and
so deserving a patriot, I cannot be altogether in his sentiments; for as to the males,
my American acquaintance assured me from frequent experience, that their flesh
was generally tough and lean, like that of our school-boys, by continual exercise,
and their taste disagreeable, and to fatten them would not answer the charge. Then
as to the females, it would, I think, with humble submission, be a loss to the publick,
because they soon would become breeders themselves: And besides, it is not im-
probable that some scrupulous people might be apt to censure such a practice, (although indeed very unjustly) as a little bordering upon cruelty, which, I confess,
hath always been with me the strongest objection against any project, how well so-
ever intended.

But in order to justify my friend, he confessed, that this expedient was put into his
head by the famous Salmanaazor, a native of the island Formosa, who came from
thence to London, above twenty years ago, and in conversation told my friend, that
in his country, when any young person happened to be put to death, the executioner
sold the carcass to persons of quality, as a prime dainty; and that, in his time, the
body of a plump girl of fifteen, who was crucified for an attempt to poison the Em-
peror, was sold to his imperial majesty's prime minister of state, and other great
mandarins of the court in joints from the gibbet, at four hundred crowns. Neither
indeed can I deny, that if the same use were made of several plump young girls in
this town, who without one single groat to their fortunes, cannot stir abroad without
a chair, and appear at a play-house and assemblies in foreign fineries which they
never will pay for; the kingdom would not be the worse.

Some persons of a desponding spirit are in great concern about that vast number
of poor people, who are aged, diseased, or maimed; and I have been desired to employ my thoughts what course may be taken, to ease the nation of so grievous an in-
cumbrance. But I am not in the least pain upon that matter, because it is very well
known, that they are every day dying, and rotting, by cold and famine, and filth, and
vermin, as fast as can be reasonably expected. And as to the young labourers, they
are now in almost as hopeful a condition. They cannot get work, and consequently
pine away from want of nourishment, to a degree, that if at any time they are

accidentally hired to common labour, they have not strength to perform it, and thus the country and themselves are happily delivered from the evils to come.

I have too long digressed, and therefore shall return to my subject. I think the ad- 20 vantages by the proposal which I have made are obvious and many, as well as of the highest importance.

For first, as I have already observed, it would greatly lessen the number of Papists, with whom we are yearly over-run, being the principal breeders of the nation, as well as our most dangerous enemies, and who stay at home on purpose with a de-sign to deliver the kingdom to the Pretender, hoping to take their advantage by the absence of so many good Protestants, who have chosen rather to leave their country, than stay at home and pay tithes against their conscience to an episcopal curate.

Secondly, The poorer tenants will have something valuable of their own, which by law may be made liable to a distress, and help to pay their landlord's rent, their corn and cattle being already seized, and money a thing unknown.

Thirdly, Whereas the maintainance of an hundred thousand children, from two years old, and upwards, cannot be computed at less than ten shillings a piece per annum, the nation's stock will be thereby encreased fifty thousand pounds per an-num, besides the profit of a new dish, introduced to the tables of all gentlemen of fortune in the kingdom, who have any refinement in taste. And the money will cir-culate among our selves, the goods being entirely of our own growth and manufacture.

Fourthly, The constant breeders, besides the gain of eight shillings sterling per annum by the sale of their children, will be rid of the charge of maintaining them after the first year.

Fifthly, This food would likewise bring great custom to taverns, where the vintners 25 will certainly be so prudent as to procure the best receipts for dressing it to perfec-tion; and consequently have their houses frequented by all the fine gentlemen, who justly value themselves upon their knowledge in good eating; and a skilful cook, who understands how to oblige his guests, will contrive to make it as expensive as they please.

Sixthly, This would be a great inducement to marriage, which all wise nations have either encouraged by rewards, or enforced by laws and penalties. It would encrease the care and tenderness of mothers towards their children, when they were sure of a settlement for life to the poor babes, provided in some sort by the publick, to their annual profit instead of expence. We should soon see an honest emulation among the married women, which of them could bring the fattest child to the market. Men would become as fond of their wives, during the time of their pregnancy, as they are now of their mares in foal, their cows in calf, or sow when they are ready to farrow; nor offer to beat or kick them (as is too frequent a practice) for fear of a miscarriage.

Many other advantages might be enumerated. For instance, the addition of some thousand carcasses in our exportation of barrel'd beef: the propagation of swine's flesh, and improvement in the art of making good bacon, so much wanted among us by the great destruction of pigs, too frequent at our tables; which are no way compa-rable in taste or magnificence to a well grown, fat yearly child, which roasted whole will make a considerable figure at a Lord Mayor's feast, or any other publick entertainment. But this, and many others, I omit, being studious of brevity.

Supposing that one thousand families in this city, would be constant customers for infants flesh, besides others who might have it at merry meetings, particularly at weddings and christenings, I compute that Dublin would take off annually about twenty thousand carcasses; and the rest of the kingdom (where probably they will be sold somewhat cheaper) the remaining eighty thousand.

I can think of no one objection, that will possibly be raised against this proposal, unless it should be urged, that the number of people will be thereby much lessened in the kingdom. This I freely own, and 'twas indeed one principal design in offering it to the world. I desire the reader will observe, that I calculate my remedy for this one individual Kingdom of Ireland, and for no other that ever was, is, or, I think, ever can be upon Earth. Therefore let no man talk to me of other expedients: Of taxing our absentees at five shillings a pound: Of using neither cloaths, nor houshold furniture, except what is of our own growth and manufacture: Of utterly rejecting the materials and instruments that promote foreign luxury: Of curing the expensiveness of pride, vanity, idleness, and gaming in our women: Of introducing a vein of parsimony, prudence and temperance: Of learning to love our country, wherein we differ even from Laplanders, and the inhabitants of Topinamboo: Of quitting our animosities and factions, nor acting any longer like the Jews, who were murdering one another at the very moment their city was taken: Of being a little cautious not to sell our country and consciences for nothing: Of teaching landlords to have at least one degree of mercy towards their tenants. Lastly, of putting a spirit of honesty, industry, and skill into our shop-keepers, who, if a resolution could now be taken to buy only our native goods, would immediately unite to cheat and exact upon us in the price, the measure, and the goodness, nor could ever yet be brought to make one fair proposal of just dealing, though often and earnestly invited to it.

30   Therefore I repeat, let no man talk to me of these and the like expedients, 'till he hath at least some glympse of hope, that there will ever be some hearty and sincere attempt to put them into practice.

But, as to my self, having been wearied out for many years with offering vain, idle, visionary thoughts, and at length utterly despairing of success, I fortunately fell upon this proposal, which, as it is wholly new, so it hath something solid and real, of no expence and little trouble, full in our own power, and whereby we can incur no danger in disobliging England. For this kind of commodity will not bear exportation, and flesh being of too tender a consistence, to admit a long continuance in salt, although perhaps I could name a country, which would be glad to eat up our whole nation without it.

After all, I am not so violently bent upon my own opinion, as to reject any offer, proposed by wise men, which shall be found equally innocent, cheap, easy, and effectual. But before something of that kind shall be advanced in contradiction to my scheme, and offering a better, I desire the author or authors will be pleased maturely to consider two points. First, As things now stand, how they will be able to find food and raiment for a hundred thousand useless mouths and backs. And secondly, There being a round million of creatures in humane figure throughout this kingdom, whose whole subsistence put into a common stock, would leave them in debt two million of pounds sterling, adding those who are beggars by profession, to the bulk of farmers, cottagers and labourers, with their wives and children, who are beggars in effect; I desire those politicians who dislike my overture, and may perhaps be so bold to attempt an answer, that they will first ask the parents of these mortals, whether they would not at this day think it a great happiness to have been sold for food at a year old, in the manner I prescribe, and thereby have avoided such a perpetual scene of misfortunes, as they have since gone through, by the oppression of landlords, the impossibility of paying rent without money or trade, the want of common sustenance, with neither house nor cloaths to cover them from the inclemencies of the weather, and the most inevitable prospect of intailing the like, or greater miseries, upon their breed for ever.

I profess, in the sincerity of my heart, that I have not the least personal interest in endeavouring to promote this necessary work, having no other motive than the publick good of my country, by advancing our trade, providing for infants, relieving the poor, and giving some pleasure to the rich. I have no children, by which I can propose to get a single penny; the youngest being nine years old, and my wife past child-bearing.

EXAMPLE 3: Satire News Article

The Onion

Professor Deeply Hurt by Student's Evaluation

Leon Rothberg, Ph.D., a 58-year-old professor of English Literature at Ohio State University, was shocked and saddened Monday after receiving a sub-par mid-semester evaluation from freshman student Chad Berner. The circles labeled 4 and 5 on the Scan-Tron form were predominantly filled in, placing Rothberg's teaching skill in the "below average" to "poor" range.

Although the evaluation has deeply hurt Rothberg's feelings, Berner defended his judgment at a press conference yesterday.

"That class is totally boring," said Berner, one of 342 students in Rothberg's introductory English 161 class. "When I go, I have to read the school paper to keep from falling asleep. One of my brothers does a comic strip called 'The Booze Brothers.' It's awesome."

The poor rating has left Rothberg, a Rhodes Scholar, distraught and doubting his ability to teach effectively at the university level.

"Maybe I'm just no good at this job," said Rothberg, recipient of the 1993 Jean- 5 Foucault Lacan award from the University of Chicago for his paper on public/private feminist deconstructive discourse in the early narratives of Catherine of Siena. "Chad's right. I am totally boring."

In the wake of the evaluation, Rothberg is considering canceling his fall sabbatical to the University of Geneva, where he is slated to serve as a Henri Bynum-Derridas Visiting Scholar. Instead, Rothberg may take a rudimentary public speaking course as well as offer his services to students like Berner, should they desire personal tutoring.

"The needs of my first-year students come well before any prestigious personal awards offered to me by international academic assemblies," Rothberg said. "After all, I have dedicated my life to the pursuit of knowledge, and to imparting it to those who are coming after me. I know that's why these students are here, so I owe it to them."

Though Rothberg, noted author of *The Violent Body: Marxist Roots of Postmodern Homoerotic Mysticism and the Feminine Form in St. Augustine's Confessions*, has attempted to contact Berner numerous times by telephone, Berner has not returned his calls, leading Rothberg to believe that Berner is serious in his condemnation of the professor.

"I'm always stoned when he calls, so I let the answering machine pick it up," said Berner, who maintains a steady 2.3 GPA. "My roommate just got this new bong that totally kicks ass. We call it Sky Lab."

10   Those close to Rothberg agree that the negative evaluation is difficult to overcome.

"Richard is trying to keep a stiff upper lip around his colleagues, but I know he's taking it very hard," said Susan Feinstein-Rothberg, a fellow English professor and Rothberg's wife of 29 years. "He knows that students like Chad deserve better."

When told of Rothberg's thoughts of quitting, Berner became angry.

"He'd better finish up the class," Berner said. "I need those three humanities credits to be eligible to apply to the business school next year."

The English Department administration at Ohio State is taking a hard look at Rothberg's performance in the wake of Berner's poor evaluation.

15   "Students and the enormous revenue they bring in to our institution are a more valued commodity to us than faculty," Dean James Hewitt said. "Although Rothberg is a distinguished, tenured professor with countless academic credentials and knowledge of 21 modern and ancient languages, there is absolutely no excuse for his boring Chad with his lectures. Chad must be entertained at all costs."

USE THE TOOLKIT

Let's use the three genre toolkit questions from Chapter 1 to examine this genre.

What Is It?

These are examples of satirical arguments, or satire. A satirical argument works by arguing the opposite case in an exaggerated way, or by using irony to point out the inconsistencies or absurdity of another argument. While it may come across as funny, satire also has a deeper purpose: to criticize problems in a social structure, institution, or government.

Example 1 criticized what the author perceived to be unreasonable fears of gender-neutral housing held by the university administration—that the housing policy would cause students to behave promiscuously. In Example 2, Jonathan Swift was criticizing the cruel attitudes of his contemporaries toward the poor in Ireland. In Example 3, the writers of the piece criticized the tendency for universities to use student satisfaction as an increasingly important criterion for decisions, including evaluations of professors.

Satire also tends to use a common set of rhetorical features. For example, word play and style choices are very important.

Who Reads It?

These satires are all directed primarily at members of a specific community—those who belong to the social institution being critiqued, but also those who might be entertained by the satire.

For instance, Swift published his satire anonymously in 1729, as a pamphlet meant to support the cause of the Irish, who were exploited by the English, dealing with famine, poverty, and the unscrupulous absentee landlords that Swift mentions in his "proposal." Swift's satire was meant to be read not only by the Irish who were suffering these conditions, but also by the British, who had the potential to change those conditions. Pia's satire mocks the administrators and parents who, she would argue, infantilize college students with their fears about gender-neutral housing.

What's It For?

The goal of a satire is to argue a point or lodge a criticism in a humorous way, often by pointing out the absurdities in news events, politics, and the like. Authors of satire use exaggerated appeals to emotions to make their points, seeking to persuade through indirect means. Readers must be able to figure out that the piece is not to be taken seriously in order to be persuaded by it. In some cases, readers may not realize that a satirical column such as this one is not meant to be taken literally. Some readers of "A Modest Proposal," for instance, have thought that Swift was actually advocating for infanticide and cannibalism! Thus, it is important for writers of satire to take into account the possibility that some readers may get the wrong idea.

EXERCISE 10.3: Analyze a Satire

Locate several examples of satire: either "fake news," such as *The Onion*, advertisements, or editorials in a newspaper or magazine (print or online). Take note of what strategies seem effective and funny, and what pieces miss the mark (either by being offensive or simply being unfunny). Then, come up with a set of criteria for an effective satire piece.

MULTIMEDIA EXERCISE 10.3: Analyze Satire across Media Forms

Locate several examples of satire from different media formats—videos, blogs, news columns, or visual advertisements. Come up with a list of strategies used in these different examples, and sort them into two groups: features that occur across different formats, and features that are unique to one format. For example, you might find that the tendency to distort a familiar logo or image occurs mainly in advertisements, while the tendency to use wordplay (such as "The Daily Voice" becoming the "Daily Vice") tends to appear in multiple formats.

E. Strategies for Argumentative Genres

So far, we have examined several different kinds of argumentative genres, starting with a visual example (an advertisement), and then considering written examples (letters to the editor and editorial), and then oral examples (a campaign speech). We then examined satire as a kind of argumentative genre that can appear in any of those types. In the process, we have identified a number of features that argumentative genres share, including appeals to logic, emotion, and character. (You'll find more information about arguments, in general, in Chapter 18.)

In this chapter, then, we'll examine how you might go about writing one of these genres. Imagine that you have been asked to contribute a satire for your college newspaper.

Let's see how one student, Pia, went about this assignment.

Prewriting (Content)

First, Pia looked at some recent articles in the newspaper (online and in print) to determine what kinds of topics seemed timely, and to identify what kinds of topics might be appropriate for a good satire. She also brainstormed a list of recent events and issues in her campus and in her local community:

- *student council elections*
- *proposal for gender-neutral housing on campus*
- *town-gown relations*
- *student parking*
- *cutting the physical education requirement*

Next, Pia tried writing out different claims (sometimes called thesis statements—see Chapter 18). Since she was writing a satire, she considered claims that she could exaggerate for effect, making a few notes about possible ideas or points she might make for satirical effect.

- *student council elections*
    - *Your posters and annoying chants totally make me want to vote for you.*
- *proposal for gender-neutral housing on campus*
    - *We should just call gender-neutral housing on campus "boy girl sexy time" housing since that's what everyone's afraid of*
- ~~*town-gown relations*~~
- *student parking*
    - *Parking lots totally beautify campus landscape so we should have more of them.*
- *Cutting the physical education requirement*
    - *"Life fit" classes are too rigorous—I couldn't finish my Melville paper because I had to study for my walking class.*

Next, Pia brainstormed more ideas for the issue she finds most compelling from her list—gender-neutral housing. She thought this issue would give her the most fodder for her satire. Here's a snippet from her notes:

- *Gender neutral housing on campus = "boy girl sexy time" housing.*
    - *"Orgies" of student studying break out late night—parody of a party (books strewn everywhere, writing indiscriminately in notebooks, etc.)*
    - *Could include interviews from students living in Garner Hall*

Of course, Pia also did research (Chapter 24) to see what others were saying about her topic.

Pia also planned her satire to address the counter-arguments (Chapter 18) that people had made against gender-neutral housing. She also framed a rebuttal.

Counter-Argument against Gender-Neutral Housing

- *What people are saying: Gender neutral housing will lead to inappropriate sexual activity. → Use idea of "orgies" and "boy-girl sexy-time housing" to lampoon this idea.*

Rebuttal

- *Implies we are children who cannot be responsible for ourselves—use a quote to parody this point?*

Drafting (Organizing)

When drafting an argument, it is important to consider how your opening will draw readers in. If you are addressing an audience that opposes your position, for example, you may want to create an introduction that first addresses their concerns, before stating your own opinion.

In the case of a satire, the opening often reads like a typical argument—that is, it poses as a serious case for or against something. The reader should gradually realize that you are writing satirically, not in earnest. Pia started out with a paragraph that might read as a serious argument:

> The University Administration and certain parent groups have shown appropriate concern about the proposed, so-called "gender-neutral" housing situation that would allow male and female university students to live in the same dorm rooms.

The reader would gradually realize that Pia was speaking satirically—that she was not actually opposing gender-neutral housing—in the next paragraph, when she introduces the term "boy-girl sexy-time housing."

The rest of the article serves to amplify the claim through additional examples and details. Pia added quotations as evidence, but for a serious argument you might also build up evidence in the form of facts, statistics, or reason chains (Chapter 18).

Revising (Style)

When you seek feedback on your draft, ask readers to highlight phrases or terms that might alienate your readers, such as inflammatory language that might seem fine for people who already agree with you, but that might turn off readers who do not agree. You should pay close attention to your tone. Sometimes, weighted language (Chapter 21) can be used selectively to emphasize your points, but you should be careful to avoid overly emotional wording.

In a satire, it is important not to take things too far. Often, there is a fine line between poking fun at an issue and offending readers, especially if you are writing about a topic that can come across as racist, sexist, homophobic, or narrow-minded.

Pia originally wrote the following quote from Susan Day (a fictional resident of Garner Hall).

> Susan Day, a resident of Garner who asked me not to use her middle name out of concern for her privacy, bore witness to this travesty: "The orgies were everywhere you turned, in every room. Some girls are studying promiscuously— they are off studying every night in a different guy's room. Then we get to watch them stumble home in the morning, still in their disheveled study clothes from the night before."

During peer review, Pia's classmates mentioned that this passage seemed over the top and that it might be drawing on sexist stereotypes. So Pia revised this quotation to read as follows:

> Susan Day, a resident of Garner who asked me not to use her middle name out of concern for her privacy, bore witness to this travesty: "The orgies were everywhere you turned, in every room. Students had books strewn all over their rooms. Pens of every color, and notebooks—these fancy composition books from places like France and Japan. And they were *writing* in them. Shudder."

Also, be careful about writing in the first person ("I think . . ."). While your personal opinions may be valid, focusing too much on yourself can make you come across as self-centered or ill-tempered. Instead, support your position with evidence drawn from other sources as well, from interviews with fellow students to facts and statistics (Chapter 24).

You might also watch out for logical fallacies, which are claims that may mislead or manipulate an audience (Chapter 18). Note that a satire, however, might actually work by drawing on fallacies, such as exaggerated appeals to pity or fear.

Editing (Design)

When you write for a newspaper or other print or online news publication, the editorial staff will exercise a lot of control over the design of your document. They will also edit your work, sometimes changing entire words or sentences that you wrote. They may also give your work a title. This is normal for a print newspaper as well as the newspaper's website.

In Pia's case, the newspaper editor suggested a new title, "Uncontrolled Study Orgies Break Out in Gender-Neutral Dorm," instead of her original title, "Let's Call Gender-Neutral Housing What it Is: Boy-Girl Sexy Time." The editor also shortened her article slightly to fit with the newspaper's standard length for opinion pieces.

If you would like to exercise more control over the final appearance of your editorial or article, you should publish it yourself, on a blog, for example, or on a flier.

Troubleshooting

Here are some common challenges that students face when writing argumentative genres.

I need help formulating my claim.   When writing an argument, you can start with the arguments of others. For a satire, you can take an opinion that you think is incorrect, and then satirize it by exaggerating the original claim. For a letter to the editor, find an article in the paper that you disagree with and start from there. (See Chapter 18 for more on how to develop claims.)

I can't find any evidence to support my argument.   A lack of evidence may mean that you need to reconsider your claim. It is unethical to argue a point just because you believe in it despite all evidence to the contrary. It is highly unethical to argue a point that requires you to ignore or twist the facts. (See Chapter 18 for more on how to locate evidence through research, personal experience, and rhetorical invention.)

I need help organizing my argument.   You can look carefully at examples of the genre you are writing, including the selections in this chapter. Pay attention to how writers tend to begin, how they order their sections or points, and how they conclude. Then, try out some of those strategies for your own document. (See Chapter 20 for more on how to organize your argument.)

My argument seems self-centered.   Sometimes, relying too heavily on your own experience can lead to an argument that seems self-centered. For example, if you are writing a letter to the editor for your college newspaper about a problem affecting you personally (say, lack of air conditioning in your dorm room), you might feel tempted to describe your own personal suffering.

However, your argument might seem more compelling if you also include the perspectives of others in your dorm. You could interview friends and use quotes to support your claims, or you could do some research to determine the prevalence of the problem and its possible effects. (How many students lack air conditioning?)

Also, consider the perspective of your audience—what aspects of the issue will they care about? School administrators might care more about the air conditioning problem if you can connect it to students' overall performance in school or their satisfaction with the university.

My argument seems boring.   Sometimes, when students write argumentative genres, they tend to get stuck in "student mode," and they end up producing something that reads more like an essay or five-paragraph theme than the genre they have been asked to write. Watch out for features of the essay genre that you use automatically, such as formal transitional words and phrases to start each paragraph (such as "In conclusion," or "Moreover,").

Often, argumentative genres use different strategies to focus each paragraph, such as providing a statistic, example, short sentence, or rhetorical question. You might also alter your tone or level of formality (see Chapter 21) to liven up your prose and make it more suitable for the genre.

Workplace Genres

Workplace genres include the variety of genres that writers compose in professional or formal settings, including emails, letters, proposals, plans, and résumés. Although these genres are typically found in the workplace, students use these genres all the time: they compose emails to professors; they write letters to scholarship committees; and they design résumés for summer internships. In business courses, students write professional letters, proposals, and plans regularly, but workplace genres might also appear in other courses that stress entrepreneurship or professional development. The ability to write workplace genres is an essential skill for success in college.

These skills are essential outside the classroom as well. For example, in the workplace, the ability to compose a professional email is essential, since the genre conveys authority and competence. Workplace genres perform much of the work of organizations, from documenting what work has been done to securing new contracts or clients.

In this chapter, we will discover three workplace genres that students encounter most often: emails, letters, and résumés. Because this family of genres shares a similar audience—professional readers in the workplace—we will keep this audience in mind as we discover the genres in this chapter.

A. Workplace Mini-Genre: Company Slogan

A company slogan is a short phrase or sentence that companies and other organizations use to capture the public's notice and draw attention to their brands.

EXAMPLE 1: Slogan for a University

FRESN◉STATE
Discovery. Diversity. Distinction.

Fresno State slogan.

EXAMPLE 2: Slogan for a Radio Station

KCRW IS MORE THAN JUST A RADIO STATION.

KCRW IS THE FUTURE OF PUBLIC MEDIA.

Slogan for public radio station KCRW.

EXAMPLE 3: Slogan for a Government Agency

Slogan for a United States Department of Agriculture program.

Let's use the three genre toolkit questions from Chapter 1 to examine this genre.

What Is It?

A slogan is a short, catchy phrase that companies use to capture consumer attention. These three examples illustrate how short slogans can be. In Example 1, for California State University, Fresno, the slogan is only three words long: "Discovery. Diversity. Distinction." Slogans tend to be presented in bold, colorful type to catch the eye.

Who Reads It?

Companies and organizations intend their slogans to be read by a wide, popular audience—the wider, the better. They hope their slogans will be instantly recognizable. Therefore, slogans need to be as simple and clear as possible. Some companies and organizations may aim for a smaller market, or niche, in which case they craft their slogans to appeal to that particular audience. The organization featured in Example 2, KCRW, is a public radio station in Santa Monica, California. It serves Los Angeles and its surrounding areas. Its target audience, then, is composed of people who live in that geographical region.

What's It For?

Slogans capture popular attention and create brand recognition. Ideally, they entice people to purchase products sold by a company or to otherwise support an organization. They also create goodwill toward a company, even among those who do not buy the company's products on a regular basis. For example, a person might not need to participate in the federal government food stamps program (Example 3), but the government would like to encourage wide support of the program among all U.S. citizens.

EXERCISE 12.1: Craft a Slogan

Suppose you are starting a public awareness campaign to address a need on your campus or in your town. Design a slogan for your campaign that helps raise awareness of the issue you are addressing.

GROUP ACTIVITY 12.1: Pitch a Slogan

Suppose your group is a marketing company hired to design a public awareness campaign to address a need on your campus or in your town. Have each person in your group pitch a slogan for the campaign; then, have the group as a whole vet each slogan. Which slogan best generates wide support for the campaign? Why?

B. Email

Email is a crucial form of communication. In the workplace, you might send dozens of emails every day. Even though email is often a casual kind of communication, certain conventions still apply when writing emails.

EXAMPLE 1: Student's Reference Request Email

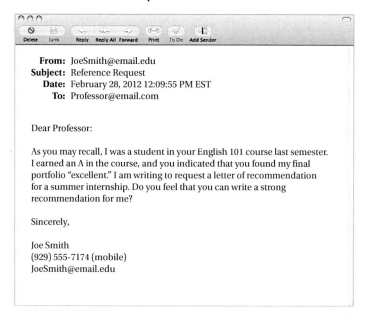

From: JoeSmith@email.edu
Subject: Reference Request
Date: February 28, 2012 12:09:55 PM EST
To: Professor@email.com

Dear Professor:

As you may recall, I was a student in your English 101 course last semester. I earned an A in the course, and you indicated that you found my final portfolio "excellent." I am writing to request a letter of recommendation for a summer internship. Do you feel that you can write a strong recommendation for me?

Sincerely,

Joe Smith
(929) 555-7174 (mobile)
JoeSmith@email.edu

EXAMPLE 2: Club Meeting Email

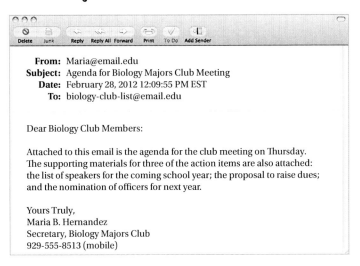

From: Maria@email.edu
Subject: Agenda for Biology Majors Club Meeting
Date: February 28, 2012 12:09:55 PM EST
To: biology-club-list@email.edu

Dear Biology Club Members:

Attached to this email is the agenda for the club meeting on Thursday. The supporting materials for three of the action items are also attached: the list of speakers for the coming school year; the proposal to raise dues; and the nomination of officers for next year.

Yours Truly,
Maria B. Hernandez
Secretary, Biology Majors Club
929-555-8513 (mobile)

EXAMPLE 3: Article Rejection Email

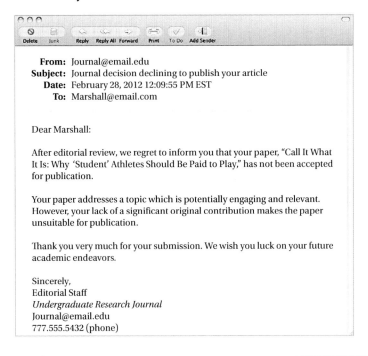

From: Journal@email.edu
Subject: Journal decision declining to publish your article
Date: February 28, 2012 12:09:55 PM EST
To: Marshall@email.com

Dear Marshall:

After editorial review, we regret to inform you that your paper, "Call It What It Is: Why 'Student' Athletes Should Be Paid to Play," has not been accepted for publication.

Your paper addresses a topic which is potentially engaging and relevant. However, your lack of a significant original contribution makes the paper unsuitable for publication.

Thank you very much for your submission. We wish you luck on your future academic endeavors.

Sincerely,
Editorial Staff
Undergraduate Research Journal
Journal@email.edu
777.555.5432 (phone)

Let's use the three genre toolkit questions from Chapter 1 to examine this genre.

What Is It?

An email is an electronic letter. The documents in the preceding examples are all emails sent by students regarding important business in students' lives. The emails share a few important qualities. First, the subject line of each email explicitly states what the email is about. Second, each email is short, limited to one to three paragraphs. Each paragraph is also concise, sometimes only including one sentence. Lastly, each email includes an email signature, information that appears after the email closing ("Sincerely" or "Yours Truly") and provides contact information about the sender of the email. This signature is the equivalent of the return address in a print letter.

Who Reads It?

Emails are read by many different audiences. In the workplace, emails are read by clients, co-workers, bosses, etc. In college, emails might be read by professors, teaching assistants, friends, group members, and family members. Remember, too, that because of the nature of email, they are easily forwarded to unintended recipients by the person that you sent the email to, so be very careful what you write in an email.

Each of the emails in the preceding examples has a different audience. The first was sent from a student to a professor, and therefore the tone is deferential. The second was sent from a student to members of a club that the student works for, and the tone is more casual. The third was sent from the student editors of an undergraduate journal to a student who had submitted an article for publication. The tone is one of explanation and kindness, to soften the blow of rejection.

What's It For?

Emails usually serve a clear purpose: they may be used to convey information, make a request, or inquire about something. While the primary purpose is informative, a secondary purpose is to maintain the goodwill of the audience. Like the slogans earlier in this chapter, these emails seek to create and maintain a positive impression of the individual or organization—even when conveying bad news, as in the rejection email in Example 3.

Proposals

A proposal is a genre that asks for something from someone. For example, in a wedding proposal, the proposer asks someone to marry him/her. The audience (the girlfriend or boyfriend) has the power to agree to the proposal—or to reject it. Proposals are characterized by this unequal relationship between the writer/speaker and the audience: the audience has the power to say yes or no.

In college, you might be asked to write a proposal to start a new student organization or to enroll in an independent study course you have designed with a professor. Or, you might write a marketing proposal for a business class. In a city and regional planning course, you might be asked to come up with a proposal for a new redevelopment project in your town.

In the workplace, proposals are a very common genre. In a number of fields, potential clients will put out a request for proposals (RFP), and businesses write proposals hoping to get the job. For example, a company might request advertising proposals for a new ad campaign. A contractor might write a building proposal for a client seeking to build a new home or office. A caterer might put together a proposal for someone seeking to host an event like a wedding or retirement celebration.

In this chapter, you will learn how to write several of the proposals that you might encounter as a college student.

A. Proposal Mini-Genre: Elevator Pitch

An elevator pitch is a short speech (usually 30 seconds to two minutes long) that you prepare in order to quickly summarize a proposal. You might prepare an elevator pitch if you are working in sales and want to be prepared for potential customers, or if you are an entrepreneur and want to be prepared in case you meet a potential investor. The term "elevator pitch" refers to the idea that you could complete your proposal during an elevator ride, in case you happen to be riding the elevator with someone who could say yes to your proposal.

EXAMPLE 1: Elevator Pitch to an Employer

"Professor Lee? I'm a first-year biology major. I'm experienced in gel elec-trophoresis and Matlab, and I'm really interested in learning more about genetic research. Would you be willing to consider me for a position as lab assistant next year? I can send you my résumé and references."

EXAMPLE 2: Elevator Pitch to an Investor

"Bananarama will be Springfield's first full-service banana stand. We'll sell fresh, hand-dipped bananas in 34 enticing flavors. The frozen fruit market is among the fastest growing in our state, since it offers a health-conscious alternative to ice cream and frozen yogurt. Would you be interested in being part of an enterprise with projected $1 million in sales over the next five years? I can send you my business plan by email."

EXAMPLE 3: Elevator Pitch to a Customer

"Hi, would you like a free sample of our Hungerfree energy bars? With each sale, we donate fifty percent of our proceeds to UNICEF to fight child hunger. Plus, the peanuts, whole grains, and honey will help you get through your next college class Hungerfree. If you like the sample, you can buy a bar for just $2."

USE THE TOOLKIT

Let's use the three genre toolkit questions from Chapter 1 to examine this genre.

What Is It?

An elevator pitch is a short request. Each one begins with an introduction—either of a person, of a business, or of a product. Then, each pitch provides a very short description—of the person's qualifications, the business's value, or the product's qualities. Each pitch also includes a request. You may begin or end with the request. You can see that in Examples 1 and 2, the request comes last, after the explanation. In Example 3, the request comes first, and the explanation second.

Who Reads It?

Elevator pitches are usually delivered orally, so instead of a reader, they have a listening audience. For each of these examples, you can imagine a different audience and situation. In Example 1, you might imagine that a student has run into a professor in the hallway or waited to speak to him after class. In Example 2, you can imagine that Bananarama's owner has met a wealthy investor at a business fair or at an event for alumni of the owner's college. And, in Example 3, we can guess that a student may have set up a display in a high-traffic area on campus. In each example, the audience is a potential employer, investor, or client, someone who has the power to grant the request.

What's It For?

An elevator pitch is primarily a persuasive genre: the goal is to convince someone to grant your request, or at least to consider it. For that reason, you can consider an elevator pitch a very short argument. In some cases, it is also an opening for further conversation or writing. You might follow up an elevator pitch with a résumé, as in Example 1, or with a longer print proposal, as the Bananarama owner did (Example 2).

EXERCISE 13.1: Write an Elevator Pitch

Prepare a short (30-second) elevator pitch for a job you would like. Imagine you are meeting a recruiter for your ideal employer at a campus job fair. How would you pitch yourself to that person? Practice your pitch several times, and then deliver it to your classmates or group.

GROUP ACTIVITY 13.1: Adjust Elevator Pitches for Various Audiences

With your group, decide on a product or service for your local community. Determine how you would make that product or service available. Then, each of you will prepare a 30-second elevator pitch for a different target audience:

- A potential investor
- A potential customer
- A potential employee
- A reporter for the business section of the local newspaper

Adjust your tone and message for each audience's concerns. Practice your pitches, then deliver them to the class.

EXERCISE 13.2: Write a Pitch   **?**

Start with an idea for a TV show, book, or film you would be interested in producing. Then, write a pitch in which you persuade an audience to support that project. You will need to do research on existing projects so that you can show how your proposed project (your book, show, or film) is unique.

C. Student Proposal

A student proposal is a document that requests approval for a new campus organization, event, course, or activity. At most universities, students can request approval (and sometimes funding) for these endeavors, but they must first complete a proposal that is approved by college administrators.

EXAMPLE 1: Student Event Proposal

Student Event Proposal Form

General Information

Name of Organization(s): __International Student Club__

Person Completing Request:_Victor Egbukichi__ **E-mail:**_victore@uca.edu___

Event Description

Description of Event: _____

Place and time: ____Mondays, 2:30-3:30 pm; Student Union Room 2010b_____

_____

Expected attendance____25 students (undergraduate)_____

Describe how this event will benefit the UCA community: International students now make up 8% of the student body at UCA, in accordance with the university's global mission. However, international students often struggle to make American friends. Many end up socializing mainly with other students from their home country, which can prevent international students from improving their language skills or learning about American culture. While international students can interact with American students in classrooms, these are high stakes situations where they may feel shy about speaking up. The weekly coffee hour will give these students a chance to meet American students in a friendly, low pressure situation.

American students who are learning a foreign language can also practice their language skills with international students, and learn more about their culture.

Describe other activities and events your student organization has held this year:

The International Student Club has thus far hosted four International Days in the cafeteria, highlighting the food and culture of China, India, Nigeria, and Russia. We plan to host four more International Days in the Spring semester (for Mexico, Ethiopia, Brazil, and Spain).

We have also participated in the Student Organization Carnival and sponsored three members in the Dance Marathon.

Describe how your student organization will publicize this event:

We have designed the attached poster, which we will put up in the Student Union, cafeteria, and in the Language & Literature buildings.

Describe how this event is unique:

This activity will help us to recruit new members who are not necessarily international students, but who would like to participate in our organizational mission. This is the first activity we know of that will specifically address the communication gap between international and American students.

EXAMPLE 2: Student Organization Proposal

Student Organization Council

Proposal for Student Organization

Name of Organization: Campus Community Garden

Name of Organizer: Leticia Garcia-Rodriguez

Contact Phone Number: 222-222-2222

Email Address: Leticia@gsu.edu

Name of Advisor: Professor Peabody

Contact Phone Number: 222-222-2224

Email Address: p.peabody@gsu.edu

Please answer the following questions as completely as possible in the space provided.

---

1. Describe the mission of your organization:
The Campus Community Garden will encourage sustainable food at GSU by providing classes, hands-on workshops, and fresh fruits and vegetables for students, faculty, and staff.

2. Describe how your organization is unique or new:
To date, no student organization at GSU focuses on growing fresh food and teaching gardening skills. Other food-related organizations, such as Local Food GSU, focus on advocating for purchasing food locally, but do not promote gardening.

3. Describe how your organization will benefit the GSU community:
Any student will be able to apply for a plot in the community garden, purchase fresh food at our weekly garden market, or volunteer for bi-weekly garden work days. Students can also sign up for free courses on topics such as composting or planting a windowsill garden.

4. Describe how your organization fulfills GSU's mission:
Sustainability is one of the key terms in GSU's mission statement. This organization will help students and faculty to promote sustainability and make a direct impact on the college's ecological footprint.

EXAMPLE 3: **Independent Study Proposal**

Independent Study Proposal Outline

Semester and Year	Spring 2016
Student Name	Tyler Williamson
Instructor Name	Professor Molly Johnson
Date Proposal Written	September 15, 2015

Project Description:
In her 1995 speech to the United Nations Fourth World Conference on Women, Hillary Clinton said: "And let us heed the call so that we can create a world in which every woman is treated with respect and dignity, every boy and girl is loved and cared for equally, and every family has the hope of a strong and stable future." Clinton has modeled her world-wide call for women's rights upon the United Nations' protection of human rights, and many others have followed. But the question remains: is she guilty of cultural solipsism when she outlines standards of women's rights based upon the lifestyle of bourgeois western women? Who decides what it means to be "treated with respect and dignity"? This independent study will examine the call for universal women's rights: is such a goal possible, and if so, what would these "rights" look like? Throughout the semester, I will work to shed my resistance to cultural perspectives from beyond the West, through readings, documentary screenings, discussions and reflections, research and presentations, and interviews with women in our community who have left their native countries to make new lives in America.

Assignments:
1. Documentary film rhetorical analysis (5 pages) 2. Interview series of immigrant women in America (5 interviews) 3. Final research paper on international women's rights (20 pages)

USE THE TOOLKIT

Let's use the three genre toolkit questions from Chapter 1 to examine this genre.

What Is It?

These proposals all relate to aspects of student life, whether it is planning an event, starting a student organization, or proposing an independent study. Like the elevator pitch, each of these proposals "pitches" something—an event, organization, or course of study. To do so, the proposal describes the goals of the activity, explains why it is unique, and outlines how it will contribute to the campus community or to the student's education. In Example 1, Victor writes that the activity will promote communication between international and U.S. students, helping international student make friends. In Example 2, Leticia writes that the garden "will encourage sustainable food" on the university campus.

All of these proposals are forms that writers download from a website and fill out. These forms give writers a clear idea of what to include, but the writers must still make rhetorical choices in order to create a persuasive case.

Who Reads It?

These proposals are read by decision makers who decide which proposals to approve or fund. The audience may be other student leaders (such as members of the Student Organization Committee), college administrators, or professors. The audience for Example 3, Tyler's independent study proposal, would include the professor whom he has asked to advise the project and the director of undergraduate studies of the political science department. The readers of the proposals decide which proposals to approve based on how persuasive the writer has been. They may prioritize proposals that are likely to help the greatest number of students, or proposals that are the most unique, or those that seem most feasible to implement.

What's It For?

The purpose of a student proposal is to persuade readers to grant the request for approval. Often, approval may entail funding. Thus, a proposal is essentially an argument: you provide good reasons for readers to support your request (Chapter 18). In Example 2, Leticia shows how her proposed organization will promote sustainability, a key goal at her university.

EXERCISE 13.3: Propose a Student Organization or Event

First, determine how students can go about proposing a new organization or event on your campus. If there is a form, download and save it to your computer. Then, write a persuasive proposal for your organization or event.

Developing a Topic

A. Genre Toolkit: What Are You Writing?

Before you can select a topic or subject for writing, you need to figure out what kind of document you are writing. A topic is different from a thesis (Chapter 18). While a thesis refers to what you will say when you write (what claim or argument you will make), your topic simply refers to what you will be writing about. For example, if you are assigned to write a film review (Chapter 9), your topic will be the movie you have chosen to write about. Your thesis will relate to your actual evaluation of that movie—whether it was good or bad, and why.

Let's see how one student, Terrence, used the three genre toolkit questions (Chapter 1) to determine what kinds of topics were appropriate for his writing project.

USE THE TOOLKIT

What Is It?

First, Terrence figured out what kind of document he was writing. Was it an op-ed or letter to the editor? A report? A research paper?

Terrence's professor assigned him to write a research paper. He read Chapter 11, "Academic Research Genres," to learn more about the genre of the research paper. He learned that a research paper presents new, interesting research on a timely topic in a particular academic field. Thus, a research paper's topic is constrained by the genre: if Terrence wanted to write a social psychology research paper, then he needed to write on a topic that is *of interest to others in the field of social psychology.*

Who Reads It?

Next, Terrence needed to figure out who was going to read his research paper. Was his research paper merely an assignment for class—and therefore to be read only by his teacher? Or was he going to present it at a conference to other students or researchers? Would it be possible to use his paper as a writing sample for a summer internship or other job application? Was it possible that he would submit the paper to a journal that publishes research by undergraduates?

Terrence identified his professor as the primary audience of his research paper, but he also thought that he might want to present his paper at the undergraduate research conference that his college hosted every year. Thus, he knew he needed to keep in mind that his research paper might have an audience beyond just his professor.

However, his professor remained his primary audience. He therefore knew that *his topic needed to satisfy his primary audience's needs.* In Terrence's case, his professor said that students' research topics needed to tie in somehow to the students' life experiences.

What's It For?

Lastly, Terrence needed to figure out what his document would *do*—that is, the document's purpose. Was it to inform? To persuade? To inquire? In the case of a research paper, the purpose is both *to inform a reader and to make an argument about the research and its significance.*

Once Terrence identified his document's purpose, he felt that he was ready to begin searching for topics. Before he began searching, he listed the answers to the three genre toolkit questions to help him stay on track:

What is it? A research paper on a topic of interest to others in the field of social psychology.

Who reads it? Primary: My professor. Secondary: Undergraduate research conference. My professor limited my topic to something I have personal experience with.

What's it for? To inform my readers (professor and conference audience) about my research and why my research is important.

B. Browse for Topics

There are many places where you can begin to find timely and important topics for documents that you need to write. Here are some places where Terrence looked to find possible topics for his research paper.

What Are You Studying?

The first place you might look for topic ideas is in your reading assignments for your classes. Look in your textbook and also at other assigned or suggested readings on your syllabus. Your class readings are useful because you've already read and likely discussed them, which means that you've already conducted some research. Class readings are useful for another reason as well: they clue you into what your professor thinks is important. You might even find that a course reading from another class gives you an idea.

In Terrence's case, his reading on parental separation from children in his child psychology course gave him inspiration for a paper on incarcerated parents being separated from their children.

What Are You Talking About?

After Terrence came up with his idea to write about incarcerated parents being separated from their children, he opened up his Twitter account and posed a question to all of his followers. Here is what he tweeted:

> What do y'all think about kids visiting their moms in prison? Helpful to kids? Too scary? For research. Pls RT.

"Pls RT" means "please retweet"—Terrence asked his friends to share his query with all of their own followers as well. Terrence received many replies to his tweeted query, some from people whom he had never met before. He even heard back from a professor at his university's law school who researches prisoner's rights. The law professor emailed Terrence some recommended reading that helped him get started with research.

What Are You Reading About?

Another strategy would be to look through online sources to see what topics seem timely or interesting. Search online news aggregators such as Google News; a web-based aggregator like Reddit or Digg; or a specialized news source (such as Science Daily.com for science). Terrence searched these online outlets for any recent events that dealt with incarcerated parents, child visitation, or other prisoner's rights issues. Terrence searched the keywords "jail and psychology" and "prisoners and psychology." He came up with a variety of news items that told him the trending topics in his area, such as the psychology of death-row inmates and the psychological ill effects of solitary confinement.

His topic, which dealt with children and their incarcerated parents, was not currently in the headlines, but many other topics were. He shared some of the other topics that he found with his classmates to help them get started with their papers. One of his classmates decided to write about the timely topic of the psychological effects of solitary confinement.

C. Narrow Topics with Initial Research

It comes as a surprise to many students that you can do research *before* finalizing a topic. In fact, doing some preliminary research often helps you to select a strong topic. Getting started with research (Chapter 23) and developing a topic work hand-in-hand. If you are writing a research paper, *before you settle on a topic*, you need to first figure out what kind of research has already been done in your area of interest.

Terrence had already decided he wanted to write about incarcerated parents being separated from their children, but he didn't know how to narrow his topic so that he could write a paper of the appropriate length for his class assignment. He turned to scholarly sources, to research articles that are of a similar genre to what Terrence himself would be writing, to figure out just what he wanted to say.

Scholarly texts are articles and books published *by* experts in a field, *for* experts in a field (Chapter 25). You can find scholarly journals through your school's library website. Many scholarly articles are available online through databases that your school subscribes to. You can also use Google Scholar, which confines your searches to scholarly sources rather than the entire Internet.

Search scholarly texts for articles about your topic using keywords. Terrence searched "parents and prison," for example. You should ask a librarian to help you narrow your search terms if your initial search returns too many results to be useful. You will want to search in journals that are in your area of study—in Terrence's case, policy journals, law journals, and psychology journals.

Suppose Terrence's initial research revealed that many states have laws that prevent children from visiting their parents in prison. But, he also found that new research was revealing that there are psychological benefits to allowing children to visit incarcerated parents—benefits to both children and parents. He would now be on his way to having a topic: the psychological benefits to both children and parents that come from allowing children to visit their incarcerated parents in prison.

Terrence still had a little more work to do. He needed to figure out what he could say that was *new* or *special* about his topic. He didn't want to simply replicate the work that another researcher had done. Terrence needed to find a gap to fill. Terrence believed, as many students do, that the notion that he might have something new or original to say seems unlikely. He is a student, after all. What could he possibly have to say that some important professor or researcher hasn't already written? Chapter 23 discusses in detail how to craft your research to fill a gap.

Prewriting

When you have a good idea of your topic, you can begin prewriting. Prewriting refers to a series of techniques that writers use to help them develop ideas. Prewriting can help you find out more about your topic—including what you *already* know (you might be surprised!). As you learn more about your topic, you will be able to narrow it down to one that is more manageable. Prewriting can also help you figure out a way to state your thesis or claim (Chapter 18) and to come up with ideas to support it. Finally, prewriting can also help you break through writer's block, by helping you get your ideas flowing again, and by helping you get those ideas from your brain and onto the page.

The point is, there are many ways that prewriting techniques can help you get your writing started and keep it moving.

A. Freewriting

Most of us have an internal editor that bogs us down when we try to write. It can be hard to free ourselves of the internal editor that tells us to correct our wording or fiddle with our sentences. Freewriting is one technique that will free you from your internal editor.

Freewriting, in some ways, is the easiest thing in the world to do. It is also very difficult to get used to. In order to freewrite, *you simply sit down and start writing.* Resist the urge to revise. Don't worry about word choice, grammar, or where you are going with your ideas.

Here are some tips for successful freewriting.

Do Not Read What You Have Written

Resist the temptation to even look at the words you have just written until you are finished freewriting. Looking at what you have written can tempt you into editing, when what you should be doing is writing.

If you can't resist rereading what you've written as you freewrite, there is a strategy that can help break this habit. When you sit down to freewrite at your computer, *turn off the monitor* before you begin. You can also change your text color to white, making it invisible. These techniques can help you focus on writing itself, the *process*, rather than focusing on what you have just typed, the *product*.

Time Yourself

Some people prefer to set a timer to limit their freewriting. This is called timed free-writing. By setting a timer—for, say, two minutes or five minutes—you can create a short period of time free of your internal editor. Keep your flow of words coming, and do not stop until the time is up.

Keep Going

The most important strategy for successful freewriting is this: *do not stop writing*. If you get to a word or concept that has you stumped, simply draw (or type) a blank line, or write the words "Come back to this," or write "What here?" And then *keep going*. It is much easier to go back later and fill in those blanks once you have a body of writing to draw from. Often, you will end up writing the words that go in the blanks later in the same freewrite.

Ask a Question

Sometimes it is easier to start freewriting if you write a question at the top of your page. Your freewriting then becomes an attempt to answer that question. Remember, though, that there is no "right" or "wrong" answer to your question—and you're not going to be graded on the answers that you *do* come up with.

For example, let's return to Terrence's proposed research paper topic on psychology and prisons (Chapter 15). He decided to focus his research on the benefits and drawbacks of allowing young children to visit their incarcerated mothers. He might begin his freewrite by typing this question at the top of a page: "Why would it be good for young children to visit their mothers in prison?" Then, using the information that he remembered from his initial research, combined with his own creativity, he might begin jotting down everything he can come up with. Those ideas may become the basis of his research plan (Chapter 23).

Looping

You can "loop" your freewriting in order to stay on track. Looping simply means freewriting for a short period of time, perhaps three minutes. At the end of the time period, read what you have written and select the most promising ideas. Use those ideas to launch into another freewrite that focuses on those ideas. Repeat this process until your freewrite is intensely focused on your topic.

B. Question–Dialogue

Sometimes, it is easier to point out all of the things you *wish* you knew. In a question-dialogue prewrite, you first write a list of questions. For example, Terrence might write:

- "What are the risks to children who visit their mothers in prison?"
- "What sorts of accommodations do prisons need to make to keep kids safe?"
- "How often should kids be allowed to visit their mothers? For how long?"

In the question-dialogue process, keep writing all of the questions that you wish you knew the answers to.

Then, go back and start writing answers. Use the freewriting techniques discussed earlier in this chapter. This kind of prewriting can help you start making notes about ideas that you need to research further. Jot down research ideas, research search terms that might be useful (Chapter 23), books and other resources you might want to look at, etc.

By the time you are finished, you might have the makings of a powerful research plan and a basic outline for your research paper.

Try the Journalist Questions

If you don't know where to start when writing down your questions, you can use the journalist questions—the five-Ws and one-H. These questions can help you get started. You'll find that they are easy to expand upon.

1. Who?
2. What?
3. When?
4. Where?
5. Why?
6. How?

Here's how Terrence wrote out the journalist questions to help his prewriting process:

Who would benefit from allowing children to visit their mothers in prison?

What is the purpose of allowing children to visit their mothers in prison? What benefits would follow from this?

When did we start imprisoning women in Western society? When did we start separating women from their children?

Where has this type of policy been implemented?

Why do people oppose this policy? Why is it a good idea?

How would this be implemented?

Try the Stasis Questions

Another set of questions that you might find useful are the stasis questions (Chapter 18). These questions help you identify the context and the conflicts in a given situation and develop a solution. You can use these questions to help start a question-dialogue prewrite.

1. What is it? (Facts)
2. How do we define it? (Definition)
3. Is it good or bad? (Evaluation)
4. What caused it? (Cause)
5. What are its effects? (Consequences)
6. What should we do about it? (Proposal)

Here's how Terrence used the stasis question to frame questions about his topic:

Facts: What is the current policy for imprisoned mothers of young children?

Definition: Would this policy count as a parental rights issue or a criminal justice issue?

Evaluation: Would this policy be fair or unfair for the children involved?

Cause: What brought about the existing policy in the first place?

Consequences: What would the effects of this policy entail for children? Mothers?

Proposal: Should this policy be enacted?

C. Audio-Brainstorming

Some people have an easy time *talking* about complicated subjects but find it difficult to *write* about them. Luckily, we are living in an age when recording our voices is easy to do. Cell phones and other mobile devices as well as computers have microphones and recording software built right in. There are many mobile apps and software programs that transcribe as you speak, creating a written transcript that you can edit later.

An audio brainstorm is basically a freewrite that you do out loud, instead of on paper. Later, you can transcribe what you have said. But for now, don't edit—just think out loud.

Just Start Talking

One way to do an audio brainstorm is to just start talking about your subject. Try using phrases like "What I'm trying to say is . . . ," or "I wish I knew more about . . . ," and then just see what comes.

Write a List of Questions First

You might find it helpful to write a list of questions to ask yourself before you start your audio brainstorm. When you run out of things to say, move on to the next question. Use the guidelines from question-dialogue to help come up with your questions. You can use the journalist questions, or the stasis questions, or both.

Post to a Social Media Network

You can always draw on the wisdom of your online networks to help you with paper ideas. If you belong to a social network such as Facebook or Twitter, you can post a question to your friends or contacts. This can be a good way to get plenty of ideas in a short amount of time. When he was researching his topic, Terrence posted messages to his followers on Twitter, such as this one: "What do you think of letting kids see their moms in #prison?" He received a lot of great responses to his tweets, including one from a law professor at his school who received a retweet from a friend of Terrence.

Bring in a Friend

Sometimes writers need to bounce ideas off friends. Find a friend who doesn't mind allowing you to record his or her voice. Say, "I just need to explain my ideas to you to see if they make sense." Then start talking. Allow your friend to point out places where your ideas do not make sense, or places where your friend wishes you could explain an idea with more depth. Later, you can go back through the recording and make notes of those places that need more research and more thought. You can even have your friend "interview" you by asking you a list of questions that you have written.

D. Concept Mapping

Concept mapping, also called clustering or even flow-charting, is a visual way to freewrite. Concept mapping allows you to connect your ideas visually, so that you can see how they relate. Generally speaking, a concept map is *a diagram or sketch of a brainstorm.*

Concept-mapping is two-dimensional. Ordinarily, we use writing in a one-dimensional way: putting ideas end to end in a one-direction line. Concept-mapping allows you to branch out in many directions to find relationships between thoughts, questions, and ideas. If you are a visual thinker, you might prefer to sketch out your ideas using a concept map, instead of using freewriting. Terrence used a concept map (Figure 16.1) to help him plan ideas for his research paper on child visitation and incarcerated mothers.

A concept map looks like circles or boxes connected by lines, and inside these shapes are sentences, phrases, or single words that represent an idea. The lines represent the relationships between these ideas.

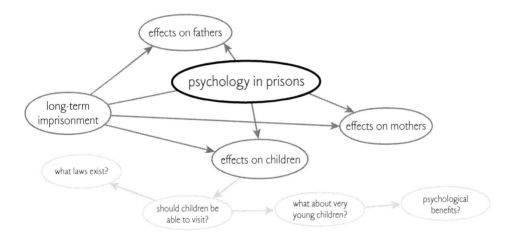

Figure 16.1. Terrence's Concept Map

You might find it helpful to include simple headings for each idea included in the map. You can even color-code the circles (or boxes) around the ideas to indicate the type of idea it represents.

One way to color-code or label your concept map might be to use some of the following:

- Question—what is the main question you will address?
- Issue—what is the broad issue at stake?
- Undisputed fact—what do we know already about this issue? What has been established by previous research?
- Disputed fact—what facts are disputed or uncertain based on existing research or opinions? (This is often where you can find a gap for your own writing.)

We included these headings in Figure 16.2.

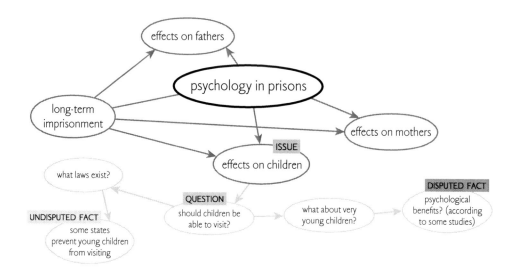

Figure 16.2. Terrence's Concept Map with Color Codes and Headings

Here are some steps to follow for creating a concept map:

1. Figure out what medium you will use to draw your map. A large piece of paper ($16'' \times 20''$) works well and gives you more space to work. A whiteboard also works really well, if you have access to one. Computer software provides another choice.
2. Start with one or more key topics or issues. Write these in the center of the page and draw separate circles around each idea. You might use some of the other invention strategies provided in this chapter to help you get started.
3. As you think of ideas that relate to the key topic(s), write them down and draw circles around them.
4. Draw lines between the circles to show relationships. Get creative, and go in all directions from the key topic.
5. Use colors and headings to indicate priority or other types of categorization.
6. Try not to worry about neatness or organization—those things come later, after you have developed your ideas.

Depth and Breadth

Keep both *depth* and *breadth* in mind while you map your ideas. *Depth* refers to how far you can take each of these initial ideas. *Breadth* refers to how many initial ideas you can invent from the original issue. If you are trying to maximize the number of ideas you can come up with, try for both.

Technology

Some software companies have caught on to the usefulness of concept mapping and have created software just for this process. Using this software is especially useful if more than one person is working on a project—the document can be emailed from user to user until the concept map is complete.

You might find online apps to create cluster maps, such as Mindmeister.com or Bubbl.us. These tools allow groups to map across the Internet. Microsoft Word and PowerPoint both include tools that you can use for concept mapping. Give it a try the next time you brainstorm arguments for a case.

Drafting

While "drafting" refers to the action of putting words on paper or screen, it also involves organizing ideas so that you can start putting them down in the first place. In most cases, you will have some pre-writing (Chapter 16) to help you, whether that includes notes from your research, a formal outline, or just some ideas you have jotted down. When you start drafting, you begin to organize this pre-writing into sentences and paragraphs (for traditional documents) or into images, sounds, and other media (for multimedia documents). In this chapter, you will learn different drafting strategies that can help you to compose effectively.

A. Try Out Different Drafting Strategies

A strong writer has a number of different drafting strategies at his or her disposal. Here are a few to get you started.

Sketch out the Genre

Your analysis of the genre you are writing should help you to begin drafting. Some genres will give you a pretty clear set of sections and even content to include. For example, a résumé (Chapter 12) typically includes a number of relatively standard sections (although you have some control over how the sections are ordered). To start writing a résumé, you can outline those sections first, and then fill in the information you have planned to include.

Other genres, such as a film review (Chapter 9) or literary analysis (Chapter 8), might be somewhat less structured—but you will still have an introduction, some kind of body, and a conclusion of sorts. If you get stuck, go back and look at more examples of the genre you are writing, and determine what kinds of sections you might use to organize your document.

As he was writing his paper, Terrence began with an outline based on articles he read in undergraduate research journals:

Terrence's Outline

- Abstract
- Introduction—begin with the conversation scholars are having about this issue and how I will add to it—what a psychological perspective adds to the issue of visitation for children of incarcerated mothers

- Body—take up main arguments against visitation advanced by scholars/barriers preventing visitation, then show how psychological research contradicts it
  - Include personal experience??
- Conclude with implications for law or policy
- Works cited list

Write around Your Evidence

One common strategy for writers is to begin by ordering the main pieces of evidence you will be using (Chapters 24 and 26). Scientists typically plan out the visual evidence they will include in a scientific article, such as graphs or tables displaying numerical data. Then, they write explanatory texts to accompany those visual representations of their results. You can do something similar even if your main pieces of evidence are textual, such as quotations from a novel or a set of interviews. Try ordering your evidence, and then writing text that introduces, explains, and evaluates that evidence. Terrence began by sketching in some of his evidence within the body section of his paper, being careful to include citation information (Chapter 28) so that he would avoid inadvertent plagiarism (Chapter 27).

Terrence's Evidence

Best interest of the child standard (article)

Costa (2003): prison "it epitomizes all that is unhealthy and dangerous." unfair for children to visit a "very bad place"; "Prison is not an atmosphere appropriate for the growth maturation of our youth. 'Ah what childhood memories these kids will have' "

Pamela Lewis (2004) on legal barriers: "the Kentucky Court of Appeals held that incarceration does not preclude or interfere with the parent's right to a hearing on the matter of visitation"; but hearing process is complicated

After listing his main pieces of evidence, he added text to elaborate on or explain key pieces of evidence. For instance, he expanded on the third point of evidence as follows:

Terrence's Elaboration

Incarcerated parents often long to maintain or mend their relationship with their children. Many mothers would want nothing more than to get the chance to see their child, and try to comfort them with love and an explanation. Yet, even if the family wants to participate in visitation, the process is not easy. Pamela Lewis (2004), a family lawyer, argues that although courts have indeed agreed that visitation is a fundamental right for people in prison to have, numerous legal barriers and prison regulations are preventing visitation from occurring as much as needed. She points out several legal factors that prohibit child visitation. First she cites the case *Alexander v. Alexander,* in which "the Kentucky Court of Appeals held that incarceration does not preclude or interfere with the parent's right to a hearing on the matter of visitation." This means that regardless of a parent's incarceration, she still has a right to petition the court for visitation. However, as Lewis describes, the hearing usually proves to be problematic, as there is limited access to legal services involving domestic issues for incarcerated parents.

Go Section by Section

It can be daunting to start a long writing project from scratch. One helpful strategy is to divide your project into different sections, such as the introduction, conclusion, and body sections, and draft one at a time. You do not necessarily need to start with the introduction. In fact, for many genres it can be easier to start in the middle, with the "meat" of the document.

Terrence began by working on the body of his paper, since he had done his research and knew how to get started with that. He was less sure about how to introduce or conclude his paper, so he left those tasks for later.

Move Things Around

Learn how to use your word processor to highlight, cut, and paste blocks of text. Do not be afraid to take advantage of those tools. You can cut sentences and paragraphs and move them around to see where they fit best in the structure of your document. When dealing with a longer draft, some writers use the highlight tool to color code common topics or ideas. Then, you can simply move similar ideas so that they are together in the text.

While Terrence was drafting the body paragraphs for his essay, he realized that his original outline did not work for the argument he was making. As he looked over his draft, he highlighted information that needed to be moved earlier in the paper. Then, he used the cut-and-paste tool to move information around.

Terrence's Cut-and-Paste

The main legal factor that prevents child visitation for incarcerated mothers is the "best interest of the child standard,". . . .

In regards to the visitation rights of incarcerated parents, especially mothers, there has been a cold stance taken that avoids the true needs of the parent's rehabilitation and the child's development. Many believe that visiting an inmate is detrimental to the child. Costa (2003), a legal scholar, discusses how prison is not a healthy environment for children as "it epitomizes all that is unhealthy and dangerous." She asserts that it is unfair for an innocent child to have to attempt to understand that her parent did something "bad" and has to stay at that "very bad place." The constant tension of visiting an incarcerated mother and the emotional trauma of having to say "goodbye" is detrimental to the child's development, Costa argues. "Prison is not an atmosphere appropriate for the growth maturation of our youth. 'Ah what childhood memories these kids will have'" (Costa, 2003).

Costa exemplifies the blanket bias that is present in our society, which in turn is re-flected in the laws. As an individual who spent a large portion of my childhood visiting my incarcerated father, I could not agree more with scholars. Although I understand that everyone has his or her own unique experiences, I always looked forward to these visits rather than having any feeling of anguish or anxiety. If more research is conducted, maybe it would be discovered that I was indeed the norm, and not the exception.

Incarcerated parents often long to maintain or mend their relationship with their children. Many mothers would want nothing more than to get the chance to see their child, and try to comfort them with love and an explanation. Yet, even if the family wants to participate in visitation, the process is not easy. Pamela Lewis (2004), a family lawyer, argues that although courts have indeed agreed that visitation is a fundamental right for people in prison to have, numerous legal barriers and prison regulations are preventing visitation from occurring as much as needed *[explain this better]*. She points out several legal factors that prohibit child visitation. First she cites the case *Alexander v. Alexander,* in which "the Kentucky Court of Appeals held that incarceration does not preclude or interfere with the parent's right to a hearing on the matter of visitation." This means that regardless of a parent's incarceration, she still has a right to petition the court for visitation. However, as Lewis describes, the hearing usually proves to be problematic, as there is limited access to legal services involving domestic issues for incarcerated parents.

Re-read, Then Write

If you get stuck, try re-reading what you have written so far. This often works best if you take a little break from writing and go back to your text with fresh eyes. By re-reading your draft, you may come up with new ideas or simply get into the mood to add more. Terrence added notes to himself (shown in bold) when he reread what he wrote, to remind himself what he should do next.

Terrence's Rough Draft

Title . . . ? Moms Behind Bars? DRAFT

[Intro—start with general topic—how many mothers are incarcerated, etc., and why legal system makes it that way . . . *Fill this in later*]

Incarcerated parents often long to maintain or mend their relationship with their children. Many mothers would want nothing more than to get the chance to see their child, and try to comfort them with love and an explanation. Yet, even if the family wants to participate in visitation, the process is not easy. Pamela Lewis (2004), a family lawyer, argues that although courts have indeed agreed that visitation is a fundamental right for people in prison to have, numerous legal barriers and prison regulations are preventing visitation from occurring as much as needed *[explain this better]*. She points out several legal factors that prohibit child visitation. First she cites the case *Alexander v. Alexander*, in which "the Kentucky Court of Appeals held that incarceration does not preclude or interfere with the parent's right to a hearing on the matter of visitation." This means that regardless of a parent's incarceration, she still has a right to petition the court for visitation. However, as Lewis describes, the hearing usually proves to be problematic, as there is limited access to legal services involving domestic issues for incarcerated parents.

Another legal factor that prevents child visitation for incarcerated mothers is the "best interest of the child standard," [. . . *expand on this using Lewis . . .*]

In regards to the visitation rights of incarcerated parents, especially mothers, there has been a cold stance taken that avoids the true needs of the parent's rehabilitation and the child's development. Many believe that visiting an inmate is detrimental to the child. Costa

(2003), a legal scholar, discusses how prison is not a healthy environment for children as "it epitomizes all that is unhealthy and dangerous." She asserts that it is unfair for an innocent child to have to attempt to understand that her parent did something "bad" and has to stay at that "very bad place." The constant tension of visiting an incarcerated mother and the emotional trauma of having to say "goodbye" is detrimental to the child's development, Costa argues. "Prison is not an atmosphere appropriate for the growth maturation of our youth. 'Ah what childhood memories these kids will have' " (Costa, 2003). *[Perhaps include an image of a visiting room to contrast with this point?]*

Costa exemplifies the blanket bias that is present in our society, which in turn is reflected in the laws. *[get more research on this].* As an individual who spent a large portion of my childhood visiting my incarcerated father, I could not agree more with scholars *[Who?].* Although I understand that everyone has his or her own unique experiences, I always looked forward to these visits rather than having any feeling of anguish or anxiety. If more research is conducted, maybe it would be discovered that I was indeed the norm, and not the exception. *[should I include this? Say more about it?]*

B. Digital Composing: Find Tools that Work for You

Writers today employ a range of tools to help them write, whether they are preparing a traditional print document or a multimedia text that incorporates images, sounds, or video. Using different digital tools can help you to compose more efficiently and to open up new possibilities for the kinds of things you can compose. Keep in mind, though, that your goal should be to make the tools work for you—try to figure out how each tool (whether it is pen and paper or a web design program) can help you to accomplish your own writing goals.

Paper and Pens Are Tools, Too

We might not think of pens and paper as technologies for writing. In fact, many students prefer to compose documents on a computer, and only use pen and paper for jotting down notes and ideas. However, it is worth trying to write out a document (or sketch out a website or plans for a video) on paper. Sometimes, switching from one medium to another can get your creative juices flowing. Writing by hand can feel very different from typing, so you might try it sometime to see how it works for you.

Many writers employ other low-tech tools, from notebooks and notecards to highlighters and Post-it notes. For example, some students write down their ideas and notes on index cards and then put them in order, moving from a set of ordered cards to a written draft. Others use Post-it notes to flag important information in books or articles. Remember that you can experiment with these kinds of tools to see what works best for your own writing process.

Terrence wrote down quotes from his research on index cards.

Terrence's Notecards

(1) Lewis, Pamela. Title: "Behind the Glass Wall: Barriers that Incarcerated Parents Face Regarding the Care, Custody, and Control of Their Children." Year: 2004 Journal of the American Academy of Matrimonial Lawyers Vol. 19 Pg. 97-116
→ visitation is a legal right.
→ legal barriers prevent visitation + prison rules (97)

(2) Lewis—"Behind the Glass Wall"
• Alexander v. Alexander—"the Kentucky Court of Appeals held that incarceration does not preclude or interfere with the parent's right to a hearing on the matter of visitation."

(3) Lewis—"Behind the Glass Wall"
→ limited access to legal services makes hearings problematic for incarcerated parents.
→ legal services often given only when parental rights are being terminated.

He rearranged them in the order he thought would work best, and then rearranged them again when he got stuck.

Terrence also wrote out some of his draft by hand. After drafting the body section, he was stuck on his introduction, so he decided to switch from his computer to a notebook to see if that would help—and it did! Here's his handwritten introduction draft:

Terrence's Handwritten Introduction

Millions of children are torn away from their mothers every day, and its perfectly legal—and not because of some loophole in the law. Over 1.5 million children in the US have ~~a parent in jail~~ an incarcerated parent, & our legal system is preventing these children from visitation with their incarcerated parents, especially mothers. Many argue that children should ~~not visit~~ not be exposed to prison, and that any visitation is emotionally unhealthy. True, prison is a cold and awful life situation for anyone . . . But, regardless of what their parents have done, they still have children who depend on them. The law ignores this fact, since courts can deny visitation if they find it would be ~~bad~~ detrimental for the child. But what factors determine that? Often, these factors are not based on <u>actual evidence</u>, but on the stigma surrounding "detriment."

Make Your Word Processing Program Work for You

Today, most writers use a word processing program such as Microsoft Word to compose texts, although there are many other programs and apps (some of them free) to try out. Most of these programs offer tools that can help you to compose more effectively. For instance, if you assign heading styles to your section headings (in Word, located under Styles), you can then tell the software program to generate a Table of Contents or to show you the Document Map (basically, a list of your main headings and sub-headings). That tool allows you to see your document at a glance.

Many of the features in a word processing program can mimic other tools: consider the actions of cutting, pasting, notes (under Review in Word) and highlighting, which all have non-digital parallels. Marking up your text using those tools can help you to keep track of your ideas and re-organize your writing as you go.

You can also use the Track Changes tool if you want a record of the changes you have made. This can be useful if you want to try out a new idea, without losing your original work in case you change your mind. Terrence did this as he was working on his introduction. He wanted to experiment with the order of his ideas, and so he used Track Changes so that he could easily see what he had changed, and remove it if he wanted to go back to the old version. He could see that everything underlined and in red was a change, and he could choose to "accept" or "reject" those changes as needed.

Terrence's Tracked Changes

<u>Over 1.5 million children in the United States have an incarcerated parent.</u> Millions of <u>these</u> children are torn away from their mothers everyday, and it's perfectly legal—not because of some loophole in the law. Our legal system is preventing these children from visitation with their incarcerated parents, especially mothers. True, prison is a cold and awful life situation for anyone, let alone a child. Many argue that children should not be exposed to prison, and that any visitation is emotionally unhealthy. But, regardless of what their parents have done, they still have children who depend on them. The law ignores this fact, since courts can deny visitation if they find it would be detrimental. But what factors determine <u>that visitation would be detrimental?</u> Often, these factors are not based on actual evidence, but on the stigma surrounding "detriment."

Try Different Software

A number of alternatives to traditional word processing programs are now available, and you might find some of them useful to you. One program, Scrivener, allows you to focus on writing without worrying about the formatting of your text. Scientists and mathematicians often compose with a program called LaTeX, which combines features of a word processor with computer code. Like Scrivener, LaTeX encourages writers to focus first on the content of their writing, and on layout and design second.

Another set of tools includes Google Docs and Adobe Buzzword, which are free, online word processors. One advantage of these tools is that you can access your documents from any computer, and they are automatically stored for you—no worrying about losing your files. Google Docs also allows multiple writers to work on a document at once, so it is great for working with a team. In fact, we composed much of this textbook using Google Docs, since it allowed both of us to write and revise simultaneously.

Since Terrence liked to work on his paper from the computer lab in the library as well as from home, he used a cloud computing storage service, Dropbox. This allowed him to open his files from any computer, without worrying about a flash drive that he might lose.

Try Audio

If you are composing an audio text, such as a podcast, you will obviously want to take advantage of audio recording and editing software. A number of free programs, such as Audacity (audacity.sourceforge.net), can help you to record and edit sounds, including music and voice recordings. However, even if you are not composing an audio text, you might like to try composing orally. A number of applications for your smartphone, tablet, or computer will allow you to speak your ideas out loud and will then transcribe them in a written document. Composing orally sometimes works well if you are stuck at a certain part of a draft, or if you have trouble typing as quickly as you'd like.

Since Terrence sometimes came up with ideas for his paper while he was walking home from campus, he used his cellphone to record reading notes (Chapter 7) and even compose sentences that he could enter into his draft later. After he read one article in the library, for example, he recorded this message to himself:

- *"That Costa article really bugs me. It's another example of . . . of a blanket bias in society against people who go to prison and their children."*

Terrence decided he liked the term "blanket bias," and included it in his essay:

- *"Costa exemplifies the blanket bias that is present in our society, which in turn is reflected in the laws"*

Audio materials might also form part of the evidence or data for a more traditional written text. For instance, imagine you were writing a rhetorical analysis (Chapter 8) of the chants and slogans used at a student protest event. You might embed an audio clip you took of those chants into a web document in order to give readers a sense of what those chants sounded like.

Try Video

As is the case with audio, you might use video for a few different reasons. Most computers now come with video recorders that allow you to use your built-in camera to record yourself. Of course, for a multimedia project you might also use the video camera on your smartphone, tablet, or a more hi-tech camera, to record scenes. Video may provide the evidence or data within a web text. For example, in a natural science class you might videotape the behavior of birds at a bird feeder, code what you see, and embed a video clip (or a still from the video) in your document to provide evidence for your claims. Terrence thought about recording a video interview with the child of an incarcerated mother, but decided that his target genre and audience did not allow for video. Or, you might compose a project that is entirely in video form, such as a public service announcement for a local organization.

Try Screencasting

One additional composing tool, screencasting, can involve audio, video, and text. A screencast uses special software to record what happens on your desktop. You can open documents and type, play videos or music clips, navigate around the web, and more. A screencast might provide a good way to create a tutorial or set of instructions (Chapter 6). But it can also be put to more experimental uses. Try out a program such as Camtasia or Jing to get started with screencasting.

C. Writing Collaboratively

In college courses, you will sometimes be asked to write a document as a team. In fact, in this textbook we have included team writing tasks in every project chapter. Writing as a team can be challenging, since you will want to make sure everyone contributes to the task and that everyone has input into the decisions you make. Here are some strategies to help you compose a document as a group:

Divide and Conquer

One way to compose with a group is to divide up your document into sections. Each person takes a shot at drafting a section. Then, you can put together your sections and edit it (Chapter 22) to make it consistent in style and tone (Chapter 21).

Co-writing

Another option is to actually sit down with your group and compose your text together, line by line. While this does not always work for a longer document, it can be effective for shorter genres, especially when you need to pay careful attention to the words you use. For example, if you are designing a brochure together as a group, it might make more sense to come up with ideas together. Appoint one person to be the recorder—that person will take charge of writing down what everyone says. Then, you can each look over the draft and finalize the language. Digital tools can also help you with co-writing. Google Docs allows multiple users to work on a document at the same time, and to see what each person is typing.

Re-writing

For some documents, it might make sense to have one person write a first draft of the whole text (or a section, as in "Divide and Conquer," mentioned previously). The next step in re-writing is for a second person to take over that section, revising and rewriting it to clarify the meaning or add ideas. You can take turns re-writing the same section as many times as you would like. When you do re-writing, you'll find that it soon becomes hard to tell who actually wrote what—each person's words will be mixed up with everyone else's.

Assign Roles

In professional writing contexts, people usually take on different roles, all of which go into producing a finalized document. For example, a website might have a content developer (the person who writes the main content), a content editor (the person who revises that writing for effective style), a layout and design editor (who fixes the text so that it appears properly on the web page), and a technical editor (who checks to ensure the accuracy of the information presented). For some genres, such as a tutorial (Chapter 6), it might make sense to assign each person in your group a different role along those lines. This way, you can draw on each group member's strengths. Someone who is good at grammar and editing can take on the role of content editor, while someone with technical knowledge can edit for accuracy, and so on.

Generating Arguments

A. What Is an Argument?

An argument makes a particular kind of claim or thesis. Both "claim" and "thesis" refer to a main point of a document. However, the term "claim" emphasizes that a main point should be argumentative—it should seek to persuade someone to adopt a new way of thinking or acting. This applies not only to argumentative genres (Chapter 10), but even to academic research genres (Chapter 11). In a research paper, you are arguing for a specific idea, interpretation, or finding. For example, a history research paper might argue for a specific interpretation of how a government policy came into being.

Here are some examples of main points that Terrence might make for his research paper:

- Prisons should provide visitation rights to incarcerated mothers because it will benefit children psychologically to maintain bonds with their mothers.
- Prisons should not provide visitation rights to incarcerated mothers because children are likely to be psychologically damaged by visiting a prison.

If you look closer, you'll see that each of these comments takes a stand on the issue of visitation rights for mothers in prison—they each make an argument.

You'll also see that each of these statements offers a reason to support the claim. The first statement argues that visitation rights should be granted *because* children will benefit psychologically, while the second argues that visitation rights should not be granted *because* children will be damaged psychologically by visiting prisons. You can think of reasons as "because-statements" that support a main claim or thesis.

In its simplest form, then, an argument consists of a claim supported by one or more reasons.

How to Recognize an Argument Genre

Much of the writing you do for your college courses will be argumentative in nature. Most academic writing includes an argument or thesis—but not always. In some genres, your claim may be more like a research question or statement of purpose, as in a scientific research report or a business memo. In other genres, your claim may be implicit rather than explicitly stated, as in a personal narrative or résumé. Only some genres, such as the ones featured in Chapter 10 (Argumentative Genres), are usually framed explicitly as arguments. But that does not mean they do not require you to make a claim and support it with good reasons.

Look for common terms for argument.   You may find that arguments get called different things by different professors or in different fields. When you get a writing assignment, look out for these words:

- Claim
- Stance
- Thesis
- Main point
- Angle

- Persuade/persuasive/persuasion
- Convince
- Argument/argue
- Editorial/opinion
- Assert/assertion

These words usually indicate that your task is to construct an argument.

Look for the word "thesis."   You may be accustomed to thinking about writing as being organized around a thesis. In fact, you might be given a writing assignment in a college course that requires you to use a thesis and support it.

You may have been taught that good writing should expand upon a statement that expresses the main point of the paper. Typically, the thesis is then supported by several "points." When you think about a thesis in this manner, the thesis is not necessarily an argument—you aren't necessarily trying to convince someone to think in a new way or to take a course of action.

A thesis that simply expresses your main point is merely a statement that sums up your ideas.

In college writing, though, it is more accurate to consider your thesis as a *claim that you must support with reasons.* Your professor will expect you to make points, yes, but also to use those points to prove a claim with well-reasoned, researched reasons. For that reason, when you see or hear the word "thesis," think "argument."

Look for opinions.   Opinions and arguments are not the same thing. We all have opinions, about everything from politics to popular culture, sports to school policy. Sometimes, we back up our opinions with arguments—but not always. Opinions tend to be more like subjective beliefs, and we often share them without trying to argue for them or persuade others to support them.

In a college course, however, if you are asked to give an opinion on something (such as a reading in a literature class or an issue in a political science class), you will usually be expected to support your opinion with good reasons—basically, you will be expected to make an argument. For example, if you are asked to write a response essay (Chapter 3) giving your opinion or thoughts on a text, think "I need make an argument about this text."

Newspapers and magazines often publish arguments under a section called "Opinion" or "Commentary." This is tricky wording, because these kinds of texts are not simply statements of what someone thinks about an issue—they are arguments that seek to persuade others to agree. By posting your opinion—plus reasons to support it—on a public forum, by writing a letter to the editor, or by starting a debate with a friend, you've entered the realm of argument.

Now that we've clarified what we mean by argument, let's consider how you can go about writing one.

B. Examining the Topic

Any argument you generate should respond to an ongoing debate or controversy surrounding your topic (Chapter 15).

When you've been assigned to write an argumentative genre, or develop a claim or thesis, it can be tempting to come up with your claim first. You may already have an opinion about this issue, so you might write up your claim first, and then set out to find reasons and evidence to support your claim.

However, a good argument should do more than set out to prove an opinion you already hold. As a college student, you will be expected to show that you've studied the topic at hand, read about it from different viewpoints, and then generated your own argument. Taking the time to research the topic at hand will also help you to make a stronger argument, since it will help you to develop better reasons and find more evidence.

It is important that you research your area of interest *before* you settle on an argument or thesis. Here are some reasons why.

Good Arguments Contribute to a Current Debate or Controversy

Imagine you are writing about child visitation rights for mothers who are in prison. You'd be unlikely to just sit down and write an article on this topic out of the blue. However, you might write a research article about this topic if it were an issue being debated in scholarly or legal circles. In that situation, you'd have a reason to write your article, and you'd be able to respond to the specific claims others have made about it. For his research paper (Chapter 11), Terrence chose to respond to a scholarly controversy over whether or not children of incarcerated parents should be allowed to visit their parents in prison.

Good Arguments Respond to What Others Have Said

Good arguments contribute to current debates in part by responding to what others have said—by agreeing, disagreeing, extending key points, or making counterarguments. Scholars tend to write articles that contribute to an ongoing research program or "conversation." In Terrence's case, legal scholars have published articles recently about child visitation rights, which means it is a topic of interest to researchers in that field.

Good Arguments Stake Out New Ground

It may seem counter-intuitive, but reading what others have said can actually help you to come up with your own claims and reasons. You'll probably find that you came up with more ideas after reading what others have written. It may seem paradoxical, but by exposing yourself to other opinions and viewpoints, you can often generate more of your own ideas—counter-arguments, extensions, and alternatives to what others have said. Terrence was able to stake out new ground by drawing on psychological studies of child visitation to address legal scholars, who had not yet considered the psychological research.

C. Researching Arguments

Reading up on an issue should help you to find new things to say, to refine your own claims, and to address your argument to a specific rhetorical situation. As you prepare to enter the conversation with your own argument, you should also do two different kinds of research:

- Researching what others have argued about your issue
- Researching the facts and evidence that support your argument about the issue

Researching what others have argued means reading up on what others have written on your topic. To find out about what others have written, you might check out the opinion pieces in newspapers and blogs, find articles about the latest developments, or even look up transcripts of speeches given at rallies or meetings. In the case of a local issue, you might check to see whether your college or town has issued official statements or policies, read editorials in the student newspaper, and perhaps also check out websites and articles beyond your own community to see what is happening elsewhere.

Researching the facts and evidence that support your argument means tracking down the data to support the arguments *that you will eventually make* on your issue, such as information from books, articles, and newspapers. (See Chapter 24 for information about how to locate these kinds of research.) It may be tempting to do this research *after* you've made up your mind about your argument—but doing so might bias your research. (Bias means a particular slant or stance on an issue to color how you interpret the evidence, which can make you less objective.) If you do some preliminary research beforehand, you'll be able to make a more valid claim in the end, one that reflects the evidence uncolored by your personal opinion.

Note that you can use the same process when you are assigned most academic writing projects. Let's see how Terrence approached his writing assignment, a research paper on child visitation rights for incarcerated mothers, once he had conducted his research. (For more on conducting research, refer to Part 4.)

D. Developing a Thesis (or Claim)

Once you have researched your issue, you can begin to determine what type of claim to make. One useful strategy can be to brainstorm many different claims before settling on one.

Using Stasis Questions

You might try an ancient technique called stasis questions to help you sort through the research you have done and to develop a claim. Stasis questions help you to pinpoint the key arguments at stake in any issue. They can also help you to identify the kind of claim you would like to make.

The stasis questions are:

- What is it? (Facts)
- How do we define it? (Definition)
- Is it good or bad? (Evaluation)
- What caused it? (Cause)
- What are its effects? (Consequences)
- What should we do about it? (Proposal)

Let's take up an example. What are some arguments Terrence might have made based on research about the psychological effects of visitations for children of mothers who are in prison? This type of question is likely to result in either a consequence claim or a proposal claim:

Consequence claim:	Granting visitation rights to incarcerated mothers would (or would not) improve the lives of their children.
Proposal claim:	Prisons should (or should not) grant visitation rights to incarcerated mothers.

You could build an argument around either of those questions. In fact, the consequence claim might turn into a reason to support the main proposal claim.

Working through the stasis questions can help you to identify a range of possibilities. Then, you can figure out which claim you'd like to choose.

Responding to Other Arguments

In addition to the stasis questions, you can also use argument templates, which usually work by responding to or extending what others have said.

For example, while conducting research for his paper, Terrence wrote reading notes (Chapter 7) about an article by a legal scholar:

Terrence's reading notes

Costa discusses how prison is not a healthy environment for children as "it epitomizes all that is unhealthy and dangerous." She asserts that it is unfair for an innocent child to have to attempt to understand that her parent did something "bad" and has to stay at that "very bad place." The constant tension of visiting an incarcerated mother and the emotional trauma of having to say "goodbye" is detrimental to the child's development, Costa argues. "Prison is not an atmosphere appropriate for the growth maturation of our youth. 'Ah what childhood memories these kids will have.' "

Terrence has a few options here. He could agree, disagree, question, or extend Costa's claims in different ways:

- **[agree] I agree that** visitation may be traumatic for some children, **but** I argue that children should be able to visit their parents as long as they do not show signs of trauma or distress.

- **[question] While Costa claims psychological** risks are associated with visitations in prisons, in this paper I question her views, investigating whether or not **psychological research supports her claim that** children may receive significant harm from visiting their parents.

- **[extend] In addition to** the effects on children Costa identifies, I argue that visitation produces negative effects for mothers as well.

- **[disagree] I disagree with** Costa's argument, and argue that research supports visitation

  rights for imprisoned mothers. For this reason, prisons should enforce regular visita-

  tions for children of incarcerated mothers.

You can try this strategy in your own writing: start by identifying some of the claims you've identified in your examination of the case or issue. Then, try out some of the patterns shown in the preceding list.

Making a Claim

Once you have generated some possible claims, take some time to weigh your options before choosing which one to pursue.

Your choice of which claim to pursue might depend on your analysis of the issue. You might consider some of these factors:

- Are people arguing this point, or have they moved on to a different point or claim? Do you want to take the debate in a new direction, or take up an issue already being discussed?
- Which claim does the evidence support best?
- Which claim seems most interesting or novel?
- Which claim will be most persuasive to your audience?

In Terrence's case, a review of psychological studies led him to choose the fourth option from his previous list, staging his argument as a refutation of Costa's claims. Note that the second option might have led to a similar response, only one framed in a slightly less straightforward manner. (The questioning approach may be a good one to use in highly controversial debates, if you want to maintain the good will of the audience before refuting their argument.)

Of course, you can always revise and sharpen your claim as you start writing. Sometimes, you'll find yourself wanting to change your claim once you've written a draft. Revision is a good thing, and it is also nearly inevitable; do not worry too much about finding the perfect argument ahead of time.

E. Finding Good Reasons

Once you have chosen a claim, work on brainstorming reasons to support your claim. Here again, you can draw on your research for ideas (Chapter 24), but once you have gathered research you can use stasis theory to help you organize them.

Using the stasis questions, try to come up with a series of potential reasons, or because-statements, that support your claim. Terrence sat down and came up with the following reasons to support his claim.

Terrence's Reasons

Children should be able to visit their mothers in prison:

- fact—**because** children of incarcerated parents are at higher risk for depression.

- definition—**because** visitation rights are human rights.

- evaluation—**because** the current system is unethical.

- cause/consequence—**because** the current system punishes children, not just their parents, leading to psychological damage.

- proposal—**because** prisons should work to support families.

This is just a starting point, of course. Terrence could generate plenty of different arguments for any of these points, especially as he continued his research.

Once again, try to come up with many more reasons than you will eventually need for your document. To make a strong argument, you should generate many reasons, and then select only the very best ones. As is the case with your main claim, you should consider:

- Which of these reasons will be most persuasive to my audience?
- Which of these reasons can I support with good evidence?
- Which of these reasons seem most, well, reasonable? Which seem far-fetched?

You can always change your reasons around once you begin drafting. As you write, you might come up with new reasons, or find out that some seem less strong than you originally thought.

G. Rhetorical Appeals: *Ethos, Pathos,* and *Logos*

While you can always find evidence through research, you can also develop evidence based on your analysis of the case at hand. To do so, you use the rhetorical appeals to *ethos* (credibility), *pathos* (emotion), and *logos* (logic).

Ethos

Ethos refers to the credibility and authority of the writer. *Ethos* can work in two ways: you can possess it, or you can earn it. For example, if you are an expert in your field, say a legal scholar or a scientist, you would possess *ethos* by virtue of your education and experience. Likewise, if a speaker has a reputation for being reasonable, honest, and reliable, he or she has *ethos*.

However, if you do not already possess *ethos*, you can earn it. In academic writing, you can earn *ethos* by doing careful research (Chapter 24), consulting credible sources (Chapter 25), and citing your sources properly (Chapter 28). You can also earn *ethos* by demonstrating that you are reasonable, honest, and reliable.

It is easier to maintain *ethos* if you take a fair position on an issue than if you are arguing a view that might be seen as radical. For example, it would be harder for Terrence to argue that mothers should be acquitted of all but the most violent crimes than to argue that mothers should be allowed monthly visitations with their children. The former argument might seem unreasonable, leading to less *ethos* on the part of the writer.

Pathos

Pathos refers to appeals to the emotions or values of the audience. In some genres, emotional appeals can be overt. In fact, we expect emotional appeals when we hear speeches at a political rally or read opinion columns about controversial issues. If you are writing a speech or op-ed (Chapter 10), you can consider how you'd like your audience to feel when they are listening or reading. You can also think about what values they might share, such as fairness, equality, or freedom.

In academic research genres (Chapter 11), we may expect fewer emotional appeals, but that does not mean you cannot appeal to the values of an audience. In our student example, the audience includes law students and scholars. What are some of the key values for that audience? A legal audience might value justice, fairness, and consistency with legal precedent. Accordingly, the writer might consider how to frame his proposal as just, fair, and consistent with legal precedent.

Logos

Much of the advice in this chapter about locating a claim, reasons, and evidence has to do with *logos*, or logic. In addition, though, rhetorical handbooks include the following logical tools. Let's see how Terrence might think about using these tools for his research paper.

Analogies   Analogies are useful because they help readers to understand a new problem or situation in terms of a more familiar one. Terrence could potentially compare depriving a child of his mother to some other type of deprivation: "Depriving a child from his mother is like depriving a fish of water. Children need their mothers to survive."

Examples   Examples are cases or instances that you use to illustrate a point. In Terrence's case, he could use an example of a particular child who was not able to visit his mother in prison. Or, he might give an example of a particular legal case.

Anecdotes   Another way to provide logical reasoning can be to use an anecdote. An anecdote is an extended example, usually told as a story or real incident. Terrence could tell a story about a time when a child visited his or her mother in prison.

Reason chains   In some cases, you may find it effective to construct a series of reasons that build on each other. We can call a series of reasons a reason chain.

Here's an example of a reason chain Terrence might use:

- Psychological evidence shows negative effects when a child cannot visit his incarcerated mother.
- Visitation yields positive effects on a child's self-esteem, lowers anxiety, and decreases risk of depression.
- Those positive effects might lead to less delinquency, higher school performance, and lower rates of incarceration among children.

H. Addressing Counter-Arguments

A good argument attempts to anticipate and address opposing claims (or counter-arguments) that readers might have. If you can address the audience's concerns, or make what is called a rebuttal, you head off disagreement and make it more likely for readers to be persuaded.

To identify likely sources of opposition, take a close look at your claim and reasons, and consider how someone might counter those claims or reasons. Or, you can also look at opposing claims that you have seen in your research.

For example, here's how Terrence anticipated counter-arguments for his argument chain:

- Counter-argument: Psychological evidence shows negative effects when a child cannot visit his mother.

  - Rebuttal: Psychological evidence that claims visitations are traumatic.

- Counter-argument: Visitation yields positive effects on self-esteem, anxiety, and depression.

  - Rebuttal: Visitation decreases self-esteem, increases anxiety and depression.

- Counter-argument: Those positive effects might lead to less delinquency, higher school performance, and lower rates of incarceration among children.

  - Rebuttal: Children of imprisoned parents are more likely to go to prison themselves.

Next, Terrence should identify strategies to address those counter-arguments in his paper. Here are a number of strategies you can use to address arguments.

Anticipating:	**Some will argue that** a prison is no place for a child. I hope readers will first consider the facts.
Acknowledging:	**Although** children of imprisoned parents are more likely to go to prison themselves, studies show that children allowed to visit their parents are more likely to break the cycle of violence.
Refuting:	**Some have claimed that** visitations are traumatic for children. **However**, those claims reflect a bias present in our society that is not supported by research.

I. Arguing Ethically: Avoiding Fallacies

As a college writer, you will be expected not just to argue effectively, but to argue ethically. There's a difference. Sometimes, arguments can be very persuasive because they manipulate us to think in a certain way. As a reader and writer, you should be on the lookout for these kinds of manipulative arguments—often called fallacies—in your own writing and in the sources you read.

We have categorized these fallacies according to the three rhetorical appeals: *pathos*, *logos*, and *ethos*. Some fallacies work by manipulating the reader's emotions (*pathos*), others through faulty or misleading reasoning (*logos*), and others through inappropriate appeals to authority or character (*ethos*).

Emotional/Values Manipulation

Appeals to emotions can be considered fallacies when they seem to distract from the main point, seem excessive or overly charged, or when they invoke prejudices. People tend to find appeals to pity, fear, and bigotry especially manipulative.

Here are some fallacies that Terrence might have encountered in his own research (Chapter 24) and writing for his academic research paper (Chapter 11). These fallacies serve to manipulate readers' emotional responses or values:

Tradition: An appeal to tradition argues that something should or should not be done because we have always done it that way. This can be a fallacy because not every tradition is worth upholding. For example, discrimination on the basis of gender or race is a societal tradition that should not be upheld.

> *Example*: We've never allowed children into prisons so we shouldn't start now.

Here, there is no reason why one should uphold the tradition that children have not previously been allowed in prisons simply because it is tradition.

Pity: An appeal to pity inappropriately preys on the reader's emotions to sway them. While not all appeals to emotions are fallacies, they can become fallacies if taken to the extreme.

> *Example*: One child never got to see her father for 10 years. She was so depressed that she ended up committing suicide.

Here, the case taken is an extreme case, ending in suicide rather than, say, disappointment or depression.

Fear: An appeal to fear, like an appeal to pity, inappropriately manipulates readers' emotions.

> *Example*: If we allow children to visit their parents in prison, we will be allowing a new generation of criminals to endanger our society.

Here, the example seeks to sway readers by appealing to their fear of criminals, but this appeal is inappropriate because it assumes (without evidence) that children will become criminals by visiting their parents in prison.

Prejudice: An appeal to prejudice relies on readers' stereotyped assumptions, or readers' pre-existing negative beliefs about a type or group of people.

> *Example*:   We should limit visitation rights for incarcerated parents because they do not make good role models.

In this case, the assumption is that prisoners are poor role models—a prejudice or stereotype not supported by evidence.

Logical Manipulation

Logical fallacies depend on errors of reasoning. Either the main claim is not supported by the reasons or evidence, or reasons and evidence are taken too far, to an inappropriate or extreme conclusion.

Here are some logical fallacies that Terrence might have encountered in his own research and writing for his paper (Chapter 11). These fallacies rely on readers' failure to locate flaws in logical reasoning:

Slippery Slope: A slippery slope argument works by assuming that an initial step (which may be true) leads to a chain of events that is not necessarily true, or is not substantiated by evidence.

> *Example*:   Allowing children to visit their parents in prison would lead to greater self-esteem, which would lead to decreased crime rates, which would ultimately break the cycle of violence in American society.
>
> *Example*:   Allowing children to visit their parents in prison would lead to exposure to the prison lifestyle, which would lead to increased crime rates, which would ultimately lead to an epidemic of violence in American society.

Here, while the first steps may be true, it is not necessarily the case that the latter chains of events will take place. One cannot take these chains of events as valid reasons to support (or not support) parental visitations in prison.

False Analogy: A false analogy occurs when an inappropriate or unsuitable analogy is given as a reason to support a claim.

> *Example*:   Depriving a child of his mother is like depriving a fish of water.

Here, the analogy is false because a fish will literally die without water, while a child will not necessarily die without his mother.

Hasty Generalization: A hasty generalization occurs when a specific fact or reason is used to support a much broader, more general claim.

> *Example*: An attempt at establishing regular visitations for children of imprisoned mothers failed. So, visitations do not work.

In this case, the conclusion "visitations do not work" is a fallacy because one example is taken as a sufficient reason to support a broad, general claim. The fact that one such program did not work does not necessarily mean that no visitation programs will work.

False Cause: A false cause fallacy occurs when a reason or fact is inappropriately assumed to be the cause of a given outcome. Usually, this involves mistaking a correlation (the co-existence of two things) with the assumption that one thing causes another.

> *Example*: Crime rates have actually gone down in areas where visitations are not allowed. Thus, visitations increase crime rates.

Here, we have a false cause fallacy because the claim ("visitations increase crime rates") is not necessarily supported by the facts. While crime rates may have gone down in those areas without visitation programs, there is no evidence to show that disallowing visitation programs caused the decrease in crime.

Straw Man: A straw man argument distorts the opponent's position, and then refutes that position.

> *Example*: Those who support visitation rights for parents in prison want to turn the prison system into a joke, where there is no accountability for illegal actions. That would be like living in a third world country. So, we shouldn't allow prison visits for children.

Here, the argument is a straw man because opponents of child visitation programs do not really "want to turn the prison system into a joke." This is a fallacy because it does not appropriately present the opposite argument.

Ignorance: An argument from ignorance assumes that lack of information or evidence about something justifies a claim.

> *Example*: There is no evidence that allowing visitations is effective, so they should not be allowed.

In this case, the argument is a fallacy because it assumes that a lack of study on child visitations necessarily means they should not be implemented.

Red Herring: A red herring argument works by distracting readers by introducing a separate topic or claim into a debate.

> *Example*: Parents who are in prison are obviously criminals. So, we should not allow them to see their children.

Here, the writer assumes that it is easier to persuade readers that prisoners are criminals, and criminals are bad, distracting them from the real issue of whether those parents have a right to see their children.

Circular Reasoning or Begging the Question: Circular reasoning (also called begging the question) happens when the main claim and reasons in an argument are essentially saying the same thing.

> *Example*:   Allowing visitations for children will make them happier. Thus, depression will be reduced if children can spend time with their parents.

Here, the claim or conclusion ("depression will be reduced . . .") is basically the same as the reason offered, "Allowing visitations for children will make them happier."

False Dichotomy: A false dichotomy occurs when readers are given a choice between only two options, when more options exist.

> *Example*:   Either we allow visitation rights for children of incarcerated parents, or we prepare to pay for an epidemic of delinquency.

In this example, readers are unfairly presented two options (visitation rights or "an epidemic of delinquency"), when more possibilities exist.

Ethical Manipulations

Ethical manipulations or fallacies involve inappropriate appeals to character and authority. They can be considered fallacies when they distract from the issue at hand, when they assume that what has always been done or thought must be correct, or when they unfairly malign individuals and groups.

Here are some logical fallacies that Terrence might have encountered in his own research and writing for his paper (Chapter 11):

Character Appeal or Ad Hominem Attack: A character appeal casts an individual or group in an inappropriately negative light, instead of addressing the issue at hand.

> *Example*:   Those who argue for visitation rights are usually children of imprisoned parents. These children have clearly been raised by criminals and have a vested interest in the issue. So, we should not listen to them.

In this case, proponents of visitation rights are unfairly maligned, and their credibility called into question.

Appeal to Authority: An appeal to authority occurs when something is taken to be true just because an authoritative person says it is so—especially if that person has no special knowledge or expertise of the issue.

Example: We should allow visitation rights in prison because Oprah Winfrey has said it is a good idea, and she is one of the most respected people in the world.

Here, the appeal to authority is a fallacy because Oprah Winfrey does not necessarily have special insight into child psychology, the law, or criminal justice.

Note that in academic writing, appeals to authority are commonly used, and are not necessarily fallacies. When you cite the claims of an established scholar in a field, who is speaking about a topic she has researched, then you can accept her claim as true—especially if other authorities agree.

Bandwagon Appeal: A bandwagon appeal is used when the actions of an admired or prestigious individual or group is used to justify a course of action for a different individual or group.

Example: Other industrialized nations allow visitation for children of imprisoned parents. It is becoming a widespread trend. So, the United States should implement it.

In this case, the example of "other industrialized nations" adopting visitation programs does not necessarily support the claim that the United States should follow suit. There may be important differences between the United States and these other countries that do not factor into this argument.

However, note that this type of appeal can be effective and appropriate in some cases. For example, colleges and universities regularly adopt programs and standards used at what they consider "peer institutions," other colleges and universities like them, if the evidence shows that such programs have been effective elsewhere.

J. Argument Troubleshooting

I Can't Find a Thesis or Claim

You can either try some brainstorming strategies (Chapter 16) or do some more reading. In the first case, you might try freewriting, concept mapping, stasis questions, or even just taking a walk to get your gears moving. In the second case, try reading some more arguments or research on your topic. You might find a jumping off point—a claim you want to counter, extend, or qualify.

I'm Not Sure How to Organize My Argument

Think about arranging your claims and reasons based on what you think will be most effective for your audience:

- Will your audience be pre-disposed against your claim? If so, you might need to address their objections first, before moving on to your own arguments.

- Will your audience be pre-disposed against you? If so, you might need to spend some time cultivating your *ethos* first. How can you show them you are a reliable person to write about this issue?
- Will your audience be confused about the issue? If so, you might need to address their misconceptions or confusion first, and then put forward your own claims.
- Will your audience lack information (key terms, definitions, knowledge) about this issue? In this case, you might want to start by giving them the background knowledge they'll need to understand your argument.
- Is your audience already predisposed to support your claim—but needs extra encouragement to act? In this case, you might summarize the issue briefly, but then move on to providing the extra impetus the audience needs to take action—perhaps in the form of emotional appeals, or *pathos.*

I Can't Find Any Evidence

You may need to look harder, in different places. Turn to Chapter 24 for more help finding research. Remember that your campus librarians are good resources for research questions. You can also ask your writing group or your instructor for help.

If you have searched for evidence to support your claim and still can't find any, that may mean that you need to revise your claim. Say you want to argue that unhealthy food causes college students to gain significant amounts of weight. However, research studies show that students, on average, only gain a few pounds during college. In order to argue fairly, you will have to adjust your claim. Perhaps you can argue that unhealthy food leads to inattention, sleepiness, or some other kind of problem—but you will need to see if the research supports it. You may end up arguing the opposite side of the case!

Using Rhetorical Modes

Writers use certain strategies, or modes, for different kinds of writing. These modes tend to work at the level of the paragraph or section, and certain modes tend to be used in certain genres.

As you are drafting a document, rhetorical modes can help you develop your ideas. Try using rhetorical modes as a form of invention—a way to come up with things to say or a way of framing your ideas. You can use Table 19.1 to help you consider how each mode might help you generate ideas based on your analysis of your audience, purpose, and genre.

Let's see how Terrence used rhetorical modes as he revised the first draft of his essay.

A. What Happened? Narration

Narration involves recounting events that have happened in the past, often using lively, descriptive language. You might use a narrative to provide support for a key point, usually by drawing on your personal experience or on experiences of others.

In his original draft, Terrence briefly related events from his own childhood in order to support his point that visiting a prison is not necessarily traumatic for a child.

Terrence's Narration

As an individual who spent a large portion of my childhood visiting my incarcerated father, I could not agree more with Stewart. Although I understand that everyone has his or her own unique experiences, I always looked forward to these visits rather than having any feeling of anguish or anxiety.

In his peer workshop, one of Terrence's group members suggested that he elaborate on this point using narration to provide a detailed account of an event that he

Table 19.1 Modes and Their Uses

	A. Narration	B. Description	C. Definition
Audience (Who Reads It?)	Would my audience find my document more interesting if I included a story? Would it help them to identify with me or the topic?	Does my audience need details in order to picture an event, person, place, or thing?	Does my audience already know this term? Do they need a definition? How detailed of a definition? Do they need a more specialized definition, or a more general one?
Purpose (What Is It For?)	Would a narrative help to support one of my points or claims?	Would detailed descriptions help me to get my point across?	Does the audience need to understand a term in order to understand my point?
Genre (What Is It?)	Are narratives usually included in this genre?	Does this genre usually feature detailed, descriptive language? What kinds of descriptions are appropriate for this genre?	What kinds of definitions are usually given in this genre? Should I provide a more specialized definition (i.e., for a research article or grant proposal)? Should I provide a more general definition (i.e., for a profile essay or news report)?

experienced personally. Terrence liked the idea and used narrative as an invention strategy to see if it would strengthen his essay.

Terrence's Revised Narration

When I was six years old, I visited my father for the first time. As my mom and I pulled up to the building, my heart was pounding in my throat, but it wasn't from fear—my heart pounded in anticipation. I couldn't wait to see my dad again—to gaze into his eyes

D. Classification	E. Compare/Contrast	F. Cause/Effect
Does my audience need to know these types of things, and how they differ?	Can I help my audience understand something by comparing it to something else that they are already familiar with?	Does my audience need to know the causes or effects of a phenomenon? Do they agree about these causes/effects, or do I need to prove it to them?
Do I need to explain these types of things to make my point?	Does my audience need a comparison in order to understand my claim?	Does describing causes or effects support my main claim or thesis?
Do classifications usually appear in this genre?	Do comparisons usually appear in this genre?	Do cause or effect elements typically appear in this genre?

and hear his chuckle. When the prison gate opened, I walked into the room and into my dad's arms. That night, I fell asleep thinking about my dad, and I could hardly wait for our next visit. Visiting my dad did not have negative effects for me—instead, it was a positive experience.

Terrence's narrative includes a chain of events—arriving at the prison, meeting his dad, and then coming back home—and ends with a short summary of what the narrative means.

You might see this type of narration in genres that appear in magazines or news-paper writing, such as a profile article (Chapter 5).

Narration can also appear in other genres where you might recount something that happened. You might consider the methods section of a research article (Chapter 11) or report (Chapter 14) to be a sort of narration, or the observation notes from a field study (Chapter 7). These narratives might be told in more formal language, but they are still narratives because they recount an event and have a beginning, middle, and end.

B. What Is It Like? Description

Description involves portraying people, places, and things in concrete language. Your goal is to get readers to picture these items, to feel that they are in on the action. Using description can make your writing more lively and interesting for readers. Terrence decided to revise his narrative to include more description.

Terrence's Description

When I was six years old, I visited my father for the first time. As my mom and I pulled up to the gray, cement block of a building, my heart was pounding in my throat, but it wasn't from fear—my heart pounded in anticipation. I couldn't wait to see my dad again—to gaze into his deep brown eyes and hear his hearty chuckle. When the prison gate clanked opened, I practically skipped ~~walked~~ into the room, ignoring the fetid smell of cigarettes, urine and bleach. That night, I fell asleep thinking about my dad, the warm touch of his hand on my shoulder, the taste of the warm orange drink we shared. Clearly, visiting my dad did not have negative effects for me—instead, it was a positive experience.

By adding sensory details (highlighted), Terrence has made it much easier for readers to picture the scene. We can now imagine what it must have been like for Terrence to visit his father.

Here are some sensory details you can add:

- Sights
- Sounds

- Smells
- Touch

- Taste

You can see that Terrence tried out a different writing style here. He used more adjectives (his dad's "deep brown" eyes and "hearty" chuckle) as opposed to the more objective language in most of his essay.

Terrence also used onomatopoeia, or a word that sounds like the thing being described, when he wrote that the prison door "clanked" open.

Descriptions tend to occur in narrative genres, such as personal essays (Chapter 4), profile articles (Chapter 5), and the like, but they might also appear in an op-ed (Chapter 10), and even in some academic research (Chapter 11). For example, an anthropologist might write a detailed description of a person she encountered while conducting research in Nepal, while a paleontologist might write a detailed description of a fossil.

C. What Is It? Definition

Definition can be useful whenever you use a term that your audience might not already understand, or when you are using a general term in a specific way. You should decide whether to define terms—and in how much detail—based on your audience, purpose, and genre.

Terrence's audience included students interested in political science, law, and public policy. Terrence thought these readers may not have familiarity with the legal term "best interest of the child standard," so he needed to provide a definition in his paper.

Dictionary Definition

The most common way of defining a term is to look it up in a dictionary, and then quote that definition.

Chances are "best interests of the child standard" will not appear in a standard college dictionary. Terrence consulted a specialized legal source to find a written definition, but its language was too complex for his purposes. Instead, he decided to use a definition on a government website intended for a more general audience. Here's the definition of the standard that he found through his research:

Terrence's Dictionary Definition

"[T]he deliberation that courts undertake when deciding what type of services, actions, and orders will best serve a child as well as who is best suited to take care of a child" (http://www.childwelfare.gov/systemwide/laws_policies/statutes/best_interest.cfm)

To find a specialized dictionary for your topic or field, consult your library website or a reference librarian.

Functional Definition

Terrence used a functional definition, defining the "best interests of the child standard" according to what it does or what it is used for.

Terrence's Functional Definition

Another legal factor that prevents child visitation for incarcerated mothers is the "best

interest of the child standard," the test used in most jurisdictions when deciding on issues

of visitation and custody (Lewis, 2004). This test allows visitation to be determined solely

by the opinion of the court.

A functional definition is useful when readers will be more concerned with what something *does* than what it *is*. In this case, readers did not need a lengthy discussion of the legal concept, because Terrence's purpose was to show how the statute was used in this specific instance, not what it is in general.

Negative Definition

A negative definition defines something in terms of what it is *not*. A negative definition of "the best interests of the child standard" would note that it is not a federal mandate, but a state-by-state standard. This may be important for readers to know, and it would help them to better understand what it is.

Synonyms

In some cases, you can provide a short, quick definition by providing a synonym. If there is another term commonly used for the term you seek to define, you can provide that term as well. For instance, Terrence considered defining the term "detriment," using the synonyms "harm" or "damage." You can find synonyms in a thesaurus.

E. How Is It Similar/Different? Comparison/Contrast

447

Example

Sometimes, the best way to help readers to understand a term is to give an example. To define "best interests," Terrence gave an example of a case where the doctrine might be used.

Terrence's Example

For instance, a court might rule that a child should live with his adoptive parents, not

his biological parents, based on the logic that the adoptive parents provided a more stable

home environment. That decision would rest on the doctrine of "best interests."

Definitions occur in almost every genre, but the type of definition given can vary. In a biology textbook, for example, you are likely to read dictionary or functional definitions, since the goal is to provide students with in-depth understanding of biological terms and concepts. In an informative newspaper article (Chapter 6) about the same concept, though, you might find a synonym or an example, since readers do not need to have a detailed understanding, just a working knowledge of the concept.

D. What Kind Is It? Classification

Classification involves placing something in a category, or sorting categories into various subcategories. For instance, Terrence might classify "best interests of the child" as a type of legal standard.

Classification often appears in textbooks, for example, where students need to learn about different types of things, such as the parts of speech in a language course, or the cultures of Nigeria in an African studies course.

E. How Is It Similar/Different? Comparison/Contrast

Use comparison or contrast to explain how two or more things are similar or different. Comparison and contrast can help you to pin down the meaning and importance of something—an event, idea, person, or thing.

In Terrence's essay, he contrasted how legal scholars view child visitation in prisons with how psychology scholars view it. In fact, he decided to organize his paper roughly by outlining, first, how legal scholars view the issue, and second, how psychology scholars offer contrasting evidence.

The comparison/contrast mode appears in a wide variety of genres. For example, in a profile (Chapter 5) of a politician, a writer might contrast the politician with another politician who holds different views.

F. What Causes It? What Are Its Effects? Cause/Effect

The mode of cause and effect involves explaining either what factors lead to a particular event or outcome (cause) or what factors result from a particular event or outcome (effects). Your analysis of your audience, purpose, and genre can help you to decide whether and when to use the cause and effect modes.

In Terrence's case, cause and effect were very important to his main claim—that children should be able to visit their parents in prison. Much of his argument has to do with the effects of these visitations on children and their mothers. While some scholars claim the effects are primarily negative, Terrence claims that there can be many positive effects if children can visit their parents in prison. Much of Terrence's essay is devoted to explaining the *effects* of visitation.

Terrence's Cause/Effect

Increased visitation will help the reunification process between mother and child. During the stressful and seemingly never-ending process of regaining custody of one's child, visitation can help motivate the incarcerated mother and encourage her not to give up her battle.

However, Terrence also devoted some attention to the *causes* of current attitudes toward visitation when he says that "Costa exemplifies the blanket bias that is present in our society, which in turn is reflected in the laws." Here, Terrence argued that a bias against incarcerated person *causes* or brings about laws against visitation for children of imprisoned parents.

A variety of genres use the mode of cause and effect. For example, in a political speech (Chapter 10), a candidate might argue that certain negative effects in society are caused by the political actions of her opponents.

Organization

Organization refers to the order in which you present the contents of a document. Different genres tend to use different types of organization. In other words, they order information in different ways.

A. Discovering Organization through Genre

The best way to determine how to organize a document that you need to write is to discover the genre itself. Often, particular genres have particular organization strategies that writers tend to follow. For example, a recommendation report tends to include a fairly standard set of sections, including an executive summary, introduction, methods, sections based on criteria or sub-topics, conclusion, and recommendation (Chapter 14).

A research paper (Chapter 11) may also have a fairly standard organization scheme, although the way the paper is organized varies by discipline. The first thing you should do is ask your teacher about the organization and structure that your teacher expects you to follow.

You can also discover how professionals write research papers in your field. If you are writing a research paper in the sciences, you should read articles in scientific journals to discover the organizational strategies that science writers employ. If you are writing in political science, then you should read political science journals. The point is, the more you study the type of document that you need to write, the easier it will be to organize that document.

In some cases, though, a genre may be more flexible in its organization, which means you can develop your own set of sections. For instance, an application to graduate school may simply require a "personal statement." Based on your study of samples and the rhetorical situation, you could develop your own organization scheme for a personal statement.

B. Outlining before Writing

Once you have studied the genre you will be writing, you can use a variety of organization strategies to help you get your thoughts in order. Outlines, flowcharts, and digital tools such as mindmaps provide ways to organize your ideas. As we study these organization strategies, we will use a political science research paper as our example.

E. Ordering Sections or Topics

For his paper, Terrence came up with an outline, or order of ideas, that was based on the logic of his argument. Each section built on the previous one to lead the reader to support his thesis. We call this type of organization logical organization.

However, there are other kinds of organization you might try, depending on your genre and purpose. Be sure to pay close attention to the kinds of organizations used in examples of your genre.

- General to specific
- Simple to complex
- Chronological

- Methodological (organized around different research methods)
- Conceptual (organized around theories or concepts)
- Problem-solution
- Compare/contrast—organize around key points of similarity or difference
- From strongest to weakest point (or weakest to strongest)
- From most to least interesting
- From least to most interesting (climactic organization)
- Put the weakest (or the bad news) in the middle
- From good news to bad news (or positive to negative)

When selecting one of these organizational structures, remember the genre toolkit questions, and use them to guide your choice: What is it? Who reads it? What's it for?

For example, a newspaper article leads with the most interesting information and progresses to the least interesting. Newspaper editors and writers know that most people aren't patient enough to read the entire article.

F. Introductions

Many genres require some form of introductory text. For example, business letters and emails require greetings (Chapter 12). Journalistic genres, such as news articles (Chapter 6) or op-eds (Chapter 10), require catchy first sentences, called "ledes." These introductory texts often serve the purpose of catching a reader's attention and clearly stating the writer's purpose.

When writing a research paper, introductory paragraphs are arguably the most important paragraphs that you write. Many readers decide whether to finish reading a research paper simply on the basis of the introduction. You want to catch your reader's interest, and earn your reader's respect, by writing a strong introduction.

Introductions to research papers typically start with an opening statement to establish why a topic is important. This statement can be an anecdote, a striking observation, a quotation, a statistic, or a statement of how the topic is of current research interest. Your opening statement announces your topic and its importance. It should rarely be gimmicky, unless that's what your genre calls for.

Terrence's Introduction

Terrence follows up this dramatic opening statement, supported by a statistic that also explains the importance of his topic.

Today in America millions of children are being torn away from their mothers, and it is

perfectly legal. Over 1.5 million children in the United States have at least one incarcerated

parent, and our legal system is prohibiting these children from being able to have visitation with their incarcerated parents, specifically mothers. Many argue that children should in no way be exposed to prison, and that any visitation of an incarcerated parent is both emotionally unhealthy and detrimental to a child. It is true; prison is a cold and awful life situation for anyone to experience. But, regardless of what incarcerated parents may have done, they still have children who depend on them. The law has ignored this fact, stating that the courts have the ability to deny visitation if they find it would be detrimental to the child. But what factors exactly determine detriment? Often, the factors used to prove detriment are not based on any actual evidence; the stigma surrounding incarceration is all that is needed to establish "detriment." The field of psychology has taken a different perspective on incarceration than that taken by the legal system. Psychological experts understand that withholding a child from her mother is often more detrimental than exposing her to the world of prison. By denying visitation, the legal field has simply been narrow-minded in its policies and perspectives on incarcerated parents. This dichotomy between the psychological and legal fields is what inspired my research. In this paper, I argue that child visitation with an incarcerated mother has positive psychological effects on both the child and the mother. First, I will examine the current barriers for incarcerated mothers to gain visitation of their children. Second, I will analyze how child visitation of incarcerated mothers affects the development of the child, parental strain, and the mother-child relationship. Lastly, I will discuss the future implications on society of the increased child visitation for incarcerated mothers and the children themselves.

> Terrence points to both the popular and the scholarly conversations that he hopes to join with his paper.

> Readers now have a sense that Terrence is going to respond to these critics, and indeed he does in the sentence that follows.

> After establishing his area of research, Terrence provides his thesis (look for the word "argue").

> He then turns to his own angle that he will use in this research paper, the "field of psychology."

> After providing his thesis, Terrence describes the methods he will use to prove his thesis.

In a later chapter, you can read Terrence's paper in full (Chapter 28). These rhetorical moves—opening statement, conversation, thesis, methods, and forecast—are the core moves for the introduction in many research papers in many different fields.

However, before you write your introduction, you should read the introductions of a few samples of your genre to get the feel for how introductions work in that genre.

G. Conclusions

Conclusions are notoriously difficult to write. For a research paper, writers typically begin by summarizing the main findings. However, a good conclusion does more than just restate what you have already written.

You can go beyond summary to tell your reader the implications of your research: what does your research *mean*? Ask yourself, "Now what?"

In Terrence's conclusion paragraph, he describes how "Our Children's Place" (a program that allows young children to live with their incarcerated mothers if the mothers' offenses are non-violent) offers one possible solution to the problems he has discussed in the body of his paper.

Terrence's Conclusion

Our Children's Place shows great promise and has had nothing but great results. It is these types of ground-breaking initiatives that have really been able to grasp the true effects of incarceration on the parent and the child. Unfortunately, current policies have generally disregarded the subject and have allowed societal perceptions of crime, rather than true academic research, to influence legislation. In recent years, the field of psychology has made great strides in assessing the true effects of incarceration on children. Experts have proven that child visitation is positive for both the parent and the child. Child visitation must be increased in order to alleviate the psychological strains that take place during incarceration. Better-informed visitation policies may even break the relentless cycle of crime.

His final two sentences draw to a close the summary of his findings. They also tie his findings to the bigger picture: how to break the cycle of crime. When you are writing a conclusion, then, consider the implications of your findings. What do they mean? Why should we care?

Conclusions may work differently in different genres. In some genres, such as a recommendation report (Chapter 14), the implications might be concrete actions readers should perform. In others, such as a literature review (Chapter 9), they may refer to future research readers should undertake. Your analysis of examples of your genre should give you a sense of how to approach the conclusion.

Developing Style

Style refers to the myriad writing choices that you make as you compose a document. Word choice, sentence length, language complexity—all of these elements make up style.

We often think of style as something you "have," not something you do. For example, you might think, "My writing style is unique or idiosyncratic." But good writers can vary their style for different genres, audiences, and purposes.

In this chapter, you will learn how to address writing style after you already have a draft. Remember: style comprises all of the writing choices that you make as you compose. Keep those choices in mind as you work.

When you begin focusing on style, first consider whether your style is appropriate for the writing task at hand. Appropriateness refers not to whether stylistic choices are grammatically correct, but to whether or not they fit the genre, audience, and purpose for your document. Again, use the three genre discovery questions from Chapter 1 to help you focus on appropriate style.

A. Matching Style to Genre, Audience, and Purpose

When working on style, your first considerations should be your genre, audience, and purpose. If you closely examine sentences in some examples of the genre you are writing, you will start to notice certain patterns or features.

Let's take a look at excerpts from some of the sources Terrence came across while doing research for his article:

EXAMPLE 1: Article in an Online Magazine (excerpt)

Maya Schenwar

The Prison System Welcomes My Newborn Niece to This World

Truthout.org

My niece—the first baby of my family's newest generation—was born last Wednesday morning at 10:52 AM. She is a superhero, although she probably doesn't realize it yet. Her path into this world was a rough, rough haul.

Here's how it went: At 4:30 a.m. Tuesday, my sister was called out of bed in the state prison where she's incarcerated with the news that she'd be heading to the hospital. Her water hadn't broken, and she hadn't started contractions. But this was the time slot in which she was scheduled to give birth. The labor would be induced.

During and after the birth, my sister was allowed no family or friends at her bedside, or even in the hospital. She endured labor alone, except for medical personnel and two prison guards, who rotated shifts, watching her at all times.

> The author uses informal language ("crying like crazy") to make the text accessible for readers.

After 26 hours, my niece finally pushed her way out—7 pounds, 5 ounces, and crying like crazy. (Wouldn't you?)

Following the birth, a guard immediately shackled my sister's ankles to the bedpost. "It made it hard to pick up the baby from the basket next to the bed," she told us afterward. "I was afraid I was going to drop her."

> The author uses reported speech to dramatize the scene.

Our state has anti-shackling laws in place, preventing women from being chained to their hospital beds during labor. But that doesn't mean they can't be chained afterward.

The ritual my sister underwent Tuesday and Wednesday wasn't an unusual occurrence. In prison, 4 percent to 7 percent of women are pregnant on arrival.

> Many of the sentences in this example are short.

The vast majority of women in prison are incarcerated for nonviolent offenses. (Plus, even those incarcerated for violent offenses aren't likely to pull a fast one while they're in labor.) Virtually none are "flight risks." In The Root, advocate Malika Saada Saar writes, "Anyone who has given birth, indeed, any person who has witnessed the birthing process, knows that the prospect of a woman in childbirth trying to run away or tackle a corrections officer is almost comical." Yet because during the wildly tumultuous hours of labor and birth, these women are outside of prison walls, they're tightly restricted, permitted virtually no contact with their loved ones.

In the preceding example, we see short sentences, descriptive language, dialogue, and a lower level of formality. We might conclude that the genre of the online magazine article employs these features for this type of story. If we think about the audience and purpose of an online magazine article, these choices begin to make sense. Readers are likely to read such sites primarily for entertainment, and they are likely to browse the magazine for interesting stories. The writer's goal is to attract and keep the reader's attention so that the serious message of the article comes across—that current practices for pregnant inmates are unacceptable.

EXAMPLE 2: Article in a Research Journal (excerpt)

Ann Booker Loper and Elena Hontoria Tuerk

Improving the Emotional Adjustment and Communication Patterns of Incarcerated Mothers: Effectiveness of a Prison Parenting Intervention

Journal of Child and Family Studies

For most inmate mothers, the most difficult prison stressors are concerns about their children's wellbeing and sadness about separation (Clark 1995; Harris 1993; Kazura 2001). Moreover, many incarcerated mothers maintain ineffective parenting styles that were developed prior to their imprisonment and struggle to communicate appropriately with their children's caregivers (Clark). Conflict with a child's caregiver can undermine a mother's interest in her child by limiting her involvement in decisions about her child's care. Although most mothers expect to resume custody of their children after incarceration (Banauch 1985; Gaudin and Sutphen 1993), lack of contact disrupts the parent–child relationship and diminishes a mother's authority to make legal and educational decisions for her child from prison (Clark 1995; Johnston and Gabel 1995).

> The author uses words that derive from the Latin roots of the English language. These words tend to be more formal.

> The author avoids weighted language in describing mothers' parenting (i.e. "ineffective" instead of "awful").

The preceding research article features denser (not necessarily longer) sentences, with more formal vocabulary. The author seems to be striving for objectivity in this text, and we do not see much vivid description or dialogue. Again, the audience and purpose for this genre help us to understand the style choices: the goal is to inform readers from a specialized field, and the writer chooses language that creates a formal, academic tone and conveys authority.

EXAMPLE 3: Article in Target Journal (excerpt)

Ashley McAlarney

Access for All: Federal Funding and Regulation of For-Profit Higher Education

Dialectics

Profit-seeking companies can provide opportunities for education that are traditionally unavailable to many citizens. However, at times, some engage in shadowy business practices that can harm students and demonstrate a misuse of public funds. The entanglement of private education and public money, associated with the for-profit sector of higher education, grows more controversial when misrepresentations of programs and inadequate training leave students unable to find employment and pay back federal loans. Recent efforts have been made by the Department of Education to impose regulations on for-profit schools to ensure that they are using fair business practices. Under these rules, if a school is not preparing students for gainful employment after graduation, it is deemed ineligible for federal funding, and attendees cannot receive federal loans and grants to pay for their education.

The preceding excerpt is from Terrence's target journal, *Dialectics*. Since Terrence hopes to publish his work in this journal, he takes a close look at this sample article. For instance, the writer uses formal verbs ("impose," "deemed," "ensure"), just like the research article in Example 2. However, Terrence notices that the writer also uses some word choices to take a stance on the issue—for example, she describes the "shadowy business practices" used by for-profit schools.

Again, the audience and purpose for this journal help to explain the style choices. As in Example 2, the author seeks an objective, academic persona, and style choices help the writer to convey authority. However, as an undergraduate journal, *Dialectics* may also seek to attract student readers. Using a more critical tone may allow the writer to attract readers by generating controversy.

Based on his analysis of the genre, audience, and purpose, Terrence decides he might be able to dramatize the issue he is writing about with some descriptive language, but that he should probably not go overboard. He incorporates more narrative elements in part of his paper (Chapter 19) to engage readers' attention, but he maintains the more objective style of a researcher in much of the paper.

Let's take a look at some specific elements to keep in mind when selecting an appropriate style.

B. Choosing a Persona

In writing, persona refers to how writers present themselves with relation to the subject or topic and audience. (Do not confuse persona with tone, which refers to the attitude the writer takes toward the subject or topic.)

It is important to note that the persona an author uses in a text is not necessarily the persona he or she uses in real life, and that you may have several different personas for different contexts. For instance, in your classes (and often, classroom writing), you take on the persona of a student, but at your job you take on the persona of an employee. In writing, persona is a rhetorical decision. For example, the persona you use to write a scientific lab report will be different from the persona you use in a profile article.

Think of your persona as connected to the role you take on as a writer. If you are writing a lab report, you will take on the persona of a scientist. Imagine yourself as a scientist—how would you write if you were in that role? In contrast, if you are writing a profile article (Chapter 5), you might imagine yourself as a freelance writer for a magazine. Picture yourself in that role. What kind of persona should you take on in this case?

Most writing that is based on research (such as research articles, reports, and grant proposals) tends toward an objective persona. That is, the writer seeks to distance himself or herself from the research, so that the research findings speak for themselves. In the sciences, especially, researchers try to write themselves out of the picture, because they want the focus to be on the results of their experiments or research. In contrast, in some genres writers strive to emphasize their involvement in the text. A magazine writer might write herself into the text, making her persona stand out, because a profile article is often a "human interest" piece—the writer can be part of the action of the text, or take a closer stance.

In Terrence's case, he thought it would be appropriate to mention his own connection to the issue of parental visitations in prisons, and to dramatize it with descriptive language (Chapter 19).

C. Choosing Tone

Tone refers to the attitude the writer takes. Is it critical? Sarcastic? Enthusiastic? Supportive? Note that for some genres, the tone is mainly neutral, as in a research article or report. In other genres, you have more room to choose a positive or negative tone, as in an op-ed piece (Chapter 10).

Terrence was careful to strike a neutral tone in his article. While he strongly disagreed with some of the studies he quoted, he was careful not to appear critical of the researchers themselves. However, he did include some elements of drama. Consider his introduction:

> Today in America millions of children are being torn away from their mothers, and it is perfectly legal. Over 1.5 million children in the United States have at least one incarcerated parent, and our legal system is prohibiting these children from being able to have visitation with their incarcerated parents, specifically mothers.

Here, Terrence strikes a slightly ominous tone in the first sentence, but balances it with an objective statistic. He considered this tone to be appropriate for his target audience and the genre he was writing.

D. Making Vocabulary Choices

Your choice of vocabulary should also fit with your audience, genre, and purpose.

One element of vocabulary choice involves the kinds of words chosen. In English, we often have two (or more) words that say basically the same thing, but some of those words sound more formal than others. Pay attention especially to verbs (action words) and nouns (words for persons, places, and things).

Compare the following two passages:

Version 1: Anglo-Saxon Verbs

> Child visitation will help **ease** parental stress while incarcerated. Being arrested can be one of the most tragic and confusing events that can occur in one's life, and having a child will certainly **make** that experience **harder** for most.

Version 2: Latinate Verbs

> Child visitation will help to **alleviate** parental stress while in prison. Being arrested can be one of the most tragic and confusing events that can occur in one's life, and having a child will certainly **complicate** that experience.

In English, verbs that come from the Latin roots of the language tend to seem more formal and scholarly than those that come from the Anglo-Saxon roots of the language. Table 21.1 shows some examples.

Table 21.1 Latinate and Anglo-Saxon Verbs

Latinate Verbs	Anglo-Saxon Verbs
Cogitate	Think
Maintain	Keep
Impose	Force
Ascertain	Learn
Receive	Get
Purchase	Buy
Accumulate	Gather

Notice that the words on the left side sound fancier, or more formal, than the words on the right. The Anglo-Saxon words tend to be shorter and to seem more casual.

The same goes for nouns. Compare the following passages:

Version 1: Anglo-Saxon Nouns

> I argue that each of these issues can increase the amount of stress surrounding the **jailing** of a mother, and perhaps delay her release by slowing the rehabilitation process. A mother's **drive** can quickly evaporate while her **child** is withheld.

Version 2: Latinate Nouns

> I argue that each of these issues can increase the amount of stress surrounding the **incarceration** of a mother, and perhaps delay her release by slowing the rehabilitation process. A mother's **motivation** can quickly evaporate while her **progeny** is withheld.

As with nouns, verbs come across as more technical and formal in their Latinate form than in their simpler Anglo-Saxon form.

Table 21.2 Latinate and Anglo-Saxon Nouns

Latinate Nouns	Anglo-Saxon Nouns
Festival	Party
Conflict	Fight
Impression	Feeling
Obstacle	Hurdle
Object	Thing

By analyzing your genre, you can determine which kinds of words seem to be appropriate. In the examples of research articles he read, Terrence noticed a preference for the more formal Latinate vocabulary, so he tried to use those kinds of words in his writing, as well.

Terminology

You should also pay attention to the specific terms used in the field or discourse community in which you are participating. If you are writing for a specific academic field (such as anthropology, sociology, biology, etc.), you will find that writers employ specific words that either do not appear in other fields or are used differently in other fields. Employing the terminology of your field shows your membership in that community.

Terrence used the term "best interests of the child" because he was writing for an audience of legal and political science scholars who would likely understand the concept. However, if he were writing about a magazine article for a general audience, not members of the community, then he would have to either define that term or choose less specific synonyms (Chapter 19).

E. Choosing a Level of Formality

Vocabulary is one element of formality, or the overall style of a text. Consider how clothing choices convey formality. If you are invited to a formal event such as a prom or wedding, you might wear your most formal clothing: a suit or gown, maybe even a tuxedo. For a professional event, such as a job interview, you would wear professional clothing: a suit and tie for men, and a skirt or pantsuit for women—not quite so formal as a prom or graduation ceremony, but not casual either. And for a casual event, like a company picnic or college party, you would likely wear something more informal—khakis, jeans, a shirt or blouse.

Similarly, you can clothe your writing in different styles, depending on the genre, audience, and purpose. You might use a high level of formality with a very formal audience, such as lawyers or scientists (picture a judge in robes, or a scientist in a lab coat). Most academic fields, such as law, sciences, and medicine, tend toward formal writing, especially for research genres.

Most business writing and persuasive writing actually functions in the middle level, mixing formal elements with a few casual elements. You might use casual writing for blogs, personal emails, personal letters—such as thank-you letters—and posts to social networking sites.

Table 21.3 demonstrates some style changes you can make to increase or decrease formality.

Table 21.3 Levels of Formality

	High	Middle	Low
Vocabulary	Technical, scientific terms, jargon specific to a discourse community or field	Balances technical terminology with everyday terms	"Everyday" terms
	Latinate vocabulary	Mixes Latinate with Anglo-Saxon vocabulary	Prefers Anglo-Saxon vocabulary
Examples	"Best interests"	"Best interests of the child, a doctrine used to..."	"what's best for the child"
	"Deoxyribonucleic acid (DNA)"	"DNA, or genetic material..."	"Genetics," "Heredity"
	"Cogitation"	"Thought"	"Thinking"
	"Appears"	"Seems"	"Looks like"
Contractions	No	Sometimes	Yes
	It is not . . .	It is not . . . or It isn't . . .	It isn't . . .
Personal Voice ("I" or "We")	No	Sometimes	Yes
	The court finds . . . The results indicated . . .	I argue that . . . We surveyed 100 students . . .	I think . . . I believe . . . You should
Grammatical Voice	Tends toward passive voice	Mixes active and passive voice	Prefers active voice
	Results were found . . .	Results were found . . . or We found results . . .	We found results . . .

F. Using Rhetorical Figures

Rhetorical figures are special language patterns you can use to express an idea in an original, eloquent, or persuasive way. You are probably familiar with some rhetorical figures already, such as metaphor, simile, and analogy. You might think about using a rhetorical figure whenever you'd like to emphasize a point in your writing.

Again, consider your genre, audience, and purpose first. Some genres are especially laden with rhetorical figures. You might expect to hear this kind of language in a presidential campaign speech, or a eulogy given at a funeral, or in a profile article.

Genres used in professional and academic language may feature fewer rhetorical figures, but you can still use them in those genres for effect.

Repetition

Repetition creates emphasis. Repetition also helps to keep an audience interested, to create memorable phrases, and to increase the emphasis or force of your statements. Here is an example of repetition of words and phrases for emphasis from the "I Have a Dream" speech by Martin Luther King, Jr., delivered in Washington, DC, in 1963.

> But one hundred years later, the Negro still is not free. One hundred years later, the life of the Negro is still sadly crippled by the manacles of segregation and the chains of discrimination. One hundred years later, the Negro lives on a lonely island of poverty in the midst of a vast ocean of material prosperity. One hundred years later, the Negro is still languished in the corners of American society and finds himself an exile in his own land. And so we've come here today to dramatize a shameful condition.

Here's how Terrence tried to work repetition into his draft. He decided the conclusion might be a good place for repetition, because he wanted to emphasize his main ideas.

First Draft

Experts have proven that child visitation is positive for both the parent and the child. Child visitation must be increased in order to alleviate the psychological strains that take place during incarceration. Better-informed visitation policies may even break the relentless cycle of crime.

Revision

Experts have proven that child visitation is positive for both the parent and the child. Child visitation must be increased in order to alleviate the psychological strains that take place during incarceration. **Better-informed visitation**

> **policies may even break the relentless cycle of crime, a cycle whose costs for society are much too high, a cycle that reduces children's potential, a cycle that must be broken.**

Parallelism

Repetition also functions on the level of grammatical structures, rather than words and phrases. By constructing parallel phrases or sentences, you create a rhythm that makes information easier for an audience to grasp, while simultaneously increasing emphasis. Here is another example from King's speech:

> We cannot walk alone.
>
> And as we walk, we must make the pledge that we shall always march ahead.
>
> We cannot turn back.

As he continued to work on his conclusion, Terrence noticed places where he could improve parallelism:

First Draft

> Unfortunately, current policies have generally disregarded the subject and have allowed societal perceptions of crime, rather than true academic research, to influence legislation.

Revision

> Unfortunately, current policies have generally disregarded the subject, have ignored true academic research, and have allowed societal perceptions of crime to influence legislation.

Metaphor

A metaphor is a rhetorical figure in which a word is used to describe a thing or action to which the word doesn't normally apply, often to create a mental image in an audience. For example, if you were to describe the sun as a "big, yellow beach ball," you would be employing metaphor to create an image.

Essentially, all of these figures work by creating mental images for readers, often in ways that create an emotional impact—in rhetorical terms, a pathos response. Here is a series of metaphors from King's speech.

> The whirlwinds of revolt will continue to shake the foundations of our nation until the bright day of justice emerges.

In his conclusion, Terrence decided to try out a metaphor to create emotional impact.

First Draft

Our Children's Place shows great promise and has had nothing but great results. It is these types of ground-breaking initiatives that have really been able to grasp the true effects of incarceration on the parent and the child.

Revision

Our Children's Place shows great promise and has had nothing but great results; it is a ray of sunshine breaking through the cloudy firmament of prison policies. It is these types of ground-breaking initiatives that have really been able to grasp the true effects of incarceration on the parent and the child.

Simile

A simile is similar to a metaphor, only it makes the comparison more explicit, usually using "like" or "as." Many similes are common phrases, or clichés, that can lose their effectiveness over time. For example, it would be a cliché to write that someone is as skinny as a rail or as happy as a clam. Try to find fresh similes that will catch the reader's attention.

In his speech, King used simile often; in the example that follows, he used the word "as" to indicate a simile—comparing cross-racial friendship to siblinghood.

> [O]ne day right there in Alabama little black boys and black girls will be able to join hands with little white boys and white girls as sisters and brothers.

In his revision of his paper, Terrence used the word "like" to indicate a simile.

First Revision

Our Children's Place shows great promise and has had nothing but great results. It is these types of ground-breaking initiatives that have really been able to grasp the true effects of incarceration on the parent and the child.

Second Revision

Our Children's Place shows great promise and has had nothing but great results. Like sunlight, these types of initiatives have helped healthy relationships grow between incarcerated parents and children.

Alliteration

Alliteration occurs when you use several words in a sentence that start with the same letter or sound. You can use alliteration to create a memorable turn of phrase, or to convey certain emotions or attitudes. Here is a sentence from King's speech that employs alliteration upon the letter "s."

> We can never be satisfied as long as our children are stripped of their self-hood and robbed of their dignity by signs stating: "For Whites Only."

Here is how Terrence revised his draft to employ alliteration upon the letter "p."

First Draft

Our Children's Place shows great promise and has had nothing but great results.

Revision

Our Children's Place shows great promise and even greater potential as a

model for future initiatives.

Notice that introducing alliteration in the revised sentence led Terrence to employ parallelism and repetition, as well.

Antithesis

An antithesis is a pattern that expresses a contradiction or relation of opposites. You can use antithesis to emphasize two opposing points or ideas. Terrence used antithesis to show how scientific research has been ignored by policy-makers who shape prison visitation rules for children.

First Revision

Unfortunately, current policies have generally disregarded the subject, have

ignored true academic research, and have allowed societal perceptions of crime

to influence legislation.

Second Revision

Unfortunately, current policies have generally disregarded the subject, have

ignored true academic research, and have allowed societal perceptions of crime to influence legislation. While academic research suggests visitation can be

positive, current legal policies have portrayed it as uniformly negative.

By emphasizing the antithesis between the current policies and the academic research, Terrence also put his sentence into more parallel form.

G. Tips for Developing Style

To improve your repertoire of style choices, try the following:

- Whatever you read, whether it is for work or pleasure, keep an eye out for effective style (vivid description, metaphor, etc.). The same goes for oral language—pay attention to effective political speeches, for example.
- Keep a computer file, blog, or notebook where you copy interesting passages from documents you read. Traditionally, rhetoricians suggested that their

Table 21.4 Matching Style to Genre, Audience, and Purpose

	Persona	**Tone**
What Is It?	What persona, or role, do writers take in this genre?	What tone, or attitude, do writers take in this genre?
Who Reads It?	What persona, or role, is most effective or expected by the audience for this genre?	What tone, or attitude, would appeal most to readers?
What Is It For?	What persona will best help me to accomplish my rhetorical goals?	What tone best matches my purpose?

students keep a commonplace book of quotations, poems, and so on. Your computer file could be a modern-day equivalent. Consider this an "inspiration file" that you can consult when you need ideas for an important document or oral statement.

- Pay close attention to examples of the genre you are producing. Even better, look for examples of that genre that are also in the target publication for your writing. If you are writing an op-ed for your student newspaper, get examples of op-eds from your student newspaper. Read your draft out loud, and then read one of the examples out loud. Do they sound about the same, in terms of style? If not, should you adopt more features of that genre?
- Picture the audience for your writing. What are they wearing? How do they act? And what would you wear if you were to speak to them directly? For instance, would you address a judge wearing jeans and a t-shirt? Or would you put on your best suit? Your language should reflect a similar level of formality, style, and tone as your dress.
- Create time in your writing process to revise your writing for style. Look for places where you can adjust your style to suit your genre, audience, and purpose. You can use Table 21.4 as a guide.

Vocabulary	Formality	Rhetorical Figures
What kinds of vocabulary do writers use in this genre? (e.g., academic jargon? Latinate words?)	What level of formality is typical for this genre?	What kinds of rhetorical figures do writers use in this genre? (metaphor? analogy?)
What kinds of vocabulary will readers find most effective or easiest to understand?	What level of formality is appropriate for my audience?	What kinds of rhetorical figures will be most persuasive to readers of this genre? What rhetorical figures will help them understand the argument or content?
What vocabulary choices will best suit my rhetorical goals?	What level of formality best suits my purpose?	What kinds of rhetorical figures could help to achieve my purpose?

Polishing It Up

After you have researched, drafted, and organized your paper, you need to revise and edit it. This chapter gives you strategies for revision, for editing by yourself, and for editing with the help of others. Let's take a look at how one student author, Terrence, revised and edited his paper.

A. Revising

Revision is the process of taking another look at your writing and thinking about what you can do better. During revision, your paper may change dramatically. Here are some strategies for revision that have worked well for other writers.

Reverse Outline

Once you have a draft of your document (in Terrence's case, an academic research paper), you may find it useful to write a reverse outline of your piece. To write a reverse outline, go paragraph-by-paragraph and write a short summary of what each paragraph is doing.

Then, consider whether you could rearrange your document for greater effect. Are there paragraphs that need to be combined or divided in two? Paragraphs that start out saying one thing but end up saying something else? Paragraphs that need to be rearranged?

Topic Sentence Outline

Another option is to write a topic sentence outline. With a topic sentence outline, you write down all of the topic sentences of your document as though they were a single paragraph. Try reading the paragraph. Does it make sense? Are some of your sentences (in other words, your paragraphs) out of order?

Terrence wrote a topic sentence outline of his paper (see Chapter 28 for his entire paper) to see if his paragraphs were in order. Here is the list of topic sentences from the beginning paragraphs of his paper:

- Today in America millions of children are being torn away from their mothers, and it is perfectly legal.
- The United States legal system prohibits these children from visiting their incarcerated parents, specifically mothers.

- The field of psychology has taken a different perspective on incarceration than that taken by the legal system.
- To conduct this study, I reviewed legal research describing the current barriers for incarcerated mothers to gain visitation of their children.

Examining these sentences, Terrence felt that his organization was strong, moving from an opening paragraph that catches the reader's attention, to a second paragraph that explains the challenging situation that his paper critiques, to a third paragraph that explains the interdisciplinary angle that his paper takes, to the fourth paragraph that describes his paper's methodology. He continued reviewing the topic sentences for the rest of his paper, ensuring that his paragraphs were in the proper order and rearranging them as necessary.

USE THE TOOLKIT

As you revise your writing, revisit the three genre toolkit questions (Chapter 1) to ensure that you have met the requirements of the genre that you are writing.

What Is It?
Have I used the expected conventions of the genre? If not, do I have a reason for deviating from the expected conventions?

Who Reads It?
Have I met the expectations of my audience? Will my audience find my document appropriate, easy to read, and useful?

What's It For?
Have I kept my document's purpose in mind? Does my document fulfill its purpose?

B. Self-Editing and Proofreading: Creating Fresh Eyes

Editing is the process of polishing your writing at the sentence level, including changing sentences to improve style, clarity, focus, and concision. Proofreading refers to the process of checking sentences for errors, such as typographical errors (typos), grammatical mistakes, or misspelled words. Many writers have trouble editing and proofreading their own work. They have trouble viewing their work with "fresh eyes."

All of the strategies described in this section will help you gain distance (sometimes called "critical distance") from your writing. Critical distance is the ability of a writer to view her own work critically and to discover problems.

Giving Yourself Time

When it comes to editing, the greatest gift you can give yourself is time. If you are able to finish a draft and let it "rest" for a few days before editing it, you are more likely to have critical distance, and therefore more likely to find errors or to spot places where you might edit the text to improve style (Chapter 21), accuracy, or concision.

Reading Out Loud

Reading your paper out loud can also help you spot stylistic flaws or errors in your writing. Take a piece of blank paper or a ruler, and hold it below the first line. Then, start reading. Blocking out the line below, combined with the slower pace that reading out loud forces you to take, helps create fresh eyes on your writing.

Recording Your Voice

In addition to reading out loud, you can record yourself reading your paper out loud and then listen to it. Use the voice recorder on your cell phone (most phones have them these days) or voice recording software on your computer. If you listen to your recording while silently reading your paper to yourself, you are likely to find errors that you might have missed or sentences whose style could be improved (Chapter 21).

C. Conducting Peer Review

An alternative to trying to edit and proofread your own work is to seek help from peers, such as your classmates or other friends. Giving (and receiving) peer feedback is a crucial process in successful writing.

Providing Useful Feedback

You might think that because you are not an expert writer that you don't have good feedback to give. This is not true. You can easily come up with plenty of suggestions for a fellow writer if you draw on your own experience as a reader and writer.

Revising at the idea level   Focus on the ideas of the document that you are reading. As you read, focus on how you respond as a reader.

First, try reading as someone who *supports* the ideas. When you read as a supporter, ask yourself the following:

- What is good about this idea?
- How could the writer make this idea clearer? Stronger?

Next, try reading as a naysayer, someone who *does not support* the ideas. Consider the following:

- How could you rebut this idea (Chapter 18)? What evidence is there against it?
- How could the writer address objections?

When you give feedback to the writer, provide both the supporter and the naysayer perspectives. Then, the writer can figure out how to make their writing even stronger.

Editing at the sentence level   If you are nervous about giving feedback for this first time, try this strategy:

For every sentence that you had to read twice or three times in order to understand it, put a question mark in the margin. Every time you spot a problem with the writing, such as a word or phrase that is unclear or clunky, put an "X" in the margin. And every time you read a sentence that you think is great, put a check mark in the margin.

Just this much feedback can really help another writer improve his or her writing. Of course, if you have further comments to make—and you will find yourself having more comments the more you critique others' work—write those down too.

Proofreading   As a peer reviewer, you will often catch small mistakes that the writer missed. Don't spend all of your time focused on these little mistakes; however, it is very useful for you to circle them so that the writer can fix them later. Your fresh eyes can often spot errors that the writer's eyes cannot.

Soliciting Good Feedback

Sometimes, students find that they do not get sufficient feedback from peer review sessions. Part of your responsibility as a group member is to actively seek out good feedback. That means that you should prompt your group members to help you with specific elements of your writing. You can do this by asking questions like these:

- How can I improve the organization of my document? Did you get lost or find the argument hard to follow?
- What do you think of my introduction? Did I capture your attention right away, or does it seem too dry?
- What are some places where I can improve the style to suit this genre?

By prompting your group members to answer specific questions, you can get better feedback than if you ask a general questions, like "What do you think of my document?" or "Does it flow?"

Critiquing with Respect

Giving useful critique is an excellent skill to have. But you must also temper your criticism with respect for the other writer. If your comments come across as mean-spirited, the recipient will either have his or her feelings hurt or just ignore your comments completely. Put yourself in the recipient's shoes and re-read all of your comments before you share them to ensure that you are critiquing with respect. Try using phrases such as these:

- "When I read this, I thought. . . . "
- "What I think you are saying is . . ."
- "As a reader, I felt . . .
- "The introduction seems to need work . . ."

Try to avoid phrases such as these:

- "You should . . ."
- "Don't. . . ."
- "This is stupid/silly/ridiculous."

Using Electronic Tools

There are many electronic tools that can make peer reviews easier. For example, simply emailing documents back and forth and making comments in the text on your computer is a fine way to collaborate without having to meet in person. Using Microsoft Word's track changes and commenting features are a great way to do this. Here is an excerpt from Terrence's draft with peer comments written using Microsoft Word's track changes and commenting features.

~~Using T~~the psychological research that is available~~, findings~~ consistently ~~conclude~~ shows

that when a child is ~~withheld~~ prevented from visiting his or her mother, negative ~~side~~ effects

occur. However, when visitation is allowed, there are numerous positive ~~implications~~ effects.

Snyder, Carlo, & Mullins (2001) found that, when a parent is incarcerated, the child has

an increased risk of suffering from anxiety, depression, sleeplessness, anger, and attention

---

deficiencies. However, these risks can be alleviated through visitation programs, and parenting classes can improve the relationship between incarcerated mothers and their children (Snyder, Carlo, & Mullins 2001). If visitation is allowed, then the problem may be prevented earlier, and the child's future will be more promising as a result (Snyder, Carlo, & Mullins 2001). [Clearly], parenting classes must be utilized [more]; the classes would be beneficial for parent, child, and other family members. And, since prison today is a business, the parenting classes will ultimately be more economical. Although it appears that adding a new program would be more expensive, the parenting programs may actually reduce the overall costs related to the incarcerated parents' mental and physical health [treatments] because of the motivation that parents will gain by having continued positive contact with their children.

Comment [1]: Perhaps avoid words like "clearly." Whenever I read words like clearly (or "obviously"), it makes me wary that the argument the author is about to make is a weak one. Otherwise, why would the author need to *tell* me that the argument is clear?

Comment [2]: Do you mean parenting classes in prison? I'm confused by the connection between parenting classes and child visitation.

Comment [3]: Great to provide a counterargument to preempt the naysayers to your proposal! This really worked for me as a reader.

Your instructor may prefer that you use a course management system to conduct peer review, perhaps using a message board or forum. You can also use real-time collaboration software such as Google Docs, which allows two or more people to write on the same document at the same time. Another option is a file sharing system like Dropbox.com or Evernote, which allows writers to share files across the Internet.

Choosing Visual Elements, Layout, and Design

In this chapter, you will learn how to employ visual elements, layout, and design effectively when you compose documents of all kinds. Visual elements refer to items such as photographs, drawings, charts, and graphs that you might include in a document. Layout refers to how those elements (along with text) are organized on the page or screen. Design refers to the visual qualities you apply to your documents. This may include colors, shapes, font types and sizes, and so on. You will learn how to choose these features based on the genre you are composing and the rhetorical situation for your document.

A. Matching Design to Genre

The first consideration when selecting visual elements, layout, and design features for a document should be the genre you are writing. Start by gathering examples of the genre.

Any genre includes some design features, even if it is a regular paper in MLA or APA format (Chapter 28). The design features for academic papers might include double spacing, headers, and a serif typeface (such as Times New Roman or Cambria). The design features for a research paper are dictated by the style guide, such as the *MLA Style Manual*. Similarly, if you submit a paper to an academic journal, the layout and design will be dictated by the journal.

In other cases, you will have a choice of design options. While résumés tend to have similar features, you can choose different options for fonts, headings, and layout (Chapter 12). Your analysis of your genre will give you a sense of the range of options open to you. While it might not be advisable to add colorful sub-headings to a research paper, you might be able to do so for a website, blog post, conference poster, or brochure.

While Terrence originally wrote his research paper (Chapter 11) on incarcerated mothers and visitation rights as a research article, for a later assignment he was asked to rework it into a one-page factsheet (Chapter 6) to summarize his findings. Unlike the article, the factsheet offered Terrence more visual choices.

Terrence started by researching examples of factsheets, and he located several to get a sense of what visual elements he could include (Figure 29.1 and Figure 29.2).

EXAMPLE 1: Factsheet on HIV/AIDS

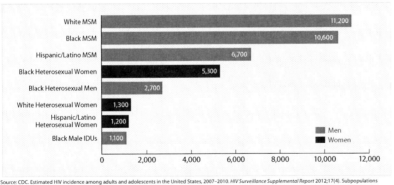

HIV Among Women

March 2014

Fast Facts
- One in four people living with HIV infection in the United States are women.
- Most new HIV infections in women are from heterosexual contact (84%).
- Only about half of women who are diagnosed with HIV are in care, and even fewer (4 in 10) have the virus under control.

At the end of 2010, one in four people living with HIV in the United States were women.[a] Black/African American* and Hispanic/Latino[b] women continue to be disproportionately affected by HIV, compared with women of other races/ethnicities.

Not all US women who are diagnosed with HIV are getting the care they need. In 19 US jurisdictions with complete reporting, of all women who were diagnosed with HIV by year-end 2009 and alive in 2010, only 53% were staying in care in 2010, and 42% had viral suppression.

*Referred to as African American in this fact sheet.

The Numbers

New HIV Infections[c]
- Women made up 20% (9,500) of the estimated 47,500 new HIV infections in the United States in 2010. Eighty-four percent of these new infections (8,000) were from heterosexual contact.[d]
- When comparing groups by race/ethnicity, gender, and transmission category, the fourth largest number of all new HIV infections in the United States in 2010 (5,300) occurred among African American women with heterosexual contact (see bar graph). Of the total number of estimated new HIV infections among women, 64% (6,100) were in African Americans, 18% (1,700) were in whites, and 15% (1,400) were in Hispanic/Latino women.

Estimated New HIV Infections in the United States for the Most-Affected Subpopulations, 2010

Subpopulation	Infections
White MSM	11,200
Black MSM	10,600
Hispanic/Latino MSM	6,700
Black Heterosexual Women	5,300
Black Heterosexual Men	2,700
White Heterosexual Women	1,300
Hispanic/Latino Heterosexual Women	1,200
Black Male IDUs	1,100

Men
Women

0   2,000   4,000   6,000   8,000   10,000   12,000

Source: CDC. Estimated HIV incidence among adults and adolescents in the United States, 2007–2010. *HIV Surveillance Supplemental Report* 2012;17(4). Subpopulations representing 2% or less of the overall US epidemic are not **reflected** in this chart. Abbreviations: MSM, men who have sex with men; IDU, injection drug user.

[a] Women are **defined** in this fact sheet as adult and adolescent females aged 13 and older.
[b] Hispanic/Latino women can be of any race.
[c] New HIV infections refer to HIV incidence or the number of people who are newly infected with HIV, whether they are aware of their infection or not.
[d] Heterosexual contact with a person known to have, or be at high risk for, HIV infection.
[e] HIV and AIDS diagnoses indicate when a person is diagnosed with HIV infection or AIDS, but do not indicate when the person was infected.

National Center for HIV/AIDS, Viral Hepatitis, STD, and TB Prevention
Division of HIV/AIDS Prevention

CDC

Figure 29.1
This factsheet uses bulleted lists, color, a graph, and photographs
to visually present information alongside text.

EXAMPLE 2: **Factsheet on Tornado Preparation**

How to get ready for tornadoes

Known as nature's most violent storms, tornadoes can strike with little or no warning, destroying entire neighborhoods in just a few minutes. But preparing ahead of time, knowing the signs of a coming tornado and familiarizing yourself with tornado warning systems can help keep you and your loved ones safe.

What's a tornado?

Photo courtesy iStockphoto--Sonja Foos

A tornado is a dangerous rotating column of air that is in contact with both the ground and a cumulonimbus cloud, which is the type of cloud involved in thunderstorms. Its violent winds can reach hundreds of miles per hour.

Tornadoes can happen anywhere in the world, but they mostly happen in the United States. Every state is susceptible to tornadoes, however they are most common in regions east of the Rocky Mountains in the spring and summer. According to the National Weather Service, the United States experiences 800 tornadoes in an average year.

Tornadoes are extremely powerful, capable of destroying even well-constructed homes and buildings, uprooting trees and hurling heavy pieces of debris.

Know the signs, be prepared

Tornado warning systems can differ from town to town, so get to know your community's tornado warning system. Know the difference between alerts for a tornado watch, which is when weather conditions mean a tornado is possible, and a tornado warning, which is when a tornado funnel has been sighted. Also, if you have children, get to know their school's tornado plan.

During thunderstorms, use a battery-operated radio to listen to weather updates and instructions from local officials. Also, be aware of tornado warning signs: dark, greenish skies; large hail; a large, dark, low-lying cloud; a visible, rotating funnel; or a loud roar.

Photo courtesy iStockphoto--Laura Young

aphagetready.org

Figure 29.2
This factsheet uses bold colors, high-contrast sub-headings,
and photographs to present information effectively.

From these two examples, Terrence learned that factsheets tend to combine text and images, often using color, contrast, visual elements, and bulleted lists to display information. Both of these examples arrange items into columns or sections, sometimes blocking off sections with borders or shading.

To come up with design ideas, you can also collect examples of other kinds of designs you like. Designers of all kinds, from web developers to fashion designers, collect materials for inspiration boards. You can keep a file of interesting designs, pin examples to a bulletin board, or you can create a digital one using online tools such as Pinterest. Terrence simply pinned flyers and magazine pages that he found interesting on the bulletin board in his room. He then came up with the following list of design features he wanted to include in his own factsheet:

Factsheet:
* *Use greys/black to convey cold/sadness of prison*
* *Contrast with a warm color (yellow/orange?) to convey hope/potential for change*
* *Use different fonts and/or colors? for headings/sub-headings*
* *Perhaps contrast risks of incarceration with benefits of visitation—use bulleted lists?*

B. Matching Design to Audience, Purpose, and Situation

In addition to genre, your layout and design choices should be guided by the audience, purpose, and context for your document.

Audience

Consider how your audience will view and use your document. For example, users of a website will expect a clear navigation scheme so that they can move from one area to another. On this website (Figure 29.3), the primary navigation scheme is a bar across the top, with tabs for articles, exhibits, and information about individual women.

EXAMPLE: **Student Website Design**

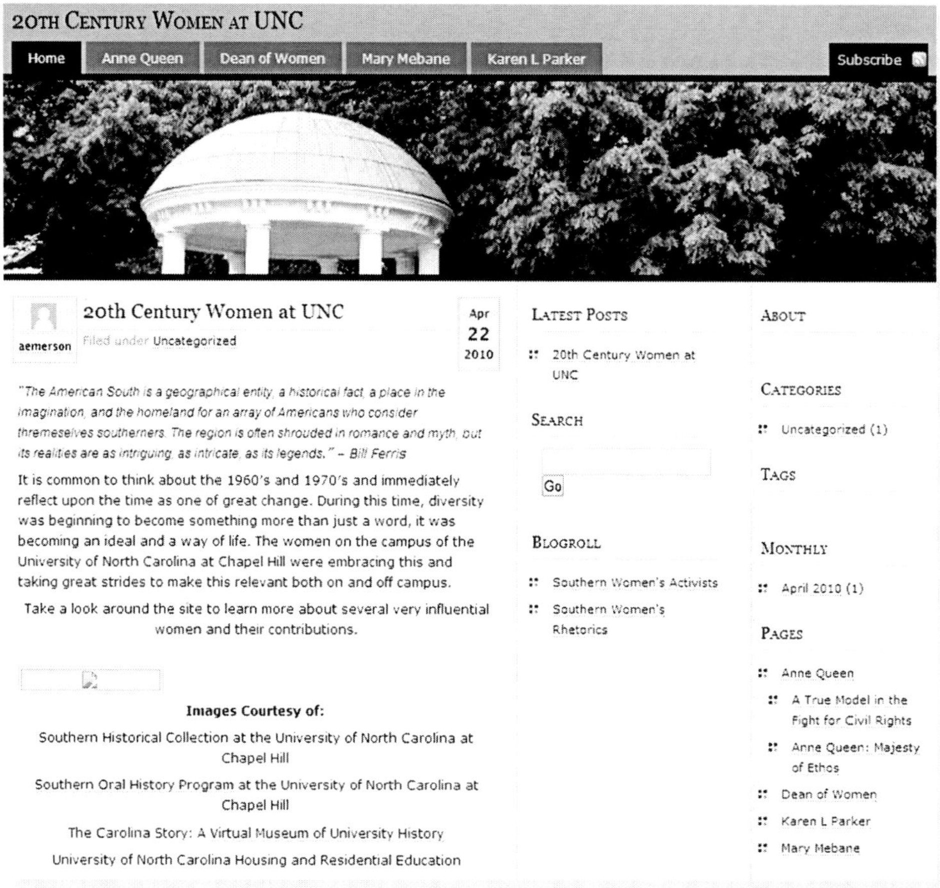

20TH CENTURY WOMEN AT UNC

Home | Anne Queen | Dean of Women | Mary Mebane | Karen L Parker | Subscribe

20th Century Women at UNC

aemerson   Filed under Uncategorized

Apr 22 2010

"The American South is a geographical entity, a historical fact, a place in the imagination, and the homeland for an array of Americans who consider thremeselves southerners. The region is often shrouded in romance and myth, but its realities are as intriguing, as intricate, as its legends." – Bill Ferris

It is common to think about the 1960's and 1970's and immediately reflect upon the time as one of great change. During this time, diversity was beginning to become something more than just a word, it was becoming an ideal and a way of life. The women on the campus of the University of North Carolina at Chapel Hill were embracing this and taking great strides to make this relevant both on and off campus.

Take a look around the site to learn more about several very influential women and their contributions.

Images Courtesy of:

Southern Historical Collection at the University of North Carolina at Chapel Hill

Southern Oral History Program at the University of North Carolina at Chapel Hill

The Carolina Story: A Virtual Museum of University History

University of North Carolina Housing and Residential Education

LATEST POSTS

:: 20th Century Women at UNC

SEARCH

[Go]

BLOGROLL

:: Southern Women's Activists

:: Southern Women's Rhetorics

ABOUT

CATEGORIES

:: Uncategorized (1)

TAGS

MONTHLY

:: April 2010 (1)

PAGES

:: Anne Queen

:: A True Model in the Fight for Civil Rights

:: Anne Queen: Majesty of Ethos

:: Dean of Women

:: Karen L Parker

:: Mary Mebane

Figure 29.3
A clear navigation scheme helps users locate content on a website.

As with a website, readers of a long print or online document might appreciate headings and sub-headings, a table of contents, and an index to help them locate information. In the following example, a United States Department of Agriculture report (Figure 29.4), you can see several design features to help readers locate information: a table of contents, bold headings, and color.

EXAMPLE: **Government Report (excerpt)**

Contents

Summary iii

Introduction 1

Consumers Fuel Market Growth but Defy Easy Categorization 3

Retailers Expand Organic Product Introductions and Private Labels 6

'Handler' Middlemen Move More Organic Products
as Shortages Are Reported.................................... 8

Organic Acres More Than Doubled From 1997 to 2005,
but Supply Still Fell Short of Demand........................... 10

Fresh Produce Continues To Be the Top-Selling Category............ 14

Dairy Products Sector Has Boomed Despite
Periodic Supply Shortages................................... 16

Organic Meat and Eggs Have Relatively Low Total Sales
but Fast Growth 18

Essential to Other Sectors, Feed Grains and Oilseeds
Face Slow Growth 20

Additional Reading 22

References 23

Recommended citation format for this publication:

Dimitri, Carolyn, and Lydia Oberholtzer. *Marketing U.S. Organic Foods:
Recent Trends From Farms to Consumers.* Economic Information Bulletin No.
58. U.S. Dept. of Agriculture, Economic Research Service. September 2009.

Summary

Organic foods now occupy prominent shelf space in the produce and dairy aisles of most mainstream U.S. food retailers, while offerings of organic meats, eggs, breads, grains, and beverages have increased. The marketing boom has pushed retail sales of organic foods up to $21.1 billion in 2008 from $3.6 billion in 1997. Supermarkets, club stores, big-box stores, and other food retailers carry organic products; many retailers have introduced lines of organic private-label products; and manufacturers continue to introduce large numbers of new organic products.

What Is the Issue?

The rapid growth of the U.S. organic industry has caused a major shift in the types and numbers of organic food retailers, manufacturers, and distributors and has widened the retail customer base. In addition, organic farmland acreage more than doubled from 1997 to 2005. With those changes has come an increased desire for research and analysis of the U.S. organic marketing system. The 2008 Farm Act allocated $5 million in initial spending for an expanded organic data collection initiative, along with an additional $5 million per year of authorized funding for researchers to:

- collect and distribute comprehensive reporting of prices relating to organically produced agricultural products

- conduct surveys and analysis and publish reports relating to organic pro-duction, handling, distribution, retail, and trend studies (including consumer purchasing patterns)

- develop surveys and report statistical analysis on organically produced agricultural products

While new data are being collected and analyzed, policymakers and other inter-ested groups have expressed particular interest in: what types of consumers pur-chase organic food; how structural change has affected the retailing, distribution, and manufacturing of organic food; and why increases in the supply of organic products at the farm level lag behind growth in demand at the retail level. This study analyzes the most recent data available to examine each level of the organic supply chain.

What Did the Study Find?

The number and variety of consumers of organic products has increased, but those consumers are not easily categorized. The one factor that consistently influences the likelihood of a consumer's buying organic products is education. Consumers of all ages, races, and ethic groups who have higher levels of education are more likely to buy organic products than less-educated consumers. Other factors, such as race, presence of children in the household, and income, do not have a consis-tent effect on the likelihood of buying organic products.

Retailing of organic products has evolved since 1997, when natural foods stores were the main outlet. By 2008, nearly half of all organic foods were purchased in conventional supermarkets, club stores, and big-box stores. Although produce remained the top-selling organic category, sales of dairy products, beverages,

Figure 29.4

To help readers navigate a print document, use a table of contents, contrast,
and consistent headings and sub-headings.

Your analysis of your audience and genre can help you to pinpoint the right type of visual elements to use. Terrence noted that factsheets about public policy issues tended to use more photographs and fewer technical images, so he planned to include photographs of women and children.

Purpose

Visual elements can help you to achieve the purpose of your document. If your purpose is to inform, you might choose visual elements that help to illustrate key concepts, provide facts or statistics, or help people to perform a task. If your purpose is to persuade, then you might choose visual elements that support your argument or attract the reader's interest.

Terrence wanted his factsheet to persuade policy makers to change visitation policies for children of incarcerated parents, so he chose photographs that he thought would attract policy makers. He thought images of mothers and their children might create an emotional connection with readers. He located images from government websites, since those are usually free of copyright. He made sure to note the source for the images, though, so that he could include a credit line for them on his factsheet.

Situation

Consider how readers will actually interact with your document. In what setting will they be reading, and how can you add elements to make it easier for them?

As he was designing his factsheet, Terrence considered where it might appear, such as on a government or non-government organization's website. Audience members might be policymakers seeking to change policies about child visitation in prisons, in which case they would want to access information quickly and easily. Terrence decided that putting information into boxes with clear headings would help them to find what they need.

C. Putting Things in Place: Layout

As you begin working on the layout for your document, you might start with a rough sketch on paper. As you work on your sketch, consider the following design principles:

Proximity: Group similar items close together. For example, on a conference poster you would probably put your name, department, and school in one place so readers can find them easily.

Alignment: Create clean lines by making sure every item on a page connects to something else on the page. Left justification tends to create the strongest alignment, while centering creates a jagged alignment that is more difficult for the eye to follow. Right justification is unusual, and can therefore attract attention, but it is also harder to read than left justification, since we read from left to right.

Repetition: To create a consistent design, repeat key elements throughout. For example, you might choose a consistent color scheme and font for each heading, varying only the size to indicate the importance of the heading. For a website, you might include a logo on each page so readers know they are on the same website when they navigate from page to page.

Contrast: Use color, bold text, or size to make important elements stand out. For example, on a conference poster you might want to bold the main headings and sub-headings using a large, bold font. Be careful not to make everything big and bold, though—if everything stands out, nothing stands out!

Let's evaluate how this draft of Terrence's factsheet uses design principles (Figure 29.5).

EXAMPLE: **Terrence's Factsheet Draft**

Photo Credit: acf.hhs.gov/programs/css/quick-fact

Figure 29.5

1. Proximity: Here, it is not clear which photograph goes with which block of text.
2. Alignment: Notice that the heading and first block of texts are centered, while the blocks of texts are not aligned with the photographs.
3. Repetition: The design uses different fonts for the main heading and the sub-headings, leading to a less cohesive look.
4. Contrast: Note that the large font sizes and colors distinguish them from the rest of the text.

After a draft workshop in class, Terrence realized that he needed to tweak his design to improve the proximity, repetition, and contrast. As shown in Figure 29.6, for his revised factsheet he chose a bold font for the headings and sub-headings, aligned everything flush left, and moved each block of text in the bottom half next to the photograph that went with it.

EXAMPLE: Terrence's Revised Factsheet

Being Mommy Behind Bars

Psychological Benefits of Childhood Visitation of Incarcerated Mothers

Terrance Bogans, University of North Carolina, Chapel Hill

66,000 women are incarcerated in the United States, leaving their children behind. Often, state laws and prison regulations violate their right to see their children, to the great detriment of both mother and child. Psychological research shows that child visitation has benefits for both mothers and their children. ①

Risks of Incarceration ③

- Disrupted family relationships
- Delinquency & risky behavior
- Risk for future incarceration
- Economic strain
- Emotional stress
- Depression & suicide

Benefits of Visitation ④

- Improves child's relationship with mother
- Improves child's understanding
- Eases parental stress
- Improves mother's rehabilitation & motivation
- Helps to break cycle of crime

Photo Credit: acf.hhs.gov/programs/css/quick-fact

Figure 29.6

1. Proximity: Here, it is clearer which photograph goes with which block of text.
2. Alignment: The left alignment makes everything connected in a straight line to something else on the page.
3. Repetition: The design uses only two different fonts, one for the main heading and the sub-headings, and one for the body text, leading to a more cohesive look.
4. Contrast: Note that the large font sizes and colors distinguish them from the rest of the text.

D. Types of Visual Elements

Visual elements refer to the types of images you might include in a design. Each type of image may work best for a particular purpose, audience, and genre. Use the three genre toolkit questions to help you determine what kinds of images to include.

What Is It?

Does your genre include images? What kinds? For example, in a profile article (Chapter 5) you might include a photograph of the person you are writing about, while a résumé (Chapter 12) would likely not include any images.

When choosing images for a project, you should also consider your audience's level of expertise and purpose for reading your document, as well as the genre you are writing. Some visual elements may be difficult for non-specialized audiences to interpret at a glance. For example, in his research paper (Chapter 28), Terrence chose a table to display numerical data because he thought it would appeal to an audience of policymakers and lawyers, and because he was writing for an academic audience. If this information were to appear in a popular magazine article, it might be simplified and displayed in a bar graph or even an infographic.

Who Reads It?

What kinds of images are best for your audience? Some images are best for technical readers, while others are more appropriate for a general audience. For example, a detailed architectural blueprint of a new house might be appropriate for the contractor who will build it, but a drawing of the house's façade might be more appropriate for potential buyers.

What's It For?

Does the image help to achieve your purpose? For example, if you would like to show readers a particular function in a computer program, you'd be better off with a screen capture of the actual program, rather than a pencil sketch. Table 29.1 can help you determine the most effective visual element for your purposes.

Table 29.1 Types of Visual Elements and Their Uses

Type of Visual Element	Purpose	Audience	Possible Genres
Graphs: Line Bar Pie Infographic	Demonstrate trends or patterns in data	Usually technical or expert audiences, depending on type of graph	Research paper Conference poster Report Factsheet
Tables and Charts: Table Flow chart Organization chart	Display information and data	Often used for more technical or expert audiences	Research paper Conference poster Report
Images: Diagram Drawing Photograph Map Screen capture	Represent a real or imagined object (person, place, thing)	Often used for those who are learning how something works or how to do something; may be used to show readers how something will be constructed (e.g., in a proposal for a new bridge). Sometimes used simply for visual interest. May be for general or specialized audiences (as in a blueprint).	Tutorials Reports Proposals Factsheet Websites Conference poster Blog

Graphs

Graphs are used to display trends or patterns in numerical data. You are probably already familiar with using and making graphs from your math or science courses. However, you may not have considered when to use them in writing assignments. Obviously, you might use a graph in a lab report for a science class, but a graph could also be used to display data in a recommendation report (Chapter 14) written for a business class or the results of a survey for a research paper (Chapter 11) in a sociology course.

There are many different types of graphs you might use in a document. Be sure to consider what types of graphs are appropriate for your genre, audience, and purpose.

Line Graphs
Line graphs are useful to indicate trends over time. In the following graph (Figure 29.7), prepared by the website WhiteHouse.gov, viewers can see that the average age at which Americans marry for the first time has increased since 1970, from around 23 for men and 20 for women, to 28 for men and 26 for women. The graph also shows that men tend to be older when they first get married than women.

EXAMPLE: **Line Graph**

Figure 29.7
Use a line graph to show trends over time.

In his research paper (Chapter 28), Terrence used a line graph to show how the number of incarcerated parents was on the rise—and also that the number of children of incarcerated parents was on the rise. He was able to import the line graph directly from a PDF copy of the source he cites in the image caption. Here's how it looked in his finished paper:

As shown in Figure 1, this number has risen by over fifty percent over the course of

the last two decades, and is likely to continue to rise as the prison population grows.

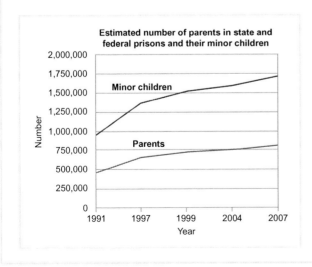

Figure 1: Number of parents in state and federal prisons, and their minor children. Adapted from Glaze, L. E. & Maruschak, L. M. (2008). *Parents in prison and their minor children.* Washington, D.C.: United States Department of Justice (p. 1).

Notice that Terrence introduced the graph in his text, referring to it as a "Figure," which is common in most citation styles. He then included a label and caption for the figure below it, and provided the source for the data he used.

Bar Graphs   Bar graphs are useful for displaying quantities of an item or measure. In the following bar graph (Figure 29.8), viewers can see how much money men and women earn, on average, according to the education they have achieved. It is easy to see that men and women earn more money each week, on average, if they have a bachelor's degree. Viewers also can see that men still tend to earn more money than women.

EXAMPLE: Bar Graph

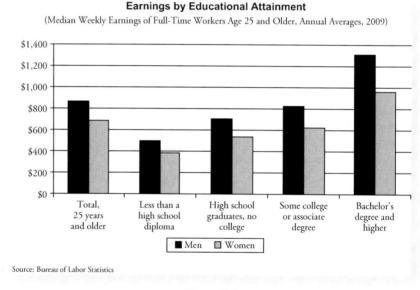

Figure 29.8
Use a bar graph to compare quantities.

Pie Graphs   Pie graphs are used to show the percentages that make up the whole. This pie graph (Figure 29.9) shows the proportion of federal spending on education that goes to instruction, support services, and other expenditures.

EXAMPLE: Pie Graph

The Cost of an Education: Breakdown of
Average Cost Per Student Expenditures
(in dollars) for Public Education

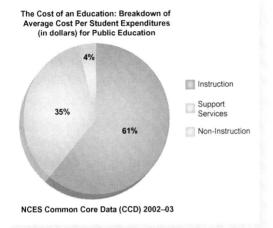

NCES Common Core Data (CCD) 2002–03

Figure 29.9
Use a pie graph to show percentages
or parts of a whole.

Infographic   An infographic is a stylized graph used to display multiple data points in one frame. In this infographic (Figure 29.10), we can see information about the effects of the national Do Not Call registry as well as a timeline of key events in its history. The infographic uses another type of graph, a bubble graph, to visualize the data.

EXAMPLE: Infographic

Figure 29.10
Use an infographic to display multiple data points in a single frame.

Tables and Charts

Tables and charts are used to display detailed information and data, or to illustrate concepts.

Tables   A table makes it easy for readers to compare numbers, especially those listed horizontally (since we read from left to right). In this table (Figure 29.11), readers can compare how much time people spend, on average, on tasks such as eating and sleeping. Unlike a graph, which would give a general sense of the trends or patterns in the data, here we get all of the numbers. This makes it harder to recognize patterns, but easier to find the exact numbers.

EXAMPLE: Table

Table 1. Time spent in primary activities [1] and percent of the civilian population engaging in each activity, averages per day by sex, 2012 annual averages

Activity	Average hours per day, civilian population			Average percent engaged in the activity per day			Average hours per day for persons who engaged in the activity		
	Total	Men	Women	Total	Men	Women	Total	Men	Women
Total, all activities [2]	24.00	24.00	24.00	–	–	–	–	–	–
Personal care activities	9.49	9.22	9.74	100.0	99.9	100.0	9.49	9.22	9.74
Sleeping	8.73	8.60	8.86	99.9	99.9	99.9	8.74	8.61	8.86
Eating and drinking	1.25	1.30	1.20	96.0	95.9	96.0	1.30	1.35	1.25
Household activities	1.74	1.29	2.17	73.7	64.5	82.3	2.36	1.99	2.63
Housework	.60	.28	.90	34.6	19.8	48.4	1.73	1.40	1.86
Food preparation and cleanup	.53	.28	.75	52.5	39.2	64.9	1.00	.72	1.16
Lawn and garden care	.18	.25	.12	9.8	11.7	8.0	1.87	2.11	1.53
Household management	.13	.10	.15	16.3	13.6	18.8	.78	.77	.79
Purchasing goods and services	.72	.60	.84	41.4	37.2	45.3	1.74	1.60	1.85
Consumer goods purchases	.35	.27	.43	37.5	34.0	40.8	.94	.80	1.05
Professional and personal care services	.08	.06	.10	7.4	5.6	9.0	1.10	1.05	1.13
Caring for and helping household members	.51	.35	.66	24.5	19.7	28.9	2.09	1.79	2.27
Caring for and helping household children	.40	.27	.53	20.4	15.6	24.8	1.98	1.71	2.14
Caring for and helping nonhousehold members	.18	.16	.20	11.2	9.9	12.3	1.62	1.59	1.64
Caring for and helping nonhousehold adults	.06	.06	.05	7.3	7.0	7.5	.80	.91	.70
Working and work-related activities	3.53	4.17	2.94	43.9	48.8	39.3	8.05	8.54	7.49
Working	3.19	3.74	2.67	41.8	46.5	37.4	7.63	8.05	7.13
Educational activities	.50	.53	.47	8.5	8.8	8.2	5.87	6.01	5.73
Attending class	.28	.30	.26	5.4	5.8	5.1	5.16	5.17	5.14
Homework and research	.17	.18	.16	6.2	6.1	6.2	2.75	2.89	2.63
Organizational, civic, and religious activities	.32	.26	.38	13.8	10.9	16.6	2.33	2.42	2.27
Religious and spiritual activities	.15	.12	.18	9.0	6.7	11.1	1.66	1.72	1.63
Volunteering (organizational and civic activities)	.13	.11	.15	6.0	5.0	7.0	2.13	2.21	2.08
Leisure and sports	5.37	5.79	4.97	96.2	96.9	95.6	5.58	5.98	5.20
Socializing and communicating	.74	.72	.76	37.2	35.4	38.9	2.00	2.04	1.96
Watching television	2.83	3.07	2.61	80.1	80.9	79.3	3.54	3.80	3.29
Participating in sports, exercise, and recreation	.32	.41	.24	19.3	21.7	17.0	1.67	1.90	1.39
Telephone calls, mail, and e-mail	.16	.11	.20	19.8	15.7	23.6	.78	.70	.84
Other activities, not elsewhere classified	.24	.23	.25	14.1	12.8	15.3	1.69	1.80	1.60

[1] A primary activity refers to an individual's main activity. Other activities done simultaneously are not included.
[2] All major activity categories include related travel time. See Technical Note for activity category definitions.
– Not applicable.
NOTE: Data refer to persons 15 years and over.

Figure 29.11
Use a table to help readers compare numerical data.

Terrence included a table in his research paper to show readers the actual numbers of incarcerated mothers and the number of children affected. Here is how it looked in his paper:

As shown in Table 1, the number of mothers in prison has risen from 1991,

when 29500 children had a mother in prison, to a total of 65600 in 2007.

Table 1 Number of Mothers in State and Federal Prisons

Number of Mothers	In State Prison	In Federal Prison	Total
2007	58200	7400	65600
2004	51800	6600	58400
1999	48500	5100	53600
1997	42900	4000	46900
1991	26600	2900	29500

Source: Glaze, L.E. & Maruschak, L.M. (2008). *Parents in Prison and Their*

Minor Children. Washington, D.C.: United States Department of Justice.

Appendix table 1.

Most of these mothers have more than one child: in 2007, a . . .

Notice that Terrence numbered the table separately from the other figures (graphs, pictures, etc.) in his research paper. He included a label and caption for the table before it appeared. He also introduced the table in the text beforehand, pointing readers to the most important information.

Charts   Use charts to show how things are organized or sequenced. Charts can be good for showing steps in a process, as in a flow chart, or how a company is organized into different departments. In this chart (Figure 29.12), viewers can see the organization of the National Oceanic and Atmospheric Association's Earth System Research Laboratory. The chart is organized hierarchically, so the person on top is the director of the whole laboratory—the boss of those below him on the chart.

EXAMPLE: **Organization Chart**

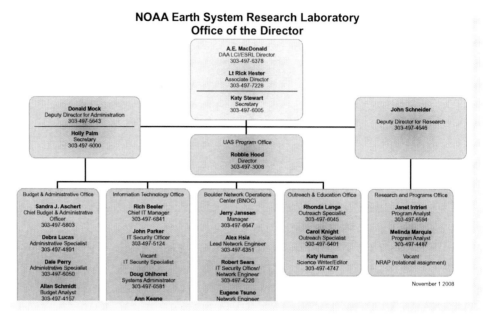

Figure 29.12
Use a chart to show how a system or organization is ordered.

Images

Images are visual representations of objects (persons, places, things). They may include images of real things, or of hypothetical things (such as a blueprint for a building that has not yet been built). Some images appeal to a wide audience, while others are used for more specialized audiences (as in a blueprint or diagram).

Diagrams Diagrams are useful for showing parts of a system or machine and their functions. In this diagram (Figure 29.13), viewers can see the parts that make up the respiratory system, and they can see a cutaway view of a normal and diseased bronchial tube. Notice that these diagrams offer an idealized view of the system, one that you cannot see in real life. (If you've ever dissected a frog in biology class, you'll remember that the actual specimen looks a bit different, and messier, than the diagrams in your textbook.)

EXAMPLE: Diagram

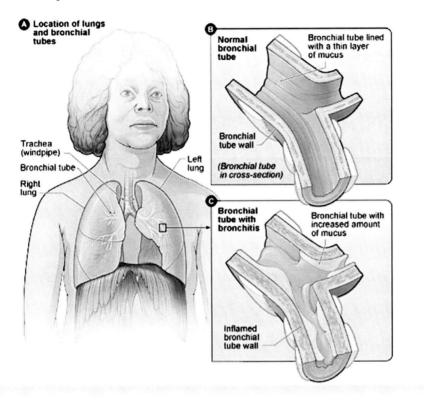

Figure 29.13
Use a diagram to show parts of a system and their functions.

Drawings   Drawings are good for displaying details, or for displaying something that does not (yet) exist in real life, such as a drawing of a new house design. This drawing (Figure 29.14) shows an early vision for the United States Capitol Building, from around 1797, before it was fully constructed.

Drawings might also include specialized architectural drawings, the sketches fashion designers make for a new design, or the courtroom sketches made when photographers are not permitted in the courtroom. Drawings might also be idealized or informal images, as in a cartoon.

EXAMPLE: **Drawing**

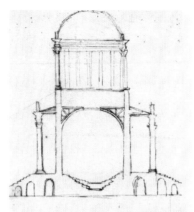

Figure 29.14
Use a drawing to display details.

Photographs   Photographs are useful for showing how something appears in real life. Viewers generally assume photographs are realistic, although the ability to edit photographs with programs such as Photoshop has led viewers to be more skeptical in some cases. This photograph displays the United States Capitol as it appears today.

You can choose photographs to create a certain impression or fulfill a purpose. Here, the photograph impresses viewers with the impressive size of the building. Note that the angle, scope, and framing of a photograph influence how it appears. In this photograph (Figure 29.15), the wide angle view offers us a different perspective than we would get from a close-up. While the wide angle allows us to see the scale and imposing size of the building, a close up might provide more detail about some aspect of the building (such as the shape of the columns). The people in the photograph also give us a sense of the scale of the building.

EXAMPLE: **Photograph**

Figure 29.15
The angle, scale, and framing of this photograph provide a sense of the imposing stature of the United States Capitol Building.

Maps   Maps are used to show where things are located, or how they are situated with relation to other landmarks. Of course, sometimes readers will use maps to actually find a place, but in other cases they will use a map just to get a sense of how an area is laid out. In this map (Figure 29.16), viewers can see where the Capitol Building lies in relation to other buildings, such as the Supreme Court. Notice that maps usually include features to help readers interpret the map, such as a legend, numbers, or symbols. The scale and angle of a map, like a photograph, can influence how viewers see it. This map employs one-point perspective so that the Capitol Building lies in the center, and buildings further away seem to recede in the distance.

EXAMPLE: **Map**

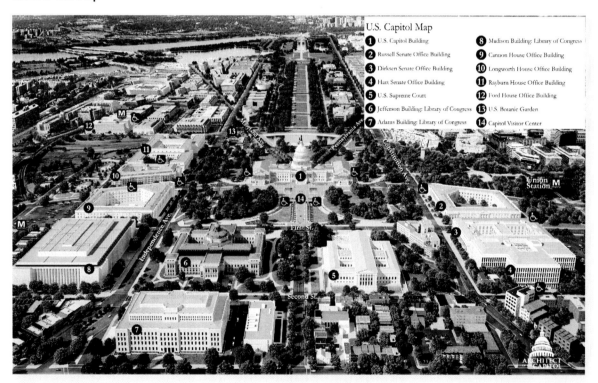

Figure 29.16
This map employs one-point perspective so that the Capitol Building lies in the center, and buildings further away seem to recede in the distance.

Screen Captures   A screen capture is useful anytime you want to save an image of something on your computer screen. For instance, you might find a screen capture useful if you are writing instructions. Say you want to explain how to edit a photograph. You might include a screen capture of the program, possibly with callouts to illustrate specific functions. Or, you might use a screen capture to show how a website looks, as in Figure 29.17. (Most computers have a keyboard command to create screen captures—check your help manual or look up the proper command online.)

EXAMPLE: Screen Capture

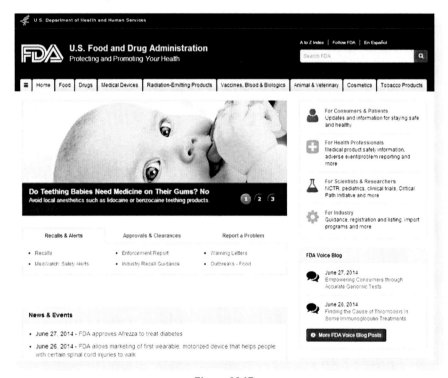

Figure 29.17
This is a screen capture of the U.S. Food and Drug Administration website.

E. Principles for Visual Elements

When selecting these types of images for your document, consider the following principles.

Follow Copyright Rules

Most images you find online are copyrighted, which means that you cannot just take them and stick them into your document. Here are a few options for finding copyright-free images:

- Make your own. Can you create your own graph in your word processing or spreadsheet program? (You will still need to cite the source for your data). Can you take your own photograph of a place? (Note that you will need permission from any people you include in a photograph, as long as their faces are identifiable.)
- Look for copyright-free images. Government images are almost always free, so try searching for images on government websites (such as archives.gov). You can also search websites such as Flickr or Wikimedia Commons for copyright-free images (look for language indicating that the content is covered by a Creative Commons license, which generally allows for free usage as long as the original source is credited). Be sure to read the terms of use for the site carefully.
- Ask. If you can contact the designer or photographer for an image, you can explain that you are using it for a class project and ask for permission to use it for free. In many cases, people are willing to grant an exception for students, as long as you are not publishing the image or making money from it.
- Investigate Fair Use. According to the United States Copyright Act, using images for non-profit educational purposes constitutes "fair use," or use for means of "criticism, comments, news reporting, teaching . . ., scholarship, or research" and is not a copyright infringement. Since Jay was commenting on the images in his rhetorical analysis (Chapter 28) and using them only for a class paper, he thought his use of the image constituted fair use. However, to publish the images in this textbook, we had to get permissions, since this textbook does not fall under the Fair Use policy. For class work, you may be able to claim Fair Use for images, as long as you do not plan on publishing them in print or online. However, check with your instructor to make sure this is okay.
- Attribute. Make sure you include a caption or footnote describing where you got the image.

Label and Caption Properly

Each image you include should have a label and caption, written according to the style guide you are using (such as MLA or APA). In most style guides, everything is labeled as a figure (Figure 1, Figure 2, etc.), except for tables, which are labeled separately (Table 1, Table 2, etc.). The labels for Figures appear below the visual, while the labels for tables appear above.

Here's an example from Terrence's research paper:

Today in America millions of children are being torn away from their mothers, and it is perfectly legal. Over 1.5 million children in the United States have at least one incarcerated parent (Glaze & Maruschak, 2010). As shown in Figure 1, this number has risen by over fifty percent over the course of the last two decades, and is likely to continue to rise as the prison population grows.

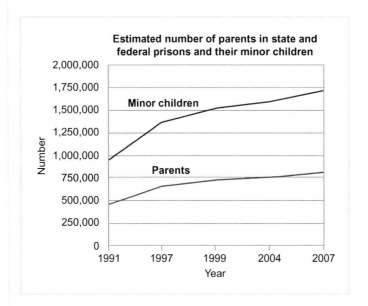

Figure 1: Number of parents in state and federal prisons, and their minor children. Adapted from Glaze, L. E. & Maruschak, L. M. (2008). *Parents in prison and their minor children.* Washington, D.C.: United States Department of Justice (p. 1).

Mothers account for a smaller proportion of these totals than do fathers; however, because female prisoners tend to receive less attention than do male prisoners, in this essay I focus on mothers.

As shown in Table 1, the number of mothers in prison has risen from 1991, when 29500 children had a mother in prison, to a total of 65600 in 2007. [8]

Table 1 Number of Mothers in State and Federal Prisons

Number of Mothers	In State Prison	In Federal Prison	Total
2007	58200	7400	65600
2004	51800	6600	58400
1999	48500	5100	53600
1997	42900	4000	46900
1991	26600	2900	29500

Source: Glaze, L.E. & Maruschak, L.M. (2008). *Parents in Prison and Their*

Minor Children. Washington, D.C.: United States Department of Justice.

Appendix table 1.

Most of these mothers have more than one child: in 2007, a total of 147,400 children had

a mother in prison, as shown. . . .

For graphs, you should also clearly label each axis and provide a legend to explain what colors or shading signify.

Introduce the Visual in the Text

In addition to a label and caption, each visual element should be introduced in the text itself before it appears. Then, if necessary, you can interpret each element after it appears. Your text signal should help readers to identify key patterns you want them to notice in the data. For example, Terrence wanted his readers to notice how the graph indicated a rise in the number of incarcerated parents in the United States. He signals the connection to the graph in the sentence beginning "As shown in Figure 1. . . ."

Acknowledge Sources

Below each table or visual element, list the source of information or the source of the visual. In the preceding example, Terrence generated his own tables and graphs, but he drew the information from a published, government source. If you use information from another study or source, you need to include that information. If you generated your own data (say, from a survey or your own calculations), you do not need to cite a source.

Use Consistent Fonts, Headings, and Colors

To create a unified design, try to employ the same fonts, colors, and headings in your images themselves. For example, for his paper, Terrence decided to use the same color scheme and fonts for all visual elements, in order to keep them consistent with the rest of the document.

Be Careful of Editing, Manipulation, and Distortion

Computer tools allow you to create and modify images in any number of ways. You may decide to modify an existing image to suit your rhetorical purpose. For example, Terrence might have used photo editing software to blur an image he included to illustrate the pain of an incarcerated mother, as in Figure 29.18.

Figure 29.18
Editing images using software can be effective, but be careful not to manipulate or distort images you are presenting as truthful representations.

In this case, the new image creates a certain effect, conveying more of the sadness and loneliness the woman pictured might feel. Since this was a government image, which carried no copyright, we felt it was appropriate to manipulate it for our own purposes. Manipulated images are often used on the web for humorous purposes as well, usually (not always) with no harm done.

However, altering photographs can also be unethical. It is unethical to take a copyrighted image and manipulate it, without seeking permission from the image's producer or owner.

It can also be unethical to alter images so as to scare or mislead readers, or to distort information. If you are using an image to demonstrate how things are, or what the facts are, be careful of distortions. For most genres and rhetorical situations for your writing, readers usually expect you to offer only truthful images. There are a few exceptions, though. For example, most readers now understand that the photographs of models used in fashion magazines have been retouched. Readers also expect to see manipulated images on humor websites, and are less likely to be misled. If you are using an image to evoke a feeling, mood, or idea, you may have more creative room.

Choose Fonts Carefully

For many genres, your choice of fonts is limited. Most academic style manuals specify a standard serif font (such as Times New Roman or Cambria). For other genres, you may have a wider range of choices open to you. Be sure to consider what font choices seem appropriate for your genre.

There are four main types of fonts:

- Serif (e.g., Times New Roman, Cambria, Garamond)
- Sans serif (e.g., Arial, Calibri, Franklin Gothic Book)
- *Italic or Script Fonts (e.g., Apple Chancery, Edwardian Script, Lucida Calligraphy)*
- Decorative (e.g., Curlz MT)

If you pay attention to the fonts used in documents you read, you'll start to notice how and when these fonts are used.

Most printed textbooks will use a serif font for the body text. That is because the extra embellishments, or feet, on each letter help readers to recognize the shapes of words. Serif fonts tend to be more readable for printed text.

However, for online documents, sans serif fonts tend to be more readable. This is because the screen resolution for most computers is still not as good as a printed page, so the extra embellishments on serif letters do not show up as easily.

Italic or calligraphic fonts are less likely to appear in academic or professional documents. They are difficult to read and tend to appear old-fashioned. For that reason, you might see a font of this type on a wedding invitation, on a menu at a fancy restaurant, or as part of a logo.

Like calligraphic fonts, decorative fonts are difficult to read in large quantities. They tend to appear informal, so they are less likely to appear in an academic or professional document. You may see decorative fonts used sparingly on a website, as part of a logo, or on a poster advertising a campus event.

As a general guideline, if you would like to use more than one font type in a document, you should choose one from each family. For example, a printed text might use a serif font for the body, and a sans serif font for the headers (Figure 29.19). The reverse might be best for a website: sans serif for the body, and serif for the headers (Figure 29.20).

Introduction

This report, prepared for the White House Council on Women and Girls, presents selected indicators of women's social and economic well-being currently and over time. The report is intended for a general audience, with the hope that it will be useful to policymakers, policy analysts, journalists, policy advocates, and all those interested in women's issues.

The indicators have been grouped into five areas of interest:

- **People, Families, and Income.** This section describes various demographic characteristics and trends in women's marriage, living arrangements, childbearing, and poverty. The Census Bureau is the primary source of the data (*census.gov*).

- **Education.** This section describes levels and trends in women's educational attainment, school enrollment, and fields of study. The data are primarily from the National Center for Education Statistics (*nces.ed.gov*).

- **Employment.** This section describes levels and trends in women's employment, earnings, and time use. The Bureau of Labor Statistics is the main source of the data (*bls.gov*).

- **Health.** This section describes levels and trends in women's life expectancy, prevalence of chronic health conditions, access to health care, and health insurance coverage. The data come primarily from the National Center for Health Statistics (*cdc.gov/nchs*).

- **Crime and Violence.** This section describes levels and trends in women's victimization, crime, and involvement in the criminal justice system. The data come primarily from the Bureau of Justice Statistics (*bjs.ojp.usdoj.gov*).

Using the Document

Each section of this report consists of a two-page narrative introduction followed by a single page for each of the indicators. Each indicator page has bullet points about the indicator, followed by a chart

Figure 29.19
A serif body text, such as Times New Roman, is easier to read on a printed page.

Figure 29.20
A sans serif body text, such as Arial, is easier to read on a screen.

F. Using Electronic Tools

When you are working on a design, determine what tools are available to you. Find out if your college has a multimedia laboratory where you can use specialized computer programs and equipment (such as scanners or digital cameras).

Use Layout Tools

Layout tools can help you to arrange items on a page (text, images, etc.) more efficiently than in a standard word processing program. Some popular layout and design programs include Adobe InDesign and Microsoft Publisher. Each program differs in its functions, but in general, you can see if your program allows you to do the following:

- Move text boxes, images, and other elements around easily
- Add design elements (boxes, shapes, etc.)
- Create a grid to align elements on the page
- Use or modify templates for your own purposes

Use Image Editing Tools

Image editing tools can help you to create and modify images. Some popular programs include Photoshop, iPhoto, and Picasa. These programs differ in functionality: some will allow you to create new images, while others are best for modifying existing images. See if your program allows you to do the following:

- Create a new image (such as a button or header for a website)
- Edit existing images for color, contrast, size, etc.
- Manipulate images using different filters (blur, posterize, etc.)
- Convert images to different file formats

Use Web Development Tools

Web development tools allow you to create websites. Some, such as Wordpress or Blogger, primarily use templates that you can easily apply yourself. These are sometimes referred to as platforms rather than web software.

Software programs, such as Dreamweaver or iWeb, allow you to create your own website from scratch, but they usually require more technical skill. To determine what type of program to use, ask the following questions:

- Does the program include templates to use/modify? Or will I need to create my own template from scratch?
- Will I need to learn some coding (e.g., HTML, JavaScript)? Or is the program a WYSIWYG editor (what you see is what you get) that requires little to no coding?
- How do I add images, text, links, and navigation elements?

Getting It Out There

In this chapter, you will learn how to get your work out into the world: how to give oral presentations, design multimedia presentations, create a portfolio of your work, submit your work for publication, or even self-publish your work (in print or online). For many college classes, you will be asked to present your work to classmates or even to outside audiences, such as at an undergraduate research conference or community event. Further, many colleges now make some kind of publication of your work, such as an electronic portfolio, a requirement for graduation. Of course, once you enter the workplace, presentations become even more common. This chapter will help you to develop strategies to use in all of these situations.

A. Delivering Oral Presentations

For many students, oral presentations represent one of the most nerve-wracking experiences of a college career. Yet, oral presentations are among the most common requirements for college courses. If you get nervous speaking in front of others (as many people do), take heart. Good preparation and practice can go a long way to alleviating nervousness.

Study the Genre

As is the case with written documents, oral presentations can also be understood as genres, in that they share common situations, purposes, and features (Table 30.1). For instance, the genre of the "opening statement" in a legal trial exists because lawyers regularly have to introduce the case for the defense or prosecution, outlining the key points they will prove. (You've probably seen examples of this genre on TV shows or in movies featuring a court case.) This type of oral presentation differs from the kind a political candidate gives while campaigning, which is known as a "stump speech." While a court case seeks to persuade an audience that has not already decided on an issue (a jury), political speeches are often targeted to the faithful "base" of a political party. The content, style, and delivery of these speeches differ accordingly.

Note that many of these oral genres have an immediate audience (those who are physically present) and a secondary audience (those who may be watching on television or the Internet). For example, presidential debates are often held at a community center or college, with audience members present from that community. However, many more audience members will watch the debate on a television broadcast or Internet feed.

Table 30.1 Genres of Oral Presentations

Genre	Audience	Purpose	Format
Spiel	Attendees on a tour or at an exhibit (e.g. at a tour of historical homes)	Provide information and background	Memorized or extemporaneous
Audio Tour	Visitors to a museum, heritage site, national park, etc.	Provide information and background	Memorized/recorded
Opening or Closing Argument	Judge, jury	Persuade the audience to acquit/convict the defendant	Extemporaneous
Conference Presentation	Conference attendees	Provide an overview of research findings; persuade audience of the importance and validity of those findings	Memorized (or read from a sheet) or extemporaneous
PowerPoint Presentation	Multiple—employees at a business meeting, students in a class, attendees at a conference	Support an oral presentation with visual elements, bulleted notes, etc.	Extemporaneous
Poster Presentation	Participants at a conference or fair	Provide information about a research project or initiative; persuade audience of the validity and importance of a project	Extemporaneous
Radio Broadcast	Radio listeners	Entertain and inform	Memorized (or read from a script), or extemporaneous, or impromptu (as in an interview)
Debate	People immediately present at a debate	Persuade the audience to accept an argument, show that one's argument is superior to the other debaters' (e.g., presidential debate)	Extemporaneous (debaters prepare with practice and notes)

continued

Table 30.1 Genres of Oral Presentations *(continued)*

Genre	Audience	Purpose	Format
Oral petition/ appeal	Members of a board or council (e.g. City Council)	Persuade audience to grant a request or appeal	Memorized, read, or extemporaneous
Eulogy	Mourners at a funeral or memorial service	Celebrate and honor the deceased	Memorized or read
Toast	Attendees at an award banquet, wedding, or other special event	Celebrate a guest of honor or award winner	Memorized, read, extemporaneous, or impromptu
Commencement Speech	Graduates, and their friends and families	Celebrate and honor the graduates' accomplishments	Memorized or read
Campaign Speech	Voters	Persuade voters to elect a candidate	Memorized or read from a teleprompter
Seminar	Students, employees	Inform audience about a topic	Extemporaneous
Roundtable or Panel Discussion	Attendees at a conference, members of a community	Provide multiple perspectives on an issue	Extemporaneous or impromptu
Interview	Public audiences (as on a tv show or radio show)	Inform audience about one's life, experiences, or expertise	Extemporaneous or impromptu (interviewees are sometimes given a list of questions to prepare)
Job Interview	Employers	Persuade audience to offer the job	Extemporaneous or impromptu

Choose a Format

Depending on the genre and assignment, you may choose from several different styles of speaking.

Impromptu Speaking

In an impromptu speech, you speak off the top of your head, without having rehearsed in advance. It takes a lot of practice at speaking, in general, in order to be a good impromptu speaker. Otherwise, you can easily lose track of what you meant to say and end up rambling or getting stuck with nothing to say.

Memorized Speaking   In a memorized speech, you write out a script and then learn it word for word. This approach tends to be used in formal occasions, such as a parent's speech at a child's wedding. A memorized speech tends to come across as more formal and polished than an impromptu speech, but can also seem too stiff for some occasions and genres.

Extemporaneous Speaking   Extemporaneous speaking lies halfway between impromptu and memorized speaking. In an extemporaneous speech, you use notes or talking points to keep you on track, but you do not memorize each word you will say. An extemporaneous speech can sound more natural than a memorized speech, but your talking points will help you to avoid rambling or getting lost.

If you choose an extemporaneous speech, be sure to keep your notes to a minimum, and practice giving your talk several times so that you do not end up simply reading your notes.

Plan Content and Organization

To get started, make sure you know the parameters for your presentation. How much time do you have? What type of presentation are you meant to give? Who is your audience? A five-minute memorized speech for city council members is very different from a ten-minute question and answer session with your classmates.

Select Key Points   Once you know the details of your speaking assignment, you can begin to plan the contents and organization for your presentation. Start by listing out the main point you want to get across to your audience. Then, sketch out an outline, such as this one:

> *Five-minute speech*
> *Min 1—introduce topic and main claim*
> *Min 2—supporting point 1*
> *Min 3—supporting point 2*
> *Min 4—example*
> *Min 5—conclude/recap*

You can see that a short speech does not give you much time. Rather than trying to cover too much ground, focus on a few key ideas that you can cover adequately in the time allotted.

Build In Signposts   Listeners can easily get lost in a long, rambling speech. To make it easier for them to focus on your key points, build in signposts. You might start by outlining the contents you plan to cover, and then use transitions (first, next, etc.) to signal each point or section.

Practice

The most important factor for a good oral presentation is practice. You should plan to rehearse your presentation several times. Try giving your presentation in front of your mirror, your roommate, or even your cat.

It can also be helpful to record yourself giving your presentation, if you have access to a webcam or digital camera. After recording your presentation, watch the video and take notes on what to improve.

Delivery

The difference between an engaging presentation and a boring one often comes down to delivery, not just to content. By delivery, we mean how you bring life to the presentation with your voice, body language, and gestures. As you practice, focus on the following:

Voice and Intonation
Practice using an authoritative, strong voice. If you normally speak quietly, imagine yourself addressing someone in the back of the room—can you make your voice reach that person? Try not to let your voice signal uncertainty. For instance, if every sentence sounds like a question, you might come across as less certain of your ideas. Try to focus on keeping your voice even, or even slightly lower than your regular speaking voice.

It might help to imagine yourself in a different persona (Chapter 21). If your assignment is to present the results of a research project, for instance, imagine yourself as a professor or scholar, not a student.

Gestures and Body Language
To convey authority with your body as well as your voice, pay attention to how you stand. You should try to look natural, not stiff. Let gestures happen naturally, if at all—if you force yourself to use certain hand gestures, you may come across as nervous or unnatural. The more you practice, the more natural you will feel.

If you videotape yourself practicing, you'll notice whether or not you have certain habits, such as brushing your hair from your eyes or putting your hands in your pockets.

Eye Contact
If you have practiced your speech enough, you will be able to look up from your notes (if you have them) and make eye contact with audience members. If you are doing a multimedia presentation or PowerPoint, try to avoid gazing at the screen or reading from the slides. Good eye contact helps to keep audience members focused and engaged.

B. Developing Multimedia Presentations

You may also choose to use multimedia to present your findings or ideas to an audience. Multimedia can accompany an oral presentation (as in a slideshow), or it can stand on its own (as in a podcast).

Choose a Format

If you are preparing a multimedia presentation, first, choose a format that suits your audience and purpose. For example, if you are presenting results from a research study, a slideshow presentation can help you to display your data visually. You might also consider how you might share your multimedia presentation online. For instance, a video can be posted to Vimeo or YouTube, where many viewers can see it.

Slideshow presentation (PowerPoint) Speakers often use a slideshow presentation to accompany an oral presentation. You can use presentation software such as PowerPoint or Prezi to illustrate key points, or show visual elements (Chapter 29) to your audience as you speak. Slideshows are especially popular among business, scientific, and medical fields, where you may need to show graphs, charts, and diagrams to the audience.

When designing a slideshow presentation, keep the following tips in mind:

- Avoid cluttering each slide with too much information. Keep bullet lists short, and avoid adding too many design features.
- Include an overview slide to focus readers.
- Avoid reading from the slides as you present—practice your presentation so that you can move seamlessly through the slides as you speak.
- Arrive early to set up your presentation, and have a back-up plan (such as a handout) in case you have technical difficulties.

Podcasts A podcast is a recorded presentation that you upload to a website or provide for listeners in some other way. (For example, some museums and art galleries now provide podcasts to visitors, who can listen to them on their cell phones or on a provided media player.)

Since listeners to a podcast will not necessarily have a visual aid, be sure to provide signposts to keep them focused—introduce the main points, and provide cues when you move from one point to another.

You might produce a scripted podcast, which you read as you go along, or you can create an extemporaneous podcast, such as an interview or debate. You should also consider what other kinds of sounds, if any, you would like to include. Can you use music or other recorded sounds to set the tone?

You can record your podcast on your computer, using audio software such as GarageBand or Audacity.

Videos   You might create a video to accompany an oral presentation, or you might create a standalone video that you upload to the web. A video might have a range of purposes or audiences. For instance, in a film class you might be asked to create a scene analysis in the form of a video you upload to YouTube (Chapter 8). Or, you might be asked to create a public service announcement (PSA) for a service learning class.

As is the case with oral presentations, there are genres of videos as well. As always, you can begin by finding examples of the type of video you wish to present. Looking at examples will give you ideas about what kinds of content to include, how to order your video, and what kinds of techniques to use.

Screencasts   A screencast is like a video that you take of your computer screen. You can use screencasting software, such as Camtasia, to record a set of actions you perform on your computer. A screencast can be useful as an instructional tool. For example, you could create a screencast to show new students how to use your online course enrolment system. Or, you can try something more creative, like a multimedia presentation with sound, video, text, and so on.

To create an effective screencast, keep the following tips in mind:

- Plan out your screencast in advance. Write down a sequence of actions and a script so that you know which action to perform and what to say, when.
- Do a practice run before you record, or plan to record a few times so that you can get it right.
- Pay close attention to pacing. When you revise, check to ensure that movements or transitions do not happen too quickly—this can make people dizzy.

Plan Content and Organization

As you plan the content for your multimedia presentation, keep in mind that you are not just writing a document users can read at their own pace—you are doing much of the pacing yourself. You will need to plan for sounds, movement, images, etc. to occur alongside a spoken text.

To make these plans, it might be useful to sketch out a storyboard: a visual and verbal description of each scene or stage in your production.

Create a Script

As you plan your script (text that will be spoken or possibly displayed on the screen), consider how you can make your text as easy for your audience to follow as possible. You should consider the following:

- Using signposts or forecasting to give readers a sense of what is coming next.
- Practicing your script out loud. Identify any stumbling points and revise the text if needed.

- If you are recording your voice, practicing and listening to the recording. Identify any quirks (such as saying "um" a lot or raising your voice at the end of sentences), then try again.
- Planning extra time to identify any technical difficulties or problems that need to be worked out.

C. Creating a Portfolio

A portfolio is a collection of your best work that you may submit in a class, as a requirement for your major or minor, or as a record of your achievements in college. The audience for a portfolio may be someone who is evaluating your work, such as your instructor or professor, or it could be something you put together for potential employers or as part of your application package to a post-college program.

Choose a Format: Print or Electronic

Take a look at some sample portfolios.

EXAMPLE 1: Digital Portfolio for a Nursing Major

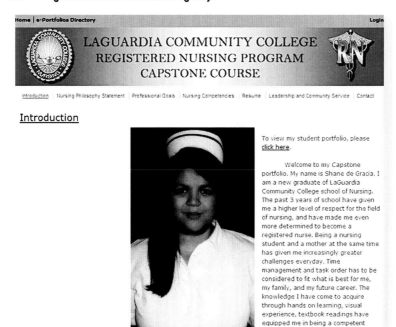

EXAMPLE 2: Digital Portfolio for an Art Major

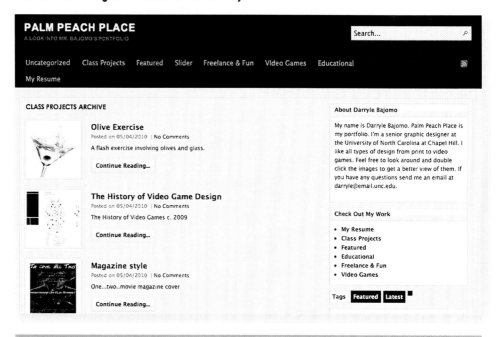

Consider Potential Audiences

Portfolios may be written primarily for evaluation purposes, or for career advancement. On the one hand, you may be submitting a portfolio in order to earn a grade in a course or to complete your major or minor. Jorge's portfolio (Example 3, below) served this purpose, and, as the title page indicates, he included polished, revised examples of writing assignments he had completed. The portfolio served as an argument that he had met his course objectives.

On the other hand, your portfolio could serve as an argument that you should be hired. Each element you choose should help potential employers to understand that you have the skills needed to perform a job effectively. Both Shane and Darryle (Examples 1 and 2) aimed for an audience of professional employers and chose content to reflect that purpose.

Determine What to Include

If you are given the choice of what to include in your portfolio, think carefully about what kinds of items will be most effective for your audience and purpose. You might consider the following:

EXAMPLE 3: **Print Portfolio for a Marketing Major**

Table of Contents

Cover Letter 3

Resume 4

Executive Summaries

Strategic Marketing (MLS Soccer) 5

Marketing Information Systems (US Men's Soccer National Team) 6

Marketing Research (Titan Classifieds) 7

Jorge Sotelo

[Home address street number and name], [City], [St], [Zip code], [Phone number], [E-mail address]

[MONTH] [DAY], [YEAR]

[NAME]
[TITLE]
[COMPANY NAME]
[ADDRESS]

Dear Sales and Marketing Department Director:

I learned about the [JOB TITLE] open position with [COMPANY] through the [WEBSITE] on May 14, 2010. I am highly interested in this position and believe my experience with the California State Soccer Association (Cal South) and leadership with the Latino Business Student Association (LBSA) makes me a strong candidate for this position.

I recently obtained my Bachelor of Arts in Business Administration with an emphasis in Marketing from the Mihaylo College of Business and Economics at California State University, Fullerton. In my marketing degree coursework, I developed marketing plans for sports organizations, such as Major League Soccer and the United States Soccer Federation.

My professional career experience includes more than two years at Cal South with some of my responsibilities providing significant experience in:

- Game-related operations and logistics.
- Community outreach.
- Conduct and interpret market research for various projects.

In addition to the aforementioned skills, I have also proved success in this industry by:

- Reaching an overall growth of 21 percent of the Los Angeles Fútbol Circuit in 2009 year to date.
- Exceeding the 2010 Los Angeles Fútbol Circuit Spring League goals by 36 percent.

I look forward to speaking with you regarding this opportunity with [COMPANY NAME]. I will inquire within a week to follow up with you and answer any questions you may have. Should you require additional information, feel free to contact me via phone or via e-mail. Thank you for time and consideration.

Sincerely,

Jorge Sotelo

Enc. Resume

- Photographs
- A biographical statement
- A résumé (Chapter 12)
- Examples of a research genre (Chapter 11)
- Examples of informative writing (Chapter 6)
- Examples of other genres, such as a profile (Chapter 5), argumentative genre (Chapter 10), etc.
- Any writing you have published
- An example of a multimedia or visual document (Chapter 29 and this chapter)
- A statement of your professional or educational goals
- A statement about your philosophy toward your major or career
- A list of key skills
- A list of volunteer or work experiences

Provide an Overview

When you put together a portfolio, your goal is to highlight your best work and give examples of projects you have completed. However, you may also be asked to (or wish to) provide an overview that explains how each item fits with your goals, what you have learned, and what skills you can apply to other tasks.

Keep your audience in mind as you prepare the overview. If you are writing for instructors, then you are essentially trying to show that you have met the objectives for your course or program. If your audience may include potential employers, though, your goal is to show that you have learned skills relevant to your potential occupation. You can refer to specific examples from your work as evidence of your claims.

Develop a Design and User Navigation

Depending on the type of project, consider what design elements you can use to create a professional look and feel for your portfolio. For an e-portfolio, a portfolio that exists online, you will have several choices to make about colors, fonts, and styles. Remember to keep your audience and purpose in mind. If your audience includes potential employers, then you should consider what visual elements will strike the right tone.

Notice that Shane (Example 1) included a photograph of herself in her nursing uniform to convey her professional authority, along with the logo from the college she attended. Darryle chose a sleek, black and white color scheme because it fits with his goal of becoming a graphic designer. Refer to Chapter 29 for more on visual design.

Regardless of whether you are putting together a print or electronic portfolio, you can consider how to help readers find what they may need. For a print portfolio, you might include a table of contents, dividers with tabs, and headings to organize the contents, like Jorge did (Example 3). For an electronic portfolio, you might add an introductory page, a navigation bar, and/or a sitemap. Shane decided to include a simple bar across the top of the page for navigation. Darryle (Example 2) included links across the top as well as a box ("Check Out My Work") to point readers to different sections.

D. Submitting Your Work for Publication

As a college student, you may be encouraged to share your writing with an audience outside of your classroom. Increasingly, students are asked to present their work at conferences, submit it to newspapers or journals, or share it with professional audiences (such as a local organization). Publishing your work with outside audiences can help you to build your résumé, and it can also give you a chance to share your ideas with others.

Choose a Venue

First, consider where you might publish your work. Your college may host its own undergraduate research conference, publish its own newspaper or literary magazine, or put out an online research journal. You can also search online for conferences, newspapers, magazines, and journals that publish student research.

Make sure your venue matches the genre you would like to publish. For instance, you might submit a personal essay or poem to a literary magazine, but probably not to a research journal. If you look up the web page for your target venue, you can see what kinds of submissions they accept.

Follow Submission Guidelines

Once you have located a publication venue, check to see if there are submission guidelines available. Take careful note of any deadlines, formatting requirements, or other information. You may need to format your bibliography using a different style guide, for instance, or condense your document to meet their word limits. Doing everything exactly according to the guidelines will increase your chances of getting published.

In some cases, you may need special permissions to publish materials included in your work. For example:

- If you have used archival materials from a library's special collection (such as unpublished letters, manuscripts, photographs, etc.), you may need permission from your library and/or from the literary executor for the collection. **Check with your library.**
- If you are publishing research results that involved human subjects (such as interviews, surveys, focus groups, or experiments), you may need permission from your college's Institutional Review Board (IRB). You may need to show proof that you have complied with the IRB's guidelines. **Check with your college's Institutional Review Board.**
- If you are using photographs, images from films, or other visual material you did not create yourself, you may need copyright permissions to publish them. **Check with whoever owns copyright for those materials.**

Create a Checklist

Once you have checked the submission guidelines, create a checklist so you can keep track of everything you need to do. Here is one students' checklist:

- ☐ Consider your genre: Is qualitative
- ☐ Change bibliography to MLA format
- ☐ Double-check quotes and citations
- ☐ Cut 750 words from article (3500 max)
- ☐ Get permissions to publish archival photos and letters from library

☐ Sign and date copyright statement
☐ Get letter from faculty supervisor
☐ Write short abstract
☐ Choose 5 keywords
☐ Create cover page
☐ Write cover letter

You may need to include additional items that you have not already written, such as an abstract (Chapter 11), a list of keywords, or a cover page. Use the genre toolkit (Chapters 1–4) to help you. Look for examples of these items, preferably in your target publication or in the submission guidelines. Try to identify the common features, and then determine how you can create your own.

Write a Cover Letter

When you submit your work for publication, you may need to include a cover letter. This could take the form of an email, a professional letter (Chapter 12), or an online form. Check your submission guidelines to make sure. Cover letters typically include the title of the work you are submitting, a short summary of your work, and a short biographical note about yourself.

E. Self-Publishing Your Work

In addition to submitting your work for publication, you may wish to self-publish your work. This means that you do not need to seek approval from anyone else, but that you will be your own editor. That is, you will decide what standard to meet, how to format your work, and how it will be distributed.

Choose a Venue

The Internet provides many different options for self-publishing your work. Depending on the type of project, you might choose one of the following:

- A website
- A blog
- A post to an existing website, such as YouTube or Scribd
- A self-published book
- An entry on Wikipedia or another "crowdsourced" venue

Consider what audience you would like to reach for your work. Then, determine which type of venue would best help you to reach that audience. For instance, you might like a printed, bound copy of your poetry just for yourself and some close friends. You could self-publish and print that volume and order just enough copies from a website such as CreateSpace or Lulu.com. Or, you might want to create a website showcasing your research for a course, one that can be seen by a wide audience.

Determine Copyright Options

Even if you are self-publishing, you will still need to follow copyright regulations, especially if you are posting materials online. Check to see who owns the copyright for any images, videos, or other materials you have not created yourself. You can write to the owner and ask for permission, or search for materials that are copyright-free.

Check Publishing Guidelines

If you are creating a website or other document yourself, then your only restrictions will involve your technical skills and the affordances of the software or platform you are using. Of course, you will want to make choices about color, layout, and so on based on your audience and purpose. See Chapter 29 for more on visual elements and design.

If you would like to self-publish your material, then you may need to pay attention to layout concerns. For instance, you might need to build in margins of a certain size to accommodate the printing and binding specifications for a self-published book or pamphlet. Check with your online publisher or copy center for more information.

How Verbs Work

A. What Is a Verb?

What do you notice about the highlighted words in these sentences?

- The candidate attacked the opposition's proposal.
- The non-profit organization feeds children across the world.
- The program will create a culture of compassion on our campus.

In each of these sentences, the emphasized word or phrase carries the action of the sentence. These words are verbs, or "action words," and they can refer to an event, action, or state of being.

B. Common Problems

Be on the lookout for the following common verb problems.

Conjugation

A conjugation problem means that you have chosen the wrong ending for a verb in its conjugated form.

Problem: He walk down the street.
Solution: He walks down the street.

Subject-Verb Agreement

Each verb has a subject—a person, place, or thing—that performs the action.

- **The candidate** attacked the opposition's proposal.
- **Charity** is difficult to define.
- **The Bahamas** is an archipelago in the Caribbean.
- **The celebration** will occur in mid-July.

A subject-verb agreement problem occurs when the subject of your sentence does not match the verb. This is likely to happen when you are misled by a series of words in between the subject and the verb.

> **Problem:** **One** of the children **are** sleeping.
> **Solution:** **One** of the children **is** sleeping.
> **Problem:** The **president**, who is the proud owner of two cats, **are** going to speak at the cat convention.
> **Solution:** The **president**, who is the proud owner of two cats, **is** going to speak at the cat convention.

Overuse of Passive Voice

Verbs can appear in the passive or active form. In the active form, the subject is the same as the person or thing that performs the action:

- I kicked the ball.
- I wrote the documents.

In the passive form, the subject and object have switched places, so that the subject of the sentence is not the person or thing who actually performs the action:

- The ball was kicked [by Frank].
- The documents were written by Jane.

You can recognize the passive voice because it always uses a conjugation of the verb "to be" plus the past participle of a verb. The passive sentence may or may not tack on "by" to show who or what performed the action.

The passive voice is not incorrect—in fact, some genres, especially types of scientific writing, may use it frequently. However, if you use the passive voice too often you make your writing more difficult for the reader to easily understand. Try to revise your sentences so that they use the active voice more frequently:

> **Problem:** By the end of the year, the amendment **had been ratified**. Prohibition **was** still **opposed**, and bootleg operations **were initiated** to provide liquor to thirsty customers.
> **Solution:** By the end of the year, Congress **ratified** the amendment. Many still **opposed** the amendment, yet a happy cast of gangsters and bootleggers **began** to provide liquor to thirsty customers.

Overuse of Nominalizations

A nominalization is a verb that has been turned into a noun. Nominalizations are not grammatically incorrect. In fact, they are necessary in some academic writing because nominalizations often express key concepts (such as "evolution," "gentrification," or "colonialism"). However, they tend to make your writing more difficult to read and understand. To revise, try to turn some of your nominalizations back into verbs.

> **Problem:** The **colonization** of Africa led to the **destabilization** of family structures and the **delegitimization** of existing political systems.
>
> **Solution:** By **colonizing** Africa, Europeans **destabilized** family structures and **delegitimized** existing political systems.

Wrong Tense

Verbs may be used in different tenses to indicate whether the action happened in the past, is happening in the present, or will happen in the future.

- I **write** the policy. [present]
- I **wrote** the policy yesterday. [past]
- I **have written** the policy. [present perfect]
- I **had written** the policy. [past perfect]
- I **will write** the policy tomorrow. [future]
- I **am going to write** the policy tomorrow. [future]

In English, you indicate the tense of a verb either by adding an ending (such as -ed for past) or by using a helping verb (such as "will" or "am going" for future, and "have" or "had" for the past).

"Wrong tense" means that you have chosen the wrong form of a verb (past, present, or future) for the idea you are trying to express.

> **Problem:** Yesterday, I **interview** Professor Steinberg about her research.
>
> **Solution:** Yesterday, I **interviewed** Professor Steinberg about her research.

Watch out for the following expressions, which are sometimes misused in the past tense.

"Used to" and "Supposed to"

> **Problem:** He **use to** work out a lot, but he doesn't any more.
>
> **Solution:** He **used to** work out a lot, but he doesn't any more.
>
> **Problem:** We are **suppose** to finish this assignment by tomorrow.
>
> **Solution:** We are **supposed** to finish this assignment by tomorrow.

"Seen" and "Been"

> **Problem:** I **seen** that movie already.
>
> **Solution 1:** I **saw** that movie already.
>
> **Solution 2:** I **have seen** that movie already.

Problem: I **been** in the library.
Solution 1: I **was** in the library.
Solution 2: I **have been** in the library.

Tense Shifts

A tense shift occurs when a writer has gone from using one form of a verb (past, present, or future) to another while writing about the same event. Try to keep the tense you are using consistent as long as you are talking about the same event or idea.

Problem: The Civil War **opened** with the Battle of Fort Sumter, when the Federal Government **attacked** the fortress outside of Charleston, South Carolina. In response, South Carolina authorities **seize** all federal property in Charleston. The situation in South Carolina soon **begins** to resemble a siege.

Solution: The Civil War **opened** with the Battle of Fort Sumter, when the Federal Government **attacked** the fortress outside of Charleston, South Carolina. In response, South Carolina authorities **seized** all federal property in Charleston. The situation in South Carolina soon **began** to resemble a siege.

Wrong Preposition

Some verbs have words that tend to follow after them, called prepositions. These kinds of verbs are called phrasal verbs. Some verbs use different prepositions in different circumstances. If you are unsure which preposition to use, use a dictionary.

Problem: I should **of** written to the professor ahead of time.
Solution: I should **have** written to the professor ahead of time.
Problem: I believe **in** it is important to keep student fees as low as possible.
Solution: I believe **that** it is important to keep student fees as low as possible.

Some verbs can go with a few different prepositions, depending on the sentence. Here are a few examples:

- Believe in (someone or something)
- Believe that (an event or occurrence)
- Try to (do something)
- Try on (an article of clothing)
- Apologize for (an act)
- Apologize to (a person)
- Hear of (a person, place, or thing)
- Hear that (an act or event)
- Argue with (a person or position)

- Argue about (an idea or theory)
- Argue that (a statement or claim is true)

Common confusions:

- Should (would, could) **of** → should (would, could) **have**
- Wanna, gonna (informal or oral form) → want to, going to (formal or written form)

Wrong Past Form

Many verbs in English do not follow the usual pattern of adding -ed to change to the past tense. For these verbs, called "irregular verbs," you use a different form to indicate the simple past tense.

> **Problem:** She **creeped** through the house.
> **Solution:** She **crept** through the house.
> **Problem**: The war **becomed** more bloody and violent.
> **Solution:** The war **became** more bloody and violent.

Here are some more examples of irregular verbs in the past tense:

- choose → chose
- cling → clung
- eat → ate
- build → built
- buy → bought
- burst → burst

To make things even more complicated, some irregular verbs use yet another form as their past participle (the form you use to write the present perfect or past perfect tenses).

> **Problem:** He **has chose** to attend college.
> **Solution:** He **has chosen** to attend college.

Here are some more examples:

- arise → arose (simple past) → arisen (past participle)
- eat → ate → eaten
- choose → chose → chosen
- give → gave → given
- begin → began → begun

If you have been told that your verb form is wrong, look in a dictionary to find the correct way to write the past participle.

How Nouns and Pronouns Work

A. What Is a Noun?

A noun is a word that identifies a person, place, or thing (e.g., professor, city, computer). If a noun *names* the person, place, or thing, then it is a *proper* noun (e.g., Professor Brown, New York City, MacBook).

B. What Is a Pronoun?

A pronoun can function like a noun in a sentence, but a pronoun *refers* to a noun that appears elsewhere in a written passage. Some common pronouns are he, they, it, you, him, mine, yours, etc. These pronouns refer to another noun; for example, "he" might refer to "Joseph" while "it" might refer to "the notebook."

C. Common Problems

Be on the lookout for the following common problems that arise with nouns and pronouns.

Capitalization of Nouns

If a noun *names* a person, place, or thing, then it should be capitalized, because the noun is a *proper* noun. All other nouns are *common* nouns.

Do not capitalize common nouns.

> **Problem:** I went to the **Store** to buy towels.
> **Solution:** I went to the **store** to buy towels.

But do capitalize proper nouns.

> **Problem:** I went to **target** to buy towels.
> **Solution:** I went to **Target** to buy towels.

Other proper nouns include the names of the following:

- languages (French, Chinese)
- religions (Islam, Buddhism)
- cities (Paris, Moscow)
- states (Nebraska, Oregon)
- countries (Japan, Indonesia)

Vague Pronoun Referents

Pronouns must refer to nouns (called "referents" or "antecedents") in order to make sense. If it is unclear from your writing what a pronoun refers to, then you have written a vague referent.

Who does the pronoun "she" refer to in the following problem sentence?

> **Problem:** Heather, Mary, and Jacinta are studying hard for the test. **She** hopes **she'll** get an A.
> **Solution:** Heather, Mary, and Jacinta are studying hard for the test. **Jacinta** hopes **she'll** get an A.

What does the pronoun "it" refer to in the following problem sentence?

> **Problem:** For the test tomorrow, I'll need my laptop, laptop charger, and textbook. I hope I don't forget **it**.
> **Solution:** For the test tomorrow, I'll need my laptop, laptop charger, and textbook. I hope I don't forget my **laptop charger**.

Pronoun Shifts

Use a singular pronoun to refer to a singular antecedent and a plural pronoun to refer to a plural antecedent.

> **Problem:** If a **student** has a problem with this course, **they** should talk to the professor.

This problem sentence has a singular antecedent ("student") paired with a plural pronoun ("they").

> **Solution 1:** If a **student** has a problem with this course, **he or she** should talk to the professor.

Solution 1 changes the plural pronoun to singular pronouns.

> **Solution 2:** If **students** have a problem with this course, **they** should talk to the professor.

Solution 2 changes the singular antecedent to a plural antecedent.

One note: using "they" as a singular, gender-neutral pronoun has become a popular usage. However, for academic writing, using "they" in this fashion is not the best choice. Use one of the preceding solutions instead, or check a style guide for your discipline for help (such as the *Publication Manual of the American Psychological Association* or the *MLA Handbook for Writers of Research Papers*).

Pronoun Confusion

Pronouns come in a variety of types:

- Subject pronouns: I, you, he, she, it, we, you, they
- Object pronouns: me, you, him, her, it, us, you, them
- Possessive pronouns: mine, yours, his, hers, its, ours, yours, theirs

When you write, you need to be sure that you are using subject pronouns as subjects of your sentences, object pronouns as objects, and possessive pronouns to indicate ownership.

In the problem sentence that follows, the writer incorrectly used an object pronoun where a subject pronoun should be used.

> **Problem:**   **Them** were working on a group project.
> **Solution:**   **They** were working on a group project.

They're, Their, and There

A common word confusion arises when writers mix up the contraction "they're" (which means "they are"), the possessive word "their," and the word "there."

Use "there" to indicate a location:

> **Problem:**   Put the graded quizzes over **their**.
> **Solution:**   Put the graded quizzes over **there**.

Use "they're" as the subject and verb ("they are") of a sentence:

> **Problem:**   **Their** hoping to find out the election results today.
> **Solution:**   **They're** hoping to find out the election results today.

Use "their" to indicate possession:

> **Problem:**   That is **there** new apartment building.
> **Solution:**   That is **their** new apartment building.

Who and Whom

Another common word confusion arises with the pronouns who (a subject pronoun) and whom (an object pronoun).

Use "who" as the subject of a sentence:

Problem: **Whom** was the fortieth president of the United States?
Solution: **Who** was the fortieth president of the United States?

Use "whom" as an object in a sentence:

Problem: **Who** does this computer belong to?
Solution: **Whom** does this computer belong to?

Your and You're

This type of pronoun confusion mixes up the possessive pronoun "your" with the contraction "you're" (which means "you are").

Problem: **Your** such a wonderful cook.
Solution: **You're** such a wonderful cook.
Problem: **You're** kitchen is amazing.
Solution: **Your** kitchen is amazing.

If you are unsure which one to use, just switch the contraction "you're" to its full form, "you are." If it does not make sense to say "you are" in the sentence, you should use "your." For example, you would not say, "You are kitchen is amazing."

Its and It's

This type of pronoun confusion mixes up the possessive pronoun "its" with the contraction "it's" (which means "it is").

Problem: **Its** a beautiful day.
Solution: **It's** a beautiful day.
Problem: That puppy keeps wagging **it's** tail.
Solution: That puppy keeps wagging **its** tail.

If you are unsure which one to use, just switch the contraction "it's" to the full form, "it is." If it does not make sense to say "it is" in the sentence, you should use "its." For example, you would not say "That puppy keeps wagging it is tail."

How Modifiers Work

A. What Is a Modifier?

A modifier is a word or phrase that gives more information about another word or phrase in a sentence. A modifier may be an adjective, adverb, or a prepositional phrase.

Adjective

Adjectives are words that modify nouns. Writers use adjectives to tell more about a noun (a person, place, or thing), such as color (a **red** balloon), size (a **small** apartment), or any other quality that a noun may possess.

Adverb

Adverbs are words that modify verbs (run **quickly**), adjectives (**brightly** colored), or other adverbs (**totally** differently, **really** well). Adverbs often end in -ly, but not all adverbs do so (such as soon, today, away, here, etc.).

Prepositional Phrase

A prepositional phrase is a modifying phrase that consists of a preposition and its object (a noun) and any words that modify the noun (such as adjectives).

Here are some examples of sentences with prepositional phrases.

- Please leave your test booklets **by the door**.
- While you are **at the store**, could you buy some milk?

Common Prepositions

above	by	over
across	during	through
after	from	to
at	in	toward
before	inside	under
behind	into	until
below	near	upon
beside	of	with
between	on	without

B. Common Problems

Watch out for these common modifier problems.

Punctuating Multiple Adjectives

When you use more than one adjective to modify a noun, you must separate the adjectives from one another with commas.

> **Problem:**   The **happy mellow** cat slept on the windowsill.
> **Solution:** The **happy, mellow** cat slept on the windowsill.

You should *not* put a comma between the final adjective and the noun.

> **Problem:**   The **happy, mellow, cat** slept on the windowsill.
> **Solution:** The **happy, mellow cat** slept on the windowsill.

Punctuating Adverbs and Adjectives

Sometimes writers use an adverb-adjective pair to modify a noun. The adverb should *not* be separated from the adjective it modifies with a comma.

> **Problem:**   My **superbly, crafted** fountain pen never leaks.
> **Solution:** My **superbly crafted** fountain pen never leaks.

Also, you should not attach any adverb that ends in -ly to an adjective with a hyphen.

Problem: My **superbly-crafted** fountain pen never leaks.
Solution: My **superbly crafted** fountain pen never leaks.

You should use a hyphen to attach an adverb that does *not* end in -ly to an adjective (so long as the adverb-adjective pair appears *before* the noun it modifies):

Problem: They are going to take a **much needed** vacation.
Solution: They are going to take a **much-needed** vacation.

However, an adverb-adjective pair should be separated from other adjectives (or adverb-adjective pairs) with commas.

Problem: Following the **old carelessly drawn** map, we quickly got lost.
Solution: Following the **old, carelessly drawn** map, we quickly got lost.

Misplaced Modifiers

Generally speaking, you should place a modifier close to the word or phrase it modifies. For example, adjectives appear adjacent to the nouns they modify.

To avoid confusion, an adverb that modifies a verb should be placed next to—or at least near—the verb it modifies.

Problem: He realized that he forgot to put his name on the test **slowly**.
Solution: He **slowly** realized that he forgot to put his name on the test.

To avoid confusion, a prepositional phrase should be placed near the word or phrase it modifies.

Problem: We had a barbecue and cleaned up quickly afterwards **in our backyard**.
Solution: We had a barbecue **in our backyard** and cleaned up quickly afterwards.

Dangling Participles

A participial phrase is a phrase that begins most commonly with an -ing verb (a present participle) and sometimes with an -ed verb (a past participle). When a sentence begins with a participial phrase, the phrase should modify the subject of the sentence (which follows the phrase). When the phrase does not modify the subject, then you have a dangling participle.

When reading the following sentences, ask yourself, "Who is walking?"

Problem: Walking home after dark, the shadows were frightening.
Solution: Walking home after dark, Sam felt frightened by the shadows.

When reading the following sentences, ask yourself, "Who is studying?"

Problem: Studying hard in the library, the chair grew uncomfortable.

Solution: Studying hard in the library, Molly grew uncomfortable in her chair.

When reading the following sentences, ask yourself, "What is dangling?"

Problem: Dangling loosely from the ceiling, Mark was afraid the light fixture might fall.

Solution: Dangling loosely from the ceiling, the light fixture looked like it might fall.

How Sentences Work

A. What Is a Sentence?

A sentence is a group of words that consists of, at minimum, a subject and a verb. A subject and verb unit can also be called a clause.

If a clause can stand on its own, it is called an independent clause.

> **Example:** George was walking down the street.

If a clause cannot stand on its own, it is called a dependent clause.

> **Example: While George was walking down the street,** he ran into his friend Julie.

If a group of words does not include both a subject and a verb, it is called a phrase.

> **Example: Walking down the street,** George ran into his friend Julie.

B. Common Problems

As a writer, be on the lookout for the following kinds of errors related to sentences.

Fused Sentence, Run-on Sentence, or Comma Splice

If you join two or more independent clauses into one sentence, you must punctuate the sentence properly. To properly join independent clauses, you can do any of the following:

- use a comma plus a coordinating conjunction (for, and, nor, but, or, yet, and so). Use the acronym "FANBOYS" to remember this list;
- use a semi-colon (or sometimes a colon);
- separate the clauses into separate sentences, ending each with a period;
- link one clause to the other, making one a dependent clause.

Often, though, beginning writers make the following kinds of errors when joining independent clauses.

Problem 1. Fused Sentence (no coordinating conjunction and no comma): The professor has not returned our **essays we** do not know our grades.

Problem 2. Run-on Sentence (no comma): The professor has not returned our essays **so we** do not know our grades.

Problem 3. Comma Splice (no coordinating conjunction): The professor has not returned our **essays, we** do not know our grades.

Each of these problems can be corrected in one of four ways:

Solution 1. Comma plus coordinating conjunction: The professor has not returned our **essays, so** we do not know our grades.

Solution 2. Semicolon (or sometimes a colon): The professor has not returned our **essays; we** do not know our grades.

Solution 3. Two sentences: The professor has not returned our **essays. We** do not know our grades.

Solution 4. Create a dependent clause: Because the professor has not returned our **essays, we** do not know our grades.

Sentence Fragment

A sentence fragment is a group of words that is missing one of the key components of a sentence (a subject or a verb) but is punctuated as a sentence. Usually, a sentence fragment is a dependent clause or series of phrases that needs to be joined to an independent clause. Or, the fragment can be turned into its own sentence or independent clause.

Here is a sentence fragment that is a dependent clause:

Problem: Over two million troops were deployed during the Iraq and Afghanistan war. **Although this number pales in comparison to the sixteen million deployed in World War II**.

Solution 1: Over two million troops were deployed during the Iraq and Afghanistan wars, although this number pales in comparison to the sixteen million deployed in World War II.

Solution 2: Over two million troops were deployed during the Iraq and Afghanistan wars. This number pales in comparison to the sixteen million deployed in World War II.

Here is a sentence fragment that is a phrase:

Problem: Over two million troops were deployed during the Iraq and Afghanistan wars. **Leaving their partners behind to cope with the emotional and economic difficulties**.

Solution 1: Over two million troops were deployed during the Iraq and Afghanistan wars, leaving their partners behind to cope with the emotional and economic difficulties.

Solution 2: Over two million troops were deployed during the Iraq and Afghanistan wars. Their partners were left behind to cope with the emotional and economic difficulties.

Lack of Variety

Lack of sentence variety occurs when a writer uses the same type of sentence too often. Lack of variety may refer to the length of your sentences as well as to their construction.

Short, simple sentences can be useful for providing emphasis, or for clarity, as when you are writing a tutorial or factsheet. However, too many short sentences may make your writing seem choppy:

Problem: Students have had enough. Our campus policies are ineffective. Our instructors are poor. Our leaders are inefficient. Our student fees are increasing. Our debts are piling up. Class sizes are growing. Administrators are enjoying fancy retreats. They are spending money on unnecessary consultants. They are raising their own salaries. It is time for a change. It is time to elect Holly Simpson for Class President.

Long, compound or complex sentences can provide detail and complexity, and are often used in narratives or research genres. However, they can easily overwhelm your reader when overused:

Problem: Students have had enough of ineffective campus policies, such as the ineffective policies, instructors, and leaders who have allowed our student fees to increase, our debts to pile up, and our class sizes to increase while administrators are enjoying fancy retreats, spending money on unnecessary consultants and raising their own salaries. It is time for a change, and it is time to elect Holly Simpson for Class President.

To revise, try to use different kinds of sentence constructions and lengths. You might combine some short sentences, or break up some longer ones.

Solution: Students have had enough. We have had enough of ineffective policies, ineffective instructors, and ineffective leaders. While we watch our student fees increase, our debts pile up, and our class sizes increase, administrators are enjoying fancy retreats, spending money on unnecessary consultants, and raising their own salaries. It is time for a change. It is time to elect Holly Simpson for Class President.

How Punctuation Works

A. What Is Punctuation?

Punctuation refers to the use of marks to separate words and sentences and to clarify meaning. Punctuation includes many types of marks.

End Punctuation

End punctuation consists of marks used to end sentences.

Period . A period is the most common mark used to end a sentence.

Exclamation mark ! Exclamation marks end sentences that express strong emotion. They should typically be avoided in academic writing unless you are quoting a strong statement made by someone else.

Question mark ? A question mark ends any sentence that poses a question.

Punctuation for Sentences

These marks are used to punctuate phrases and clauses in sentences.

Comma , A comma is used to separate parts of a sentence or to separate items in a list or series.

Semicolon ; A semicolon is used to link two independent clauses or to separate complex items in a list or series.

Colon : A colon is used to introduce a list or a quotation and to connect two independent clauses when the second clause builds upon or expands the first clause.

Dash — A dash can be used to separate out text that interrupts the main thought of a sentence and—in typically less formal occasions—to connect two independent clauses.

Parentheses ( )   Parentheses are used to separate less-important material from the main part of a sentence or to indicate citations in certain citation styles, such as MLA and APA.

Other Marks

The following punctuation marks typically change the meaning of individual words, rather than the meaning of whole sentences.

Apostrophe '   An apostrophe is used to indicate possession or to form a contraction. Contractions tend to make writing less formal, so they are not suitable for every genre. Your analysis of the genre you are writing can help you to decide whether a contraction is appropriate.

Brackets [ ]   Brackets are most commonly used to alter quotations.

Hyphen –   A hyphen is commonly used to join a compound word, such as a compound number ("twenty-one") or a compound modifier ("well-made").

Quotation marks " "   Quotation marks indicate when a writer is using the words of another, when a word is slang or its usage is uncommon, and sometimes to indicate sarcasm. In academic writing, you should avoid using quotation marks to indicate sarcasm.

B. Common Problems

Punctuating a List or Series

When you write a list of items in a sentence, you should separate the items in the list with commas:

> **Problem:** Michael went to the store and bought **pita hummus cucumbers and lettuce**.
>
> **Solution:** Michael went to the store and bought **pita, hummus, cucumbers, and lettuce**.

The comma before the "and" in the preceding sentence is called the "final comma." Some fields, such as journalism, prefer that the final comma be left off. Although the final comma is not required for your series to be punctuated properly, if your discipline allows its use, then you can always use the final comma to ensure clarity.

Sometimes, you should use semicolons instead of commas to punctuate a series, especially if the items in your list contain internal punctuation or complex items:

Problem: Michael went to the store and bought hand-made pita, hummus imported from Lebanon, organic, hydroponic cucumbers, and bibb lettuce.

Solution: Michael went to the store and bought hand-made pita; hummus imported from Lebanon; organic, hydroponic cucumbers; and bibb lettuce.

Punctuating a Quotation

Punctuating quotations can be tricky. You have to figure out (1) where to place your quotation marks, (2) how to separate the quotation from the rest of the sentence, and (3) how to punctuate the end of the quotation.

In general, you place quotation marks around the words of another. In the U.S., we use double quotation marks (not single).

Problem 1: Martin Luther King, Jr., once said, **I have a dream**.
Problem 2: Martin Luther King, Jr., once said, '**I have a dream**.'
Solution: Martin Luther King, Jr., once said, "**I have a dream.**"

In general, you should separate the quotation from the rest of the sentence with a comma (or sometimes a colon).

Problem: Martin Luther King, Jr., once **said "I** have a dream."
Solution: Martin Luther King, Jr., once **said, "I** have a dream."

But do not separate the quotation from the rest of the sentence with a comma if the quotation "goes with the flow" of the sentence.

Problem: Abraham Lincoln said **that, "our** fathers brought forth on this continent a new nation."
Solution: Abraham Lincoln said **that "our** fathers brought forth on this continent a new nation."

You can test whether a quotation "goes with the flow" by removing the quotation marks and seeing if you would use a comma. Since you wouldn't put a comma between "that" and "our" in the preceding sentence, you should not use one with the quotation.

In writing U.S. English (as opposed to British English, which you might encounter in texts you read in college), the final comma or period of a quotation always appears inside the quotation marks.

Problem: Abraham Lincoln said that "our fathers brought forth on this continent a new **nation".**

Solution: Abraham Lincoln said that "our fathers brought forth on this con-
               tinent a new **nation."**
Problem: Some believe that the Cold War was just a war of "ignorant
               armies", but others disagree.
Solution: Some believe that the Cold War was just a war of "ignorant
               armies," but others disagree.

If you are using in-text citations (Chapter 28), the period may appear after the citation information in parentheses, depending on the citation style you are using:

Problem: Abraham Lincoln said that "our fathers brought forth on this
                    continent a new **nation." (22)**
Solution: Abraham Lincoln said that "our fathers brought forth on this
(MLA Style)   continent a new **nation" (22).**
Solution: Abraham Lincoln (1863) said that "our fathers brought forth
(APA Style)   on this continent a **new nation."**

Be sure to check the guidelines for the citation style you are using so that you punctuate cited quotations correctly.

   If your quotation is a question, then the question mark should be placed inside the
quotation marks (just like a period). However, if the sentence containing the quotation itself is a question, and the quotation is *not* a question, then you should place
the question mark outside the quotation marks. Do not use two end punctuation
marks, such as a period and a question mark.

Problem 1:   Did the professor really say, "No class **tomorrow?"**
Problem 2:   Did the professor really say, "No class **tomorrow."?**
Solution: Did the professor really say, "No class **tomorrow"?**

Question Marks and Indirect Questions

Generally speaking, you should end a sentence that is a question with a question
mark.

Problem: Are you going to the performance **tonight.**
Solution: Are you going to the performance **tonight?**

However, if the sentence contains an indirect question, then you do not end the
sentence with a question mark. An indirect question is a question that is merely reported in a sentence that is not, itself, a question.

Problem: You should ask our professor whether we need to bring a pencil
               for the exam **tomorrow?**
Solution: You should ask our professor whether we need to bring a pencil
               for the exam **tomorrow.**

Apostrophes and Possession

In English, we use apostrophes to create contractions (such as "can't" or "won't") and to show possession.

When using an apostrophe to create a possessive noun, you should usually place an apostrophe plus -s at the end of a noun.

> **Problem:** Did you listen to the **senators** speech?
> **Solution:** Did you listen to the **senator's** speech?

If the noun is a plural noun ending in -s, you should only add an apostrophe—no -s.

> **Problem:** Did you listen to the **senators** speeches?
> **Solution:** Did you listen to the **senators'** speeches?

If the noun is a singular noun ending in -s, you can add *either* an apostrophe plus -s *or* just an apostrophe. You should follow the style guide for the discipline in which you are writing to determine how to pluralize nouns ending in s.

> **Problem:**   Did you listen to our **boss** speech?
> **Solution 1:** Did you listen to our **boss's** speech?
> **Solution 2:** Did you listen to our **boss'** speech?

Placing Dashes Properly

A dash can be used to separate out text that you wish to emphasize or to connect parts of a sentence. However you use the dash, you must place it properly in your text—and ensure that you are using the correct punctuation mark in the first place. Most word processing programs will automatically create a dash when you type two hyphens between two words.

Do not confuse a dash (which is long) with a hyphen (which is short).

> **Problem:** My favorite dog-the poodle-is a highly intelligent breed.
> **Solution:** My favorite dog—the poodle—is a highly intelligent breed.

Be sure to place the dash directly adjacent to the words that surround it; do not surround the dash with spaces.

> **Problem:** My favorite dog — the poodle — is a highly intelligent breed.
> **Solution:** My favorite dog—the poodle—is a highly intelligent breed.

Selecting Brackets or Parentheses

Many students confuse brackets [ ] with parentheses ( ). These two sets of punctuation marks are not interchangeable in academic writing.

Use parentheses, not brackets, to set off less-important (parenthetical) material from the main part of a sentence.

Problem: This video [one of the first to appear on YouTube] demonstrates the power of online communication.

Solution: This video (one of the first to appear on YouTube) demonstrates the power of online communication.

Use brackets, not parentheses, to do minor alterations to quotations. (You should not do major alterations to quotations—paraphrase instead).

Problem: Lincoln said at Gettysburg, "(Eighty-seven) years ago our fathers brought forth on this continent a new nation."

Solution: Lincoln said at Gettysburg, "[Eighty-seven] years ago our fathers brought forth on this continent a new nation."

How Usage Conventions Work

A. What Are Usage Conventions?

Usage conventions are patterns of word choice and sentence structure that are dictated by custom or tradition. Sometimes, these patterns differ between disciplines or fields, and often they are described in a style guide (such as the *MLA Handbook*). These style guides describe conventions for punctuation, word choice, verbs (such as when to use present or past tense), and more. If you are unsure if you are using the right word or sentence structure, check the style guide for your field, such as the *MLA Handbook for Writers of Research Papers*, the *Publication Manual of the American Psychological Association*, or the *Chicago Manual of Style*.

B. Common Problems

Beware these common usage problems that arise in academic writing.

Inclusive Language

Most style guides recommend that you use words that do not exclude individuals on the basis of race, sex, gender, sexuality, age, or ability.

Avoid using masculine words (he, him, fireman, policeman) as defaults.

> **Problem:** Every **man** should thank **his** local **fireman** for **his** dedication.
> **Solution:** **Citizens** should thank **their** local **fire fighters** for **their** dedication.

Be sure to refer to disabilities only when relevant. Do not define people by their disability, but rather as people, first:

> **Problem:** The film will be shown with closed captioning so that **deaf people** can watch.

Solution 1 (no disability mentioned): The film will be shown with subtitles.
Solution 2 (people first): The film will be shown with closed captioning so that **people with hearing loss** can enjoy it.

Avoid singling out individuals for their gender, race, ability, sexuality, or age when it is not necessary or relevant:

Problem: Both James, **a gay psychology professor**, and Stewart, **a Black historian**, commented on the proposal.
Solution: Both James, **a psychology professor**, and Stewart, **a historian**, commented on the proposal.

Avoid making assumptions about sexuality:

Problem: Sorority members are welcome to bring their **boyfriends** to the event.
Solution: Sorority members are welcome to bring **dates** to the event.

Avoid making assumptions about competence based on gender, race, ability, sexuality, or age:

Problem: Mr. Jones is remarkably sharp **for a senior employee**.
Solution: Mr. Jones is one of our sharpest employees.

Weak Nouns and Verbs

To make your writing more powerful, look for places where you can replace weak, vague nouns with more specific ones, and weak verbs with stronger ones.

Look for nouns that refer to vague ideas ("thing," "notion," "person," "idea," etc.) rather than concrete nouns:

Problem: Poor nutrition **is one of the things** that causes tooth decay.
Solution #1 (stronger noun): Poor nutrition **is one cause of** tooth decay.
Solution #2 (stronger verb): Poor nutrition **can cause** tooth decay.

Look for the verbs "to be" ("is," "are," etc.) and "to have" ("has," "have," etc.) and see if you can replace them with verbs that carry more impact. Changing the passive voice to active voice (Chapter S1) can also create more impact:

Problem: Costa's work **is an example** of the blanket bias **that is present** in our society, which in turn **is reflected in** the laws.
Solution: Costa's work **exemplifies** the blanket bias **present** in our society, which the law **reflects** in turn.

You can also look for noun and verb clusters that can be condensed with a single, strong verb or noun:

> **Problem:** Increased visitation **will also have a positive impact on** the broader society by helping break the cycle of crime.
>
> **Solution:** Increased visitation **will benefit** the broader society by helping break the cycle of crime.
>
> **Problem:** Child visitation is also impeded by the "best interest of the child standard," the test used in most jurisdictions when deciding on **issues of visitation**.
>
> **Solution:** Child visitation is also impeded by the "best interest of the child standard," the test used in most jurisdictions when deciding on **visitation**.

Long Lead-ins

Sentences are more difficult to read if the subject and the verb appear later in the sentences. To make your sentences easier to read, try to put the subject and verb together, early in the sentence.

> **Problem:** Once we determine the factors involved, test each one experimentally, and distinguish key trends in the data, **we can** identify potential causes of bus delays on campus.
>
> **Solution:** **We can** identify potential causes of bus delays on campus once we determine the factors involved, test each one experimentally, and distinguish key trends in the data.

To get rid of long lead-ins, go through your draft and circle the main verb for each sentence. If the subject and verb appear toward the end of the sentence, try to rearrange the sentence so the verb and its subject come sooner.

You can also look for "dummy" or impersonal clauses, which tend to create long lead-ins and make readers wait for the main point of the sentence:

> **Problem:** **It is important to note that** not all politicians are corrupt.
>
> **Solution:** Not all politicians are corrupt.
>
> **Problem:** **Another interesting factor involved in** the Vietnam War protests was music.
>
> **Solution:** Music **catalyzed** the Vietnam War protests.

Separating Subject and Verb

A sentence may be more difficult to read if the subject and verb are separated.

Problem: **Another legal factor** that prevents child visitation for incarcer-
             ated mothers **is** the "best interest of the child standard," the test
             used in most jurisdictions when deciding on issues of visitation
             and custody.

Solution 1: **Child visitation is** also impeded by the "best interest of the child
             standard," the test used in most jurisdictions when deciding on
             issues of visitation and custody.

Solution 2: **The law also impedes** child visitation through the "best interest
             of the child standard," the test used in most jurisdictions when
             deciding on issues of visitation and custody.

Weak Openers

When we read a sentence, we tend to focus on the first part for key information. If
you start sentences with "This is," "It is," "There are," and so on, you are not taking
advantage of the reader's focus.

You can either revise the weak opener itself, or connect the sentence to a previous one:

Problem: Increased visitation will also have a positive impact on the
             broader society by helping break the cycle of crime. **There are**
             studies that find that a child's risk of one day being incarcerated
             is increased if that child had a parent who was at some point
             incarcerated.

Solution: Increased visitation will also have a positive impact on the
             broader society by helping break the cycle of crime. **Many** studies
             find that a child's risk of one day being incarcerated is increased
             if that child had a parent who was at some point incarcerated.

Clutter

Try to revise sentences that use lots of prepositions: to, of, that, so, by, at, etc. Go
through your draft, and circle any preposition you see. Then, see if you can revise
sentences that have more than two or three prepositions.

Problem: In recent years, the field **of** psychology has made great strides **in**
             assessing the true effects **of** incarceration **on** children.

Revision: In recent years, **psychologists** have demonstrated **how** incarcer-
             ation **affects** children.

Doublings

Look for places in your writing where you say the same thing twice, or provide two
words where one would do.

Problem: The child will have a better **understanding and concept** of her parent's situation, have a possibility of **a stable and steady** relationship, and can reach a **more mature and grownup** mental state.

Revision: The child will have a better **understanding** of her parent's situation, have a possibility of a **stable** relationship, and can reach a **more mature** mental state.

Printed in the USA/Agawam, MA
August 7, 2015

621054.006